The Concept of Analytic

The Concept of Analytic Contact presents practitioners with new ways to assist the often severely disturbed patients that come to see them in both private and institutional settings. In this book Robert Waska outlines the use of psychoanalysis as a method of engagement that can be utilized with or without the addition of multiple weekly visits and the analytic couch.

The chapters in this book follow a wide spectrum of cases and clinical situations where hard to reach patients are provided with the best opportunity for health and healing through the establishment of analytic contact. Divided into four parts, this book covers:

- The concept of analytic contact
- Caution and reluctance concerning psychological engagement
- Drugs, mutilation, and psychic fragmentation
- Clinical reality, psychoanalysis, and the utility of analytic contact

Analytic contact is demonstrated to be a valuable clinical approach to working analytically with a complicated group of patients in a successful manner. It will be of great interest to all practitioners in the field of psychoanalysis and psychotherapy.

Robert Waska MFT, PhD has worked in the field of psychology for the last twenty-five years. He has published over fifty articles and reviews in various psychoanalytic journals, many of which have appeared in his five published books. Dr. Waska was certified as both a psychoanalyst and a psychoanalytic psychotherapist from the Institute of Psychoanalytic Studies and he currently maintains a full-time psychoanalytic practice in San Francisco and Marin County.

The Concept of Analytic Contact

The Kleinian Approach to Reaching the Hard to Reach Patient

Robert Waska

Routledge
Taylor & Francis Group

LONDON AND NEW YORK

First published 2007 by Routledge
27 Church Road, Hove, East Sussex BN3 2FA

Simultaneously published in the USA and Canada
by Routledge
270 Madison Avenue, New York, NY 10016

Routledge is an imprint of the Taylor & Francis Group, an informa business

© 2007 Robert Waska

Typeset in Times by Garfield Morgan, Swansea, West Glamorgan
Printed and bound in Great Britain by MPG Books Ltd, Bodmin, Cornwall
Paperback cover design by Lisa Dynan

This publication has been produced with paper manufactured to strict
environmental standards and with pulp derived from sustainable forests.

British Library Cataloguing in Publication Data
A catalogue record for this book is available from the British Library

Library of Congress Cataloging-in-Publication Data
Waska, Robert T.
  The concept of analytic contact : the Kleinian approach to reaching the
hard to reach patient / Robert Waska.
        p. ; cm.
  Includes bibliographical references and index.
  ISBN 978-0-415-42291-8 (hbk.) – ISBN 978-0-415-42292-5 (pbk.) 1. Klein,
Melanie. 2. Psychoanalysis. 3. Psychotherapist and patient. 4. Analysands.
I. Title.
  [DNLM: 1. Klein, Melanie. 2. Psychoanalytic Therapy—methods.
3. Psychoanalytic Theory. WM 460.6 W319c 2007]
  RC506.W3746 2007
  616.89'17–dc22
                                                            2007006405

ISBN 978-0-415-42291-8 (hbk)
ISBN 978-0-415-42292-5 (pbk)

Contents

PART III
Drugs, mutilation, and psychic fragmentation:
is analytic contact still possible?

PART IV
Clinical reality, psychoanalysis, and the
utility of analytic contact

Acknowledgments

First, I must thank the patients I work with. While I am confident I help some of them some of the time, I always learn something about myself and about the human condition by spending time with them. I am grateful to encounter and experience a wide range of individuals who are all struggling to better their lives. It is a privilege to be a part of that journey. All case material has been disguised, altered, or censored in a manner that maintains confidentiality.

I am grateful to my wife, Elizabeth, who has helped in innumerable ways, providing helpful suggestions and doing all the things that make her a patient, understanding, and loving partner.

I want to thank the *International Forum for Psychoanalysis* for use of material in Chapters 1[1] and 2,[2] the *American Journal of Psychoanalysis* for use of material in Chapter 8,[3] *Psychoanalytic Review* for material in Chapter 9,[4] the *Bulletin of the Menninger Clinic* for material in Chapter 10,[5] *Issues in Psychoanalytic Psychology* for material in Chapter 11,[6] the *International Journal of Applied Psychoanalysis* for material in Chapter 12,[7] and the *Bulletin of the Menninger Clinic* for material in Chapter 13.[8]

Notes

1 Originally published as Waska, R. (2006) Has Analytic Contact Been Established? Refocusing Political, Organizational, and Theoretical Debates into a Clinical Issue: Part One, *International Forum of Psychoanalysis*, 15: 4, 233–43.
2 Originally published as Waska, R. (2006) Has Analytic Contact Been Established? Refocusing Political, Organizational, and Theoretical Debates into a Clinical Issue: Part Two, *International Forum of Psychoanalysis*, (2007) 16: 28–37.
3 Waska, R. (2005) Addictions and the Quest to Control the Object, *American Journal of Psychoanalysis*, 66: 1, 43–62.
4 Waska, R. (2002) Mutilation of Self and Object: the Destructive World of the Paranoid-Schizoid Patient and Their Struggle for Containment and Integration, *Psychoanalytic Review*, 89: 3, 373–98.
5 Waska, R. (2003) Fragmented Attachments: the Paranoid-Schizoid Experiences of Loss and Persecution, *Bulletin of the Menninger Clinic*, 67: 1, 50–64.

6 Waska, R. (2000) Experiences of Intrapsychic Loss within the Paranoid-Schizoid Position, *Issues in Psychoanalytic Psychology*, 22: 2, 19–33.
7 Originally published as Waska, R. (2005) Two Tales of Loss and the Search for Solution: New Thoughts on Acting Out, Sadomasochism, and Working Through, *International Journal of Applied Psychoanalysis*, 3: 1, 101–10.
8 Waska, R. (2006) Psychoanalysis or Psychoanalytic Psychotherapy: Shifting the Debate from Theoretical to Clinical with the Concept of Analytic Contact, *Bulletin of the Menninger Clinic*, 70: 2, 145–59.

Introduction

This book presents the variations and complexities of psychoanalytic patients who want help and desire change, but also turn away from the painful emotional exchange that must take place with the psychoanalyst as they face their internal conflicts. The exploration of transference, defenses, phantasies, and internal bargains regarding love and hate are all part of an interpersonal, intra-psychic, object-relational exchange that can be termed analytic contact. This is a term that describes the clinical method of investigation that makes up psychoanalytic treatment as opposed to theoretical issues or external criteria such as frequency or use of couch. There are countless ways patients avoid analytic contact and attempt to turn what is analytic into something less than analytic. Patients who consistently act out strive to shift analytic contact into something either more superficial, more intellectual, more action-orientated, more suggestive, or more of a repetitive acting out.

The chapters in this book follow a wide spectrum of cases and clinical situations where hard to reach patients are provided the best opportunity for health and healing through the establishment of analytic contact. Then, the case material follows their phantasies, defenses, and internal conflicts (the transference) which work to oppose, neutralize, or destroy analytic contact.

Chapter 1 reviews the current crisis in psychoanalysis in terms of the profession's decline, the apparent lack of patients, the ongoing debate over what constitutes psychoanalysis versus other therapies, and the lack of clinical focus in those debates. The concept of analytic contact is introduced and clinical material showcases this concept as a bridge from the circular political debates to a more meaningful examination of what truly is psycho-analytic. In addition, case material explores how patients tend to fight off the establishment of analytic contact in favor of safer, less threatening modes of relating. The author suggests that most patients fight off analytic contact, trying to shift the treatment into something less analytic. It is up to the analyst to detect this, interpret it, and notice any counter-transference collusion that may occur.

While the state of psychoanalysis as a profession is less than stellar in the eyes of the public and the profession is apt to sabotage itself with endless debates about what constitutes true analytic work, the end is not necessarily near. Chapter 1 proposes analytic contact to be the more useful focus of research and the more productive area of clinical exploration. If the decline of our field is to turn around, it will be on the clinical battlefront, not the theorizing among disagreeing groups of territorial analysts afraid of losing their political high ground. The concept of analytic contact assumes that deep exploration of intra-psychic phenomena, conflicts, and defenses, all within the realm of the transference, is the best clinical method of helping the mentally troubled individual. This genuine chance of change is best administered by a trained psychoanalyst. This simple idea is something the profession has contaminated with its often pointless arguments over frequency, analyzability, couch, and so forth. Clinical material shows that what happens in the room between analyst and patient is what best defines the true psychoanalytic treatment.

Chapter 2 continues the exploration of the clinical phenomenon of analytic contact. The author demonstrates, through case material, the essential ingredients of psychoanalysis to not be frequency or use of couch, but rather the moment-to-moment analysis of the patient's transference state and various phantasies of meaning regarding establishment of relational contact with their objects and with themselves. The nature of the treatment can be shaped, prevented, perverted, or fostered by the patient's phantasies and unconscious conflicts into something more analytic or less analytic. Interpretation needs to include the exploration of the patient's attempts to change the treatment into something that is often a replica or repetition of archaic object relations. The typical patient in psychoanalytic treatment is struggling with rather profound pathology and as such tends to create a significant standoff with the analyst when analytic contact is forming. Analytic contact is often threatening to these patients in very primitive and alarming ways that must be gradually understood and interpreted if the treatment is to survive and remain a primarily analytic journey rather than be transformed into a more supportive counseling or a pathological reenactment of conflictual phantasy states.

Extensive case material is used in Chapter 3 to illustrate the variation in clinical technique available within a Kleinian framework. The process of projective identification is examined as a central factor in the transference, and therefore important in the exploration of analytic contact. Ways of interpreting projective identification and other associated mental mechanisms are discussed. The way analytic contact becomes stabilized and enhanced or stagnant and derailed is shown to be influenced by projective identification and the manner in which the analyst effectively or ineffectively interprets its place in the therapeutic relationship.

There are similarities between what occurs in everyday life and what occurs in the psychoanalytic setting. At the same time, the analytic process seeks to take normal, expectable human discourse and shift it in the direction of a discovery process and a journey toward change. In day-to-day dialogue, people are often not honest or direct with one another. Psychoanalytic therapy seeks to be clear and curious about everything in the person's mind and within the analytic relationship. In the treatment setting, we strive to understand the nature of the unconscious phantasy world and how it dictates the theme of the transference. In addition, we search for how, when, and where to interpret the transference. This is based on the essential psychoanalytic belief that the best way to help the patient is to interpret the transference. In Chapter 4, comparisons are made of some everyday life encounters to several clinical cases. In doing so, the author shows how certain projective identification and transference dynamics lead to a corruption and a decline of analytic contact unless properly interpreted and explored.

The mind, in all of its urges and anxieties, is in constant relationship to the external world. In this context, the mind is regularly affecting the environment and this ever reshaped world is then affecting the mind. In other words, perspective↔experience, experience↔perspective. Phantasy and projective identification are the cornerstones of this reciprocal bond. It can strengthen and expand or corrupt and damage the capacities of the ego and the reality principle. Phantasy is an attempt to relationally organize and structure internal and external experiences and is the mind's primary method of struggling toward homeostasis. Chapter 5 examines the different reactions patients had to an announced office move. All patients were given four weeks' notice and told where the new location would be, literally twenty feet next door. Their reactions highlight the fragile and volatile nature of external↔internal, transference, and the always changing nature of analytic contact. Analytic contact is often derailed, complicated, or contorted by interpersonal and external factors. These situations and the subsequent emotional fallout must be interpreted, explored, and worked with if analytic contact is to be maintained or strengthened.

Most analysts encounter a wide variety of private practice patients and many of these individuals present complicated and difficult transference situations. Projective identification is often the primary vehicle in which persecutory and primitive depressive phantasies are played out in the interpersonal and intra-psychic realm of the transference. With the more regressed and defensive patient, there can be chaotic and confusing moments in which acting out by both patient and analyst is common. This fragments the foundation of analytic contact. The analyst can easily stumble within the counter-transference, falling into a mutual object-relational enactment. More than any other time, the tool of analytic interpretation is most crucial with these difficult patients. Interpretation of projective identification and the defensive manifestations of the death instinct is key to the resolution of core transference conflicts. With these hard to reach cases, the analyst must try to work in-the-moment and consistently interpret the immediate relational situation, since the flow of interaction tends to be rapid and unpredictable.

Through projective identification and a variety of transference acting-out dynamics, some analytic treatments are strongly marked by the patient's avoidance of any exploration or working through of core depressive anxieties and paranoid fears. Through counter-transference acting out, the analyst can become part of this unconscious effort to not explore the internal life and nullify analytic contact. Chapter 6 illustrates how the analyst can be supportive of the patient's external, environmental struggles, but collusive to the avoidance of more psychological, intra-psychic matters. In other words, counter-transference problems can unbalance or cancel potential analytic contact. Several cases are used to illustrate the patient's need to not only avoid ownership of unacceptable psychic experiences, but to push the analyst to be the translator, holder, and spokesperson for their unconscious conflicts. This is the result of psychological conflicts involving desires to reveal, express, and work through difficult object-relational issues that are matched by intense convictions about the danger or distaste to do so by oneself. So, the patient, via projective identification, enlists the analyst to do the undoable or the undesirable. This chapter highlights the importance of consistent interpretation of these transference efforts. Ongoing interpretation helps to maintain analytic contact and avoid counter-transference acting out of this translation role to the exclusion of analytic exploration. Various degrees of success are achieved, depending on the analyst's level of enactment and the patient's level of emotional standoff.

Chapter 7 explores patients encountered in psychoanalytic practice who demonstrate a strong transference desire for the analyst to serve as parent, so that they do not need to take responsibility for their own desires, phantasies, or thoughts. While it is common for a patient to wish for an idealized parent/analyst, these patients are skilled at pushing the analyst to be their private spokesperson or mouthpiece for all things unpleasant or unwanted in their moment-to-moment phantasy experience. Chapter 7 uses case material to further explore those patients who unconsciously wanted to be parented instead of being analyzed. This is a specific type of parenting, wherein the analyst is enlisted, often through projective identification dynamics, to own, feel, and express those things the patient would rather pass off to someone else to deal with. As already shown in previous chapters, there are multiple layers of internal struggle that emerge within these types of analytic relationships. Control, manipulation, therapeutic standoffs, sadomasochism, and conflict avoidance become central to the transference picture and as such constrict the potential for analytic contact. Counter-transference is particularly important to follow in these cases, as the analyst can become part of a strong interpersonal and intra-psychic invitation to act out, verbally and relationally, the projected conflicts of these patients. Being parented becomes the force against analytic contact in these cases and the analyst must interpret this desire in order to reestablish or maintain the analytic process.

Most patients come into psychoanalytic treatment engaged in some form of repetitive, destructive behavior that is an externalization or projection of their internal struggles. One form of this object-relational acting out is the addictions, be they to alcohol, gambling, drugs, sex, procrastinating, or other variations. The patient's experience is a "must do-can't stop" one that leaves them both relieved and desperate.

Patients come to us wanting help in refraining from these addictive patterns. Sometimes, they are attending a twelve-step program or a day treatment recovery program, but need additional assistance in remaining free from their addictive behaviors. Others seek out psychoanalytic treatment while still involved in their addiction, but wish to stop the behavior and build a more positive plan for their lives.

Chapter 8 examines the deeper object-relational issues that lie behind the addictive process and the way these issues become organized within a transference that stands in opposition to analytic contact. This transference is often colored by acting out, by sadomasochistic dynamics, by projective identification, and by phantasies of persecution and loss. Case material will be used to explore these specific problems as well as the patient's general difficulties with paranoid-schizoid and depressive functioning.

These particular patients, who resist the progressive, integrative aspects of analytic contact and who appear to not want to change, can be understood by many theoretical perspectives. Chapter 8 identifies these patients as still grappling with paranoid-schizoid turmoil, but also trying to navigate the choppy seas of the depressive position without yet being emotionally capable. Developmentally, these are patients who were forced to face the burdens of excessive depressive issues. As children, they tried to care for their objects when they, as children, really needed to be cared for. Feelings of unresolvable loss or abandonment as well as an urgency to forgive their objects when anger was more appropriate were just some of the problems created by primitive and premature experiences within the depressive realm. As a result, these individuals have problems with allowing goodness, growth, dependence, change, and reliance on the good object of the analyst. The good object ends up representing something manipulative and persecutory, rather than healthy, restoring, and soothing.

These patients often have an allegiance to a bad object, experienced as a rejecting other, which leaves them feeling angry, abandoned, and persecuted. This also results in a strong belief in a bad self. Clinically, this comes out of a strong oral demand for an all-knowing, perfect, and completely caring parent. The search for a more utopian object overshadows the more available good object with its natural mix of gratifying and frustrating traits. So, these patients cry out for idealized relationships and reject more available, realistic good objects. Authentic contact with the good, normal object is rejected, dismissed, and devalued. Therefore, establishment of analytic contact is experienced as painful or threatening. In addition, many of these patients have had a historical lack of good object experiences which would have led to a healthy counterbalance. Instead, the lack of internalized goodness has left them all the more dismissive and disbelieving of the good object and its value. This pathological dynamic fuels the addictive feelings, phantasies, and behaviors which in turn create a vicious self-destructive cycle.

Chapter 9 continues the exploration of borderline patients and psychotic patients, including those who have a history of substance abuse. The cases presented in this chapter also involve various forms of self-mutilation. Many experts, including a portion of psychoanalytic practitioners, view these patients as especially in need of "ego-supportive" interventions, directive and prescriptive measures, and behavioral and interactive procedures. The author feels that while these parameters to psychoanalytic technique are at times unavoidable, the psychoanalytic method is still the treatment of choice. This stance is based on the idea that self-destructive behaviors are the sum outcome of numerous unconscious phantasies. Several cases are offered to illustrate the use of psychoanalytic principles and the resulting analytic contact as the vehicle for reconstitution in these more primitive patients. These case examples include several derailments and failures of "proper technique" that seem to be inevitable in the work, but critically valuable to analyze with the patient.

Continuing the examination of three phases of functioning that occur in the psychoanalytic treatment of hard to reach patients, Chapter 10 explores the use of analytic contact with patients who come into treatment dealing with chronic paranoid-schizoid personality struggles. Externally, these patients' struggles manifest in self-destructive behaviors, generalized anxiety, and depression. Internally, these patients feel overwhelmed by experiences of primitive loss, persecutory guilt, and phantasies of abandonment and rejection. These phantasies and feelings are heightened by pathological projective identification dynamics. Intra-psychic tensions spill out externally through acting out, usually in ways destructive to the self and to others. A sadomasochistic pattern of relating is common. In analytic treatment, ongoing containment and constant interpretation of these patients' paranoid-schizoid dilemmas is crucial in order for analytic contact to be successful.

Eventually, some of these borderline, narcissistic, or psychotic patients are able to settle down and participate in analytic work. A second phase of treatment emerges. Continual focus on the transference as well as the external manifestations of internal phantasies reveals a destructive projective identification process in which the death instinct and the life instinct battle for control of the patient's mind. Harshly unrealistic superego demands and a combination of persecutory and depressive tensions serve to constantly destabilize and attack the ego. These superego problems bring on a defensive reaction from the death instinct, aimed at stopping the push for an idealized self. This war within the ego colors the transference and creates difficult counter-transference problems. Ultimately, the third phase of treatment with these patients reveals they are defending and retaliating against primitive phantasies of loss and persecutory guilt in a part-object, part-self world. Case material is used to explore the clinical and theoretical aspects of these difficult analytic cases.

Chapter 11 examines paranoid-schizoid patients who are yet to deal with whole-object depressive fears of harming one's object. Their paranoid-schizoid anxiety is more a combination of dread, paranoia, and fear of destroying one's object with neediness, envy, and other oral desires. In this part-self and part-object world, destruction is absolute. Ego functions and object-relational capacities such as guilt and grief are not yet fully consolidated. The part-object is not only destroyed, but equally capable of magically resurrecting itself to seek revenge. Fear of annihilation of the self and object, as well as desperate attempts at keeping each other alive, are the primary focus of this early anxiety state. These infantile fears are at the root of many uncertain and difficult treatment situations in which analytic contact is problematic.

The clinical issues of primitive guilt and paranoia are discussed in regards to more disturbed patients who experience internal fragmentation and psychic chaos. Case material includes a psychotic patient who struggled with experiences of paranoid-schizoid guilt and intense persecutory phantasies. These obstacles to full analytic contact, the working through of the transference and the object-related phantasies and conflicts, are examined. Technical approaches to working analytically in such a situation and how to maintain analytic contact in such a circumstance are illustrated.

Within the transition from paranoid-schizoid to depressive, the ego struggles with highly exaggerated and distorted phantasies of persecution, loss, and primitive guilt by resorting to crude and often self-destructive mechanisms. These include splitting, projective identification, and idealization. These fears and the defenses against them emerge as either abrupt or chronic reactions to analytic contact.

Chapter 12 examines two movies, *Secretary* and *Mostly Martha*. Using these seemingly unrelated movies, the author draws a parallel between two stories of loss, focusing primarily on two women's struggles with troubled father–daughter relations. On one hand, the case can be made for a simplistic profile of a healthy working-through process in *Mostly Martha* versus a pathological solution in *Secretary*. However, the author shows how normal mourning and aspects of paranoid-schizoid pathology can overlap, providing certain internal bargains that work adequately and serve to maintain a functioning ego. The corresponding psychoanalytic concepts of acting out, sadomasochism, and working through are reviewed.

This cinematic comparison and psychoanalytic perspective of the films' deeper message is useful in understanding the place of analytic contact in the healing process. Part of establishing analytic contact is viewing the exploration of transference, defense, phantasy, and conflict as essential to treatment, regardless of frequency, diagnosis, or use of couch. In addition, the clinical concept of analytic contact includes the important need of the analyst's acceptance in our stance with patients. There can be an optimal degree of analytic contact, but that is always changing, always fluid, because of the patient's involvement or lack thereof. Each patient's level of ego functioning during the course of treatment as well as at termination will never be fully integrated, perfect, or finished. We must accept this in order to provide our best assistance to each person. However, we do our best to be psychoanalysts, interpreting the patient's feelings and phantasies about their experience of analytic contact and their methods of retreat from it. The clinical encounter that takes place within the realm of analytic contact provides each patient with the best opportunity for psychological healing, integration, and a sense of personal balance in the world. How the patient interacts with and reacts to the experience of analytic contact is something we can try to navigate through interpretation. Ultimately, the patient's transference will determine the course of treatment and its outcome. Much like the two movies this chapter explores, the interface between a psychoanalyst practicing their craft to the best of their ability and the patient's phantasies, defenses, and transference state produces a compromise in which some new ground is established and some old ground remains.

Over the years, there have been numerous books, papers, panels, and debates regarding the differences and similarities between psychoanalysis and psychoanalytic psychotherapy. In Chapter 13, the author shifts this often circular and political argument from a theoretical tug-of-war to a clinical focus. Clinical material is used to show that frequency, diagnosis, and use of the couch are at best external enhancements to a process of analytic exploration. The case material illustrates the concept of analytic contact, in which the aim of treatment, regardless of setting, is to establish an ongoing investigation into the patient's defenses, phantasies, and internal conflicts that come out of the patient's object-relational experiences. Analytic contact is evoked, established, maintained, and protected by the consistent interpretation of transference and extra-transference experiences that occur in the treatment relationship. External issues and life circumstances cannot be avoided and must be given equal focus, but always in the pursuit of understanding their associated underlying object-relational phantasies. Clinical matters must take precedence over theoretical ideals in the struggle to establish analytic contact. The analyst consistently seeks, sometimes failing and sometimes succeeding, to understand how the patient either builds on genuine analytic contact or seeks to dismantle it.

Part I

The concept of analytic contact

Chapter 1

Defining psychoanalytic treatment

ORGANIZATIONAL ISSUES

Kernberg (1996) has explored the many ways psychoanalytic training institutes prevent, punish, and work against the creativity and individuality of candidates. He points to the abuse of power, political rigidity, pathological narcissism, competitiveness, and the general need of the institutional authority to control the candidate's contribution to the point of making sure there is no contribution, only unquestioning allegiance.

Kernberg has explored the ways psychoanalysis manages to sabotage itself within the training society atmosphere. In a similar manner, I notice the psychoanalytic community as a whole managing to work against its own identity, growth, and potential by conducting a self-destructive debate about what is analytic. Without covering the long history and the many contributions in the debate, this struggle to define what constitutes "true psychoanalysis" has been going on for decades, while the integrity and strength of the field crumbles. In many varied ways, the field of psychoanalysis seems to be in conflict about how to interact with society, with its own members, and with the patients who should be at the heart of Freud's invention rather than part of theoretical debates on analyzability. In this chapter, I will touch on these self-defeating manners of relating to the public and relating to its own professional identity and suggest an alternative focus that realigns the profession to a more therapeutic standard. Specifically, there needs to be a rededication to the clinical process that we all call psychoanalysis, rather than competitive, academic debates taking the place of our mission as clinicians helping the sick and troubled.

The almost religious battleground that the field of psychoanalysis has created over what constitutes true, authentic, proper analytic treatment can be understood as a primitive, self-destructive act. I will examine a few aspects of this problem, but mainly concentrate on why the theoretical and political battle that alienates candidates, the public at large, and the prospective patients who need the help a trained analyst can provide is very much out of touch with and overshadows what actually occurs in the clinical setting.

Most of the general public has no idea what the difference is between a counselor, a psychologist, a psychiatrist, or a psychoanalyst. What the analytic profession fails to realize is that analytic training enables the psychotherapist, from whatever background, to provide the best psychodynamic, therapeutic encounter possible to every patient that comes to them for help. The bickering, backbiting, and territorial squabbling between analysts blinds them to the value of what we have to offer. Therefore, the importance of educating the public about the unique and skillful therapy we have to provide is lost.

The dramatic posturing, the arrogant debates, and the devaluing of anything that doesn't fit the idealistic notion that rarely exists in clinical reality demeans the valuable work all psychoanalysts do and the special expertise we provide to our troubled patients. The obsessional focus on frequency and use of couch, the fear of sibling rivals in forms of counselors, medications, and managed care companies, the need to appear superior and omnipotent, and the religious worship of theoretical ideals that fly in the face of clinical data leave the psychoanalytic profession adrift.

Twenty-five years ago, Der Leeuw (1980) stated, "Anyone who is familiar with the practice of psychoanalysis and psychotherapy today can distinguish two trends: a steady decline in the number of psychoanalysts engaged in full-time psychoanalytic practice" and "a diminished demand, or social need, for psychoanalytic treatment. Young psychoanalysts complain that it is difficult to get patients." He goes on to note the reasons for this that include "the many kinds of psychotherapy that have been developed since psychoanalysis began, the high costs, the long duration of treatment, the time required daily for therapy, and the difficulty in predicting and testing the results in a reliable way" (pp. 137–8).

This lament is still with us three decades later. Many in the profession would say it has merely gotten worse.

The American Psychoanalytic Association has pondered how to generate new members especially when the average age of current members is now in the seventies. Many mental health professionals seek psychoanalytic training in some capacity, but when exploring the official routes, they often are met with off-putting arrogance and rigidity.

On the internet discussion group of the International Psychoanalytic Association, the audience's reaction to Kernberg's (1999) article on the differences between psychoanalysis, psychoanalytic psychotherapy, and supportive psychotherapy brought out many voices within the analytic community. Many of these reactions illustrate the changing tide within the profession to what has been a restrictive, rigid, and idealistic vision of psychoanalysis and an overfocus on politics, territoriality, and theory rather than the clinical outcome of psychoanalytic work with patients.

Galatariotou (2000) has summarized in his review many of these responses to Kernberg's article and the more contemporary views of what psychoanalysis really is in its modern practice. Jose Silberstein sees the debate as mostly political and points out that most patients suffer rather severe pathology and don't attend sessions with the frequency usually considered "analytic" for financial and cultural reasons. Ray Poggi clarifies that psychoanalysis and psychoanalytic psychotherapy both aim for structural change and use expressive means to do so. Poggi thinks psychotherapy is merely a modified form of psychoanalysis that is much more applicable to the usual patients whom analysts treat. Echoing the political aspect of Kernberg's debate, Poggi notes that the profession's need to find organizational clarity and alleviate professional anxieties hinders more important clinical issues. In the same article by Galatariotou, Howard Levine noted how a debate about psychoanalysis versus psychoanalytic psychotherapy seems to come up every twenty years or so because of a perceived threat by whatever the latest wave of innovative thinking brings to the theoretical and clinical stage, such as the Sullivanians, Self Psychology, Relational Analysis, and the Kleinian Movement. Leo Goldberg, in the same article, points out that the distinctions Kernberg and others make between psychoanalysis and psychoanalytic psychotherapy are artificial and break down when the clinical process is examined.

I think this is at the heart of the problem. Goldberg sees psychoanalysis as the analysis and interpretation of psychic phenomena, with couch and frequency not a defining factor. She believes psychoanalysts should serve all patients, not just the rapidly vanishing mild neurotic sector of the population. This brings us back to Freud's mission, healing the wounded psyche.

The debates over frequency of sessions, acceptable patients, and the differences between psychoanalytic psychotherapy and "true" analysis all destroy the efforts to demonstrate to the public and to our own community how we actually help people in distress.

At a conference in 2003, Otto Kernberg talked about this matter. He told the audience that he had been on a committee several decades earlier that had voted on the specific number of sessions per week which were to be deemed proper for a "true" psychoanalysis. He said he now regrets being a part of something that became so religiously deified and rigid to the point of dismissing the actual clinical work of psychoanalysis and to focusing on numbers instead. Also, he pointed out that these now unmoving frequency rules were invented only as a standard of training, not as a standard of actual practice. This has obviously been lost in the translation. Finally, he said most of the major psychoanalytic organizations today resist any major change, in frequency or any other now sacred rule, out of fear of psychoanalysis being seen as no different than any other therapeutic treatment. All of Kernberg's comments make sense from a clinical standpoint. Interestingly, they all contradict what he said in his 1999 paper on supposed differences between psychoanalysis and psychoanalytic psychotherapy. I think this is because his paper was formulated from a narrow, theoretical perspective and not within a clinical context.

I believe that one crucial step in changing all of these self-destructive debates that plague the field of psychoanalysis is to study the clinical reality of psychoanalytic work. After graduation, most certified psychoanalysts see an average of one patient four times a week for on the couch treatment. When looking at the research, some analysts simply have no patients that fit that criterion. Cherry (Cherry *et al.* 2004) has noted that the modal number of analytic cases for graduates of analytic institutes was zero and the mean number was one. Their research showed that newly graduated analysts had a mean of three patients in twice-a-week treatment, with most not using the couch. The most common form of treatment was once-a-week psychother-apy. So, out of a forty-hour work week in private practice, a well-trained psychoanalyst may spend four hours "doing analysis" by textbook criteria and the other thirty-six hours doing "something other than analysis" by that same criterion.

We analysts have put ourselves in a constrictive mindset in which we collectively feel negative and pessimistic about the future of psychoanalysis. Because of this self-inflicted inertia, the profession has blinded itself to the fact that as a result of our psychoanalytic training, we provide a quality of treatment that is unique: the analytic approach. Whether it is in the form of once-a-week couples therapy, four-times-a-week analysis on the couch, or twice-a-week individual analysis face to face, we offer a superior, sophis-ticated, time-tested psychodynamic therapy for mental conditions.

ANALYTIC CONTACT: THE CLINICAL QUEST

When psychoanalysts engage in the now predictable and tiring debates over the differences between psychoanalysis and psychoanalytic psychotherapy, there is usually a central assumption, either spoken or unspoken. This is the idea that as the doctor and authority, we decide what form of treatment is best to apply to the patient. In one sense, this seems right. We are the professional with the knowledge of what sort of treatment would be best for what sort of ailment. But, this is a view based in medical metaphor rather than a psychological perspective. This skewed view is noticeable in debates over the indications or contraindications of psychoanalysis versus psychoanalytic psychotherapy versus supportive counseling. Various authors propose that certain diagnostic categories are best dealt with by one form of therapy over another. This type of outlook is not only narrow-minded and often flavored by an authoritative stance. Most importantly, it is very removed from the clinical reality of the analytic setting. In previous writing (Waska 2005), I have stated that the bottom line for psychoanalytic theorizing should always be based on what goes on in the room with the

patient. Regardless of what we recommend or prescribe, the patient ultimately decides what form of therapy will be administered. This decision
occurs through both conscious and unconscious channels and is actualized
both interpersonally and intra-psychically. The analyst can attempt to
influence this, by means of interpretation and working through of defenses,
toward the direction of something more analytic, promoting more *analytic
contact*. Or, the analyst can be pulled by the patient's transference stance,
often with counter-transference acting-out fueling the fire, into something
less analytic and away from genuine analytic contact.

In a conscious, reality-based, or situational realm, the patient can take
our recommendation regarding the type of treatment, the frequency, the use
of couch, and so forth and simply agree or refuse. In other words, we can
offer ourselves to the patient as a skilled and trained psychoanalyst and
make whatever recommendations we want, but the patient's conscious,
verbal response will shape what the treatment is or becomes. This goes
either way. Some patients may not accept the analyst's recommendation of
supportive counseling and instead want to come in more often, bring in
dreams, make associations, ask about using the couch, and so forth. Likewise, patients who are told they would benefit from a "full" psychoanalysis
can balk, only attending once a week and refusing to use the couch.

Another factor is the external circumstances that a patient brings to the
setting. It is common enough that patients who would be suitable for a
psychoanalysis cannot partake because they don't have the funds, don't have
the time, or don't have third party coverage that will pay for it. Unless we
simply refuse to see the patient, we must find a way to still work analytically
within these difficult confines. Some would say that is impossible. However,
I think it is rare that we are operating under optimal settings and most
analytic work is done under duress of one sort or another. So, I see analytic
contact as the clinical goal, with the understanding that this may not always
be possible.

The main way the patient shapes what clinical treatment is taking place
clinically is from their internal world. The patient's intra-psychic landscape
ultimately determines the nature of the treatment. Regardless of how badly
we want to conduct a psychoanalysis with a particular patient because we
decide they would benefit from it, that patient's particular phantasies and
internal object relations may force that treatment into an interactive,
supportive counseling situation. So, I think that it is simple-minded to
argue over the differences between psychoanalysis and psychoanalytic
psychotherapy if that argument presupposes that we can exert the power to
apply whatever aid we wish to the passive entity. This theoretical mistake is
perhaps a reliance on the medical model in which the all-knowing doctor
applies the bandage of his choosing to the passive finger of his compliant
patient. In saying this I don't mean to say the patient should come up with
their own diagnosis and treatment and that somehow analysis should be a

completely mutual co-construction. This is not the case. We are the trained professional and should determine what sort of problem is before us and how to proceed. But, I am asserting that as psychoanalysts, we need to believe that the psychoanalytic approach is the best treatment and if we attempt to engage the patient in an analytic exploration, we are trying to foster a comprehensive path toward healing. However, the patient's internal world will either enhance our attempt to establish analytic contact or seek to distort or destroy it.

I will present various cases in which the transference and sometimes the counter-transference were responsible for shaping the work into either what could be termed psychoanalytic contact or something less than analytic contact. Circumstantial and external environmental factors play a significant role in some of these cases. But ultimately, it was the transference, the phantasies, and the associated defensive structure of the patient that molded the treatment into something either more analytic or less analytic.

The cases I use may seem extreme, too brief, "untraditional", or even outright failures. I make it a point to use all clinical situations I encounter in my psychoanalytic practice as illustrations in my writing and not just the "classic", well-running, successful ones that seem to fit the norm because I believe analytic contact, and the struggle to find and maintain that contact, occurs in all our cases. In previous writing (Waska 2005, 2006), I have noted how research shows that actual psychoanalytic practice in the US and internationally consists mostly of stormy, "untraditional", often brief, and often "unsuccessful" cases with patients suffering severe pathology and rarely achieving any full cure. However, if the psychoanalyst uses the psychoanalytic method to try and establish analytic contact, the same research also shows a great deal of successful work can take place which leads to significant internal and external change for the patient, with subsequent increase in ego integration and functioning.

Case 1.1: An ever so brief analytic contact

John was a middle-aged manager for a software company. He had worked there five years when the company was purchased by a larger entity. John and his company were aware they were facing a period of several months in which there would be an increased workload to bring themselves in line with the larger, new company. For John, this meant some longer hours and increased paperwork. However, when this transition began, John felt overwhelmed, anxious, and unable to sleep. He sought help for this sudden tension and we began meeting regularly, using the analytic couch.

My immediate impression was of an obsessive man wound up in a manic quest to appease and please his object. John talked rapid-fire and kept things very concrete. His goal was "to get back to normal" and "find a way to do all the extra work without feeling so overwhelmed". His way of relating to me was to use me as a path back to efficiency. I asked him, "Are you curious about why this has thrown you so much?" When I introduced more reflective questions like this, John would first respond reflectively but quickly bring it back to the more concrete.

Answering my question, he said, "I am not sure. I feel like I have to make sure to do everything and make sure I deliver it all exactly on time." I said, "So, there is a way you make yourself feel pressured and rushed, trying to get it done exactly?" He replied, "Yes, that is right. But, I think it is normal to want to put your best foot forward and, after all, they do own us now so we need to comply." I said, "Owning you sounds like you feel you're a slave and better do as you're asked or else." He said, "Oh no. That isn't true. It is just a job like any job. You have work given to you and then you need to deliver." Then, John would launch into a pressured monologue of various business matters and work issues and how he was trying to comply in a timely way.

I asked John about the way he was using me and the treatment setting. I said, "You seem to want to use our meetings as an opportunity to become a better worker. Is that maybe easier than also looking at why you feel so much pressure to deliver and please?" Here, I was aware that John's transference, object relations, and defenses were unconsciously shifting our relationship into more of a counseling situation, a rebalancing station for wayward workers, rather than an exploratory, analytic experience. I was trying to build analytic contact through my investigation and interpretations, but I was aware of being pushed away from that contact in a particular manner. In noticing how he was pushing us away from establishing analytic contact, I assumed he was used to doing this to himself as well, pushing himself away from his actual feelings and more into trying to conform to others' and his ideas about what they wanted. Of course, the danger here was that he could begin trying to comply with me and falsely engage with me in a pseudo-analytic manner. In the counter-transference, I felt lonely for the analytic journey and rushed, tense, and taken over by this work demand focus. I assumed my counter-transference was a result, at least in part, of projective identification dynamics in which I was feeling the same loneliness and pressure that John did.

My interpretation led him to say, "Well, I do try and please the company. I guess I do that quite a bit. I want to try and not disappoint anyone. This is something I have always done." I tried to take his comments a bit further by saying, "I notice you are polite and hard working with me too. Do you think you are trying to not disappoint me? In other words, are you trying to please me?" John said, "No. I just am here to sort out why I became so anxious and get myself back to normal. I am focused on figuring that out." I said, "The way you say that it is as if you are also saying, 'so I can get back to work and be a productive worker bee'." He replied, "Well, yes. I guess I see what you mean. I don't just want to be a productive worker, but at the same time I am concerned about how this big change shook me up so much and I do want to be a reliable worker. I like my job and I want to be able to support my family, so I do want to get back to the way I used to be." Here, John was spelling out his conscious goals and showing how he momentarily could engage with me about deeper issues, but then had to retreat to more reality-based matters. He was able to make momentary analytic contact, but then retreated into something less analytic. His comments illustrated the manner in which he related to me, the transference. He unconsciously tried to maintain us in a more superficial, symptom-reduction model of treatment and avoided deeper analytic relating, to me and to his own dynamics.

At one point, I realized how much John was using the phrase "parent company" in describing his new boss. So, I said, "You use the term parent company quite a bit. I wonder if you feel like a worried boy trying to please your parent?" Here, I tried to evoke a symbol or metaphor to help John consider the possibility of deeper dynamics and conflicts. In other words, I was trying to reestablish analytic contact. He said, "No. I don't feel like a child, trying to please my parents. I just want to please my boss and do the work I am asked to do." Again, I can't quite replicate it in writing, but what John actually said took up the next five to ten minutes because it was this pressured, rapid, intense talk that became more and more logical, rational, and concrete as he went. I thought that my interpretation might have brought him in touch with deeper anxieties that he now had to ward off. To do so, he had to be right, do right, and be seen as right. Again, when I asked him if he felt as worked up and tense as he sounded, he said no without much other elaboration. So, he kept us caged, close to the freedom of analytic explora- tion, but out of reach.

John's careful, delicate tasting of the deeper, more intimate aspects of his experience was rapidly followed by a restriction and a blocking out. He repeated this pattern in the fifth session, the last that was covered by insurance. When I asked what he planned to do, noting my counter- transference feeling to urge him to continue doing more analytic work just like he felt pressured to do extra work at his office, he said, "I feel much better, actually completely better. But, I think I would like to continue for one or two more sessions to make sure everything is alright. It probably isn't good to leave the minute you feel good in case there are some other things I don't see right now." So, John kept coming and was open to more exploration, but still was maintaining a goal of getting back to being a normal worker, so as to not disappoint the parent company.

After four more sessions, John told me, "I feel much more centered now. You helped me get back on track. I want to thank you. I will return if I get into the same trouble again, but right now I feel happy to be my old self again. Also, you gave me quite a bit to think about. If I need to, I will give you a call." Here, he described how he had been successful in using the treatment to return to how he usually experiences and manages life. There was no fundamental change or new perspective on himself and others, but he was glad to be back to "his old self". This is a good example of how the psychoanalyst can always utilize the psychoanalytic method, attempting to establish analytic contact. But, it is ultimately how a patient reacts to that offer that determines what type of treatment takes place.

This brief case well illustrates the gentle to-and-fro, back-and-forth that was the transference to the object of the analyst. John was interested in experiencing analytic contact in small doses, but then needed to dilute it or shift our relationship into something less than analytic and more of a repetition of phantasies and conflicts he was struggling with. Unconsciously, John tried to manage and control the anxiety he felt when working analytically by retreating from analytic contact. He was able to engage and tolerate analytic contact long enough to rebalance his usual relationship to his objects, to minimize his symptoms, and to restore himself to the psychological position he felt most comfortable and in control with.

Case 1.2: Analytic contact in couples treatment

Jack and Leslie came to me for help with the lack of helpful communications they were having around career issues. In the first session, Leslie made it clear that she thought her husband was a "coward" for not being assertive and landing a promotion. In addition, she was angry that they weren't going to take their usual summer vacation, because he had to attend a business seminar. My impression during the session was that she was a bully and he was quite passive. I guessed that his passive, non-direct mode of communication left her frustrated and angry, leading to her being more of a bully. And, her pushy, aggressive stance probably left him feeling intimidated and wanting to withdraw. I made this interpretation during the second session. But, here in this first visit, I mostly listened and tried to gain a beginning perspective on what was possibly going on in their relationship and what type of dynamics were at play. At the end of this first session, I said we would meet again to continue our investigation. Leslie became irritated and confrontational. In a condescending tone, she said, "You haven't said anything about what we should do! Don't you have any recommendations?!"

In the counter-transference, I felt assaulted, demeaned, and surprised. It was difficult to respond without throwing some of that hostility back at her. But, I did my best and said, "No, I don't have any suggestions. That is not the way this works. I need to get to know you and then together we may be able to figure out some answers. But, that will take time, probably months, not one or two sessions." My last comment about "probably months" was a leak in my hostile feelings I was trying to hold back, but overall I think I managed myself adequately.

Later, I gave the session a good deal of thought. My evaluation was that Leslie was treating me like she treats Jack, in a pushy and demanding manner. I speculated that Jack normally tries to hold back his anger and does his best to appease her, much like I did. So, I was assessing this couple in a psychoanalytic manner and thinking about the unconscious dynamics that were at play in the transference as well as within the couple's relationship to each other.

In the second visit, we started out discussing our schedule and looking at the times we could meet in the upcoming weeks. Out of the two times I had available, one didn't work at all for either one of them. The other time was fine for Jack. Indeed, he was OK with just about any time, showing himself to be very accommodating. I said this to him. He said he has noticed that about himself and "actually has feelings about things but doesn't say much in order to avoid conflicts". For Leslie, neither time was preferable and she became agitated. She said, "Therapy may not be what I need. This doesn't look like it works. I don't see any benefit." I asked her why she was so angry with me. I said, "You are unhappy with me right now. What is going on?" In other words, I engaged in analyzing the transference to promote analytic contact. Leslie challenged me about whether or not I was telling the truth about what times I had available. She said, "Why can't you see me at the time that works for me? I don't believe that is the only time you have open." I asked her why she thought I would lie to her and she said it might be that I wanted to control things. I said, "Could it be that you feel anxious or angry when you feel things are not in your control, not going your way?" She replied, "Yeah. I don't like that feeling. I know I have a quick temper when things like that happen, but I have always been that way." I said, "Since you are that way with me so fast and we only have met twice, I wonder if it is not also an issue in the marriage." Here, I went on to add the part about the bully–passive dynamic I had speculated on during the first visit. Both of them thought it was a valid point and we began exploring the various aspects of that way of their relating.

The frequency of visits, once a week, has been determined by my available time, their trouble finding childcare, their concern over finances, their combined work schedules, and no doubt some degree of resistance on both their parts to exploring the underlying issues that have created the marital tension. My sense about the case is that it is one of those that could go either way. At that point, I thought they might establish themselves in the treatment and gradually take a look at what makes each other tick as well as how they individually shape the marriage. Or, this might be one of those cases in which the treatment is aborted rather early on, based on the patients' dissatisfaction with me, often a final, devaluing comment made on the phone without a chance to ever discuss it. Or, it might be a quick and early termination based on money, scheduling, or other resource problems that all provide a convenient vehicle to not discuss negative feelings.

The point this brief vignette provides is that as a psychoanalyst, I was able to work in a psychoanalytic manner, providing this couple with the opportunity to understand and possibly master certain unconscious psychological dynamics in their lives. Should we call this psychoanalysis, psychoanalytic psychotherapy, psychodynamic counseling, or analytically informed therapy? My point is that it doesn't really matter. In fact, I think it is a symptom of group pathology that we even have that sort of debate. If psychoanalytic therapy means a procedure in which transference and defense analysis take precedence, a treatment in which self–object relating is carefully studied and interpreted, and an exploration of unconscious phantasy states is attempted, then this couple's therapy is a psychoanalytic situation in which I began to make analyst contact with each party.

Coming back to this case a few weeks later, things look both the same and a little different. During one of the couple's sessions, Leslie revealed how she was feeling angry and upset about her family and her homeless, drug-addicted sister. Crying, she said she "doesn't know what to do about her guilt and a sense of abandonment" regarding her family and sister. I suggested she might want to see me privately to talk more about those matters. She said, "OK, but only if my husband can't make it. I don't think I need to have any special treatment." I said, "You are feeling very upset over something that has bothered you for a long time. You say you don't know what to do. When I offer some help, you jump back and say you don't really need me. Maybe you feel guilty receiving help or 'special treatment' and you are used to only giving it, but then resenting how alone you end up feeling." She said, "Well, I really do feel alone. You made a good point."

The next visit, her husband couldn't make it and she came alone. She told me she was feeling better because she spoke to her family and told them that they all needed to help her sister and that she wasn't going to be the only one that acted responsible anymore. Leslie said this "freed her up and things were good now". I said, "You are acting like all that sadness and anger suddenly went away. I am sure it helped to talk to your family, but I am interested in how your mood just switches like that." She said, "I am moody. I don't know why but I always am pretty moody. Yesterday, I tried to turn the washing machine on and it didn't start. I started screaming at it and kicked it a few times. My neighbor and I are friends and she ended up calling me to ask if everything was OK because she heard me. It's that kind of thing. I get moody and I have no idea why." I said, "In that example, and in here with me, it looks like you want something a certain way and you want it NOW. If that doesn't happen you get impatient and moody." She said, "That sounds right, yeah."

I inquired, "Where do you think that kind of thing comes from?" Leslie said, "I don't know. Maybe from when I was a kid. I got picked on quite a bit. I was the fat little girl with glasses and braces. I wasn't pretty." "Maybe that experience has followed you into adulthood", I said. Leslie replied, "Well, at work I often feel picked on. I see myself as the lowest person on the ladder and that everyone probably looks down on me and thinks poorly of me. But, then I get home and all hell breaks loose!" I said, "Maybe that is your reaction to feeling picked on. You turn the tables and become the bully. I think that has happened here before. You think I am picking on you and not giving you a good schedule time to come in. Then, you get angry and bite back." She said, "I think that could be. I will think about that. So, what am I supposed to do about all this? Can't you give me tools to deal with it? I want to walk away from this today with some tools to deal with all this so I can change it. What do you suggest?" I interpreted, "Right now you are picking on me. You are saying we haven't done anything worth while and you are demanding some magic answers immediately. Let's look at this, I think it is important. You are being a bully just like you think your co-workers are and putting us down for doing nothing this session. Everything you explored, said, and felt gets thrown out as useless." She replied, "I see what you mean. I don't think what we did was useless, but I don't have anything to take with me. I want something I can use when I leave!" I said, "Again, you are discounting what you figured out today and what we worked on together. Maybe it is painful to remember and reflect on everything we looked at. Tools are something out there, something not about you. Maybe safer and easier to control. I think you have plenty to take with you today. You started to put together quite a bit about your past and your current life." She said, "OK. I will see what happens. See you next time."

This type of devaluing, combative stance is common with patients like Leslie, struggling with paranoid-schizoid (Klein 1946) experiences of self and the world. A great deal may be achieved in a session or over the course of several months, only to be discounted and attacked by the patient. This is a deliberate pushing away and canceling of the painful and intense analytic contact that was established.

Case 1.3: Exploring the avoidance of contact

Maria has been in analytic treatment for five years now. Her frequency has been on average once to twice a week, with rare periods of three times a week. The frequency has to do with her wish to control the degree of vulnerability and honesty between us as well as issues of finance and time restrictions. The other way she demonstrates her need to be in control of our relationship is by her refusal to even try using the analytic couch. Maria says, "I feel better knowing where you are." This communicates her combined worry of me being a threat, her wanting to have knowledge of "where I am at" in terms of how I feel toward her, and her wanting to keep tabs on me in a controlling, managing manner.

Maria was quite reluctant to share any feelings, positive or negative, with me for the first few years and this reluctance is still a core aspect in the analysis of her transference and phantasy life. During the first two years she focused mostly on her ongoing problems with her alcoholic boyfriend, whom she finally broke up with in the third year of treatment. Much of my work during the first two years was on interpreting her efforts to have me and her boyfriend comfort her, understand her, and rescue her without her having to do much. She took a passive stance in the transference that mirrored her home life, waiting for things to get better and hoping I would show her the way. I interpreted this as a way of controlling her object by allowing the object to control her. In other words, through the vicissitudes of projective identification, which is often the base of the patient's transference stance (Waska 2004), Maria created an internal object-relational bargain (Waska 2005) in which she phantasized her desire for a caring object who would be her spokesperson and do the dirty work of feeling, thinking, and saying the things she felt, thought, and kept silent about. The cost of this was she had no voice, no mind, and no right to feel.

So, in the transference, Maria controlled me by placing me in the role of translator and spokesperson and she got to sit back and do nothing. Also in the transference, this meant she was with a person who took over, said what would be, and generally ran the show. She controlled and forced me to be a certain way, but in doing so I became the controller and dominated her. This is exactly the problem Maria was having with her abusive, alcoholic boyfriend. And, when she would describe the latest alcohol-fueled crisis she had endured and tolerated, I was put in the position of bully by having to always say, "So, how did that make you feel", "What are you thinking about that?", "Why aren't you telling me how you feel?", and so forth. And, if I wasn't doing that, I was bullied by her silence into being spokesperson and saying things like, "You must feel afraid and angry about that." Over time, I better under-stood my counter-transference reactions and I was able to step out of this sort of psychic engagement with Maria, making deeper and more effective interpretations. Technically, this meant I was able to call Maria's attention to how she was drawing me into a dynamic in which I had to feel and speak what she avoided. Bit by bit, she acknowledged her handoff or discharge of unwanted feelings and desires onto me, leaving her safe, in control, but ultimately powerless and without her own voice. This was pretty much the type of relationship she had with her boyfriend as well.

During the third year of treatment, she had been able to take ownership of some of these states of mind because of our increased level of analytic contact. This emotional shift was enough to allow herself to speak out and take actions in her life to make things a little better. Part of this improvement was to break up with the boyfriend. During the third and fourth years, she settled into a new phase of treatment that still contained aspects of her old way of relating. Maria avoided any references or direct discussion of our relationship. By exploring this avoidance of the transference (Gill 1979), we restored the level of analytic contact and came to see that Maria tried hard to protect me and others from her feelings, especially angry ones. I interpreted that on one hand she was scared about being too aggressive and hurting me so she kept these destructive feelings to herself. But, in fact, what she was really doing was ejecting those feelings onto me and not dealing with them. Then, as a result of projective identification, she saw me and others as angry, stern, and in need of deference. The working-through process was easy to see in that once I made these interpretations, we shifted from a more paranoid, masochistic type of transference to a more depressive, loss-focused investigation. However, Maria was usually reluctant to maintain this path of exploration and easily reverted back to being quiet and withholding. This is an example of the transference-influenced ebb and flow of analytic contact. Maria would place me, via these interpersonal aspects of projective identification, in the role of bully analyst who would once again pull out what she was really feeling. Once I did, she could then pick up the ball and make some headway on her own, but not without that sadomasochistic warm-up.

So, maintaining analytic contact with Maria was really a touch-and-go process in which she avoided deeper analytic contact and through her projective identification dynamics shifted us into more of a suggestive, supportive counseling that enacted these sadomasochistic and paranoid ways of relating. She avoided analytic contact and tried to establish us in a particular set of roles based on phantasies of controlling parental objects and submissive children who waited to be told what they felt and thought. By continuously interpreting these transference modes, I was able to bring us back into a more analytic method of working, but Maria would resist taking up that effort and maintaining the analytic focus. So, analytic contact was fought against, built back up, restored, and then attacked again. However, more often, Maria was able to tolerate this intimate contact and she engaged in the psychoanalytic process without having to react so defensively.

Some examples of Maria's depressive fears emerged in the fourth year. One month I was away for a week and she was to be away another week. We scheduled an extra session on a day we usually don't meet. When that day came, she didn't show up. I tried to leave a message at her home but there was no service. A week later, I was waiting for another patient to show up and Maria came into the waiting room. I told her she was off by one week. She seemed flustered and looked at her calendar and realized what she had done. She apologized and confirmed our next regular appointment two days from then. When she came in the next time, she didn't say anything about it. But, during our conversation about her wanting more consistency in her life, I brought up that she might be referring to her non-appointment. Maria was silent for a bit and then began crying. She said, "I can't believe I messed up like that. I was scared to show my face today. I am horrified that you might think I am so insensitive or careless about your valuable time. I normally don't act like that, but in the rush of getting away that week I wrote it down backwards. But, I want you to know that I sincerely would never disrespect you that way. I hope you understand that I really mean it! Please don't hold it against me." I interpreted that Maria was feeling trapped with two intense feelings. She was convinced that she had broken the rules and committed a fundamental offense toward me, her object. Her phantasy was that she hurt me, offended me, and completely discounted my importance. This painful depressive phantasy then turned into a more paranoid one (Waska 2002) when she became convinced that I was so offended I could not possibly understand, forgive, or forget. In fact, she was very worried I would "hold it against her" and possibly retaliate somehow.

It took a few sessions and much more exploration before Maria could forgive herself and begin to trust me to care for her again.

The other example of her depressive (Klein 1935) state took place when she was having some financial trouble. One day she announced she would "have to come in less often, because I have this sudden money problem. As soon as I can clear it up, I will be able to come in like usual." First, I pointed out how matter of fact she was and there wasn't much explanation or talk about options. She said, "What kind of options would there be? I can't pay you for a while. I wish I didn't have this problem, but it was sudden and there is no way around it." I interpreted that she was controlling us in the moment by the way she had already pre-decided on how things should be between us. I went on to say that if her finances were temporarily low, we could discuss a temporary reduction in the fee. Also, I interpreted that she had prevented that possibility by pre-deciding what to do. I wondered if she did not want to see us as being able to negotiate or work out a problem together. Maria said, "There is no negotiation to make. You are a professional and you have your fee. That is that, so I didn't think of any options." I said, "You make me out to be a rigid person who wouldn't give you a break." Maria started crying, "I see you as an authority figure that I look up to and need to respect. I don't value myself at all. I don't think I deserve to disturb you and ask you for a break. I feel very insignificant in your shadow and can't imagine being worthwhile enough to ever ask you for such a favor. It seems crazy." Here, Maria again showed the terrible inner struggle she had with her objects. She felt unlovable and with an object that she didn't feel she deserved love from and that if she did, there was the threat that I would be disturbed, offended, or put out.

During the fifth year of treatment, she had completed a graduate level degree in a field that she genuinely enjoyed. This was a major accomplishment for her, both academically and emotionally. As the date of graduation came closer, she had to make final arguments for her thesis project, plans for her graduation in which her family would attend, and a long-anticipated trip to Europe as a gift to herself for completing this goal. What became very noticeable was that Maria made virtually no references to the joy, excitement, or pride she must have felt. Rather than sharing some of these positive feelings she no doubt had, Maria seemed to make a point of only sharing the stress and tension she felt about planning the graduation party, finding the research for the thesis, and the hassles of packing and planning the trip to Europe. I interpreted that she was hiding her joy from me because she felt she didn't deserve it. She agreed and added that it "makes her angry when she sees other people having a good time and talking about their excitement". I said she must think they are getting away with something she can't have or won't dare to have. Maria said, "I want you to see me as doing my job and working hard, I don't want you to think I am selfish or only after a good time.

I try really hard. That's why I get frustrated here when I don't think I am making progress. I want to change and I try!" I interpreted that she wants to control me by making sure I see her as serious, suffering, and working hard, so I don't think she is greedy or selfishly out for her own joy. But, this means she is really working hard for me, for my benefit, not hers. So, she would ultimately feel resentful, especially if I don't give her exactly the response she wants.

These moments in the treatment were certainly analytic. We were maintaining a strong contact to the transference, to her phantasies, and to the exploration rather than the acting out of her object-relational wishes and conflicts. So, while Maria continues to push the treatment to something less than analytic at times, more and more she is able to stand within the intra-psychic and relational focus of analytic contact, and be able and willing to mutually investigate the times she retreats from that or attempts to push us away from that contact.

Case 1.4: Slippery contact but contact nevertheless

Peggy was in her late twenties when she came to me for help with "a lack of direction in life". We met once a week because she hadn't been working in six months and was low on funds. At the same time, she was able to afford some art classes so I wondered about her wish to control us and the frequency in some manner. She used the analytic couch as I felt she also was too focused on our interactions and eye contact to truly turn to herself for reflection. This is an example of something I noticed but waited to interpret because we didn't have enough genetic, interpersonal, or transference history to organize it around yet. The context was not there yet to place such an interpretation in, so using the couch helped this matter until I could address it later on.

During the first few sessions, she told me about how she felt like the "outcast of her family" and how she felt isolated and "distant from any friendships". She talked about how she grew up in a family where emotion was never talked about and "everyone was on their own". Peggy had a brief marriage when she was twenty-two and it fell apart after her husband's depression "rendered him inaccessible and far from anything like a real partner". As I listened to Peggy, I noticed that everything she told me should have left me feeling sympathetic and interested, but in fact I was more bored and unsure of what my role would be with her. The more we met, the more distant she seemed and I began to realize that she was alienating me in a narcissistic manner that was on one level quite polite and demonstrative, but at a deeper level rather aloof and self-absorbed. I started to see why she felt her family and others "gave her the cold shoulder". Bit by bit, I came to see that much of what she talked about was her desire to be self-sufficient and she had come to me because that was not a complete success.

After the sixth visit, she canceled the next one by phone message with no explanation. She didn't say why and she didn't mention the following meetings already scheduled. I left several messages which were not returned. But, I did say I would expect to see her at the next time we had already agreed on. Peggy showed up for that session and announced she was terminating. She told me she was feeling much better, "finding herself more self-sufficient and able to follow her heart". She went on about feeling "solid and auto-nomous" and thanked me for helping her to "get back on the right track, her own track".

I felt Peggy's statements rang false and dismissive of our work together and her general state of mental health. I said, "I think there is something else going on. You came to me only a little while ago and wanted help because you felt lost, aimless, and depressed. It doesn't make sense that you feel so great right away. I think you are running away from something you feel in our rela-tionship, something we are beginning to look at together." Peggy paused and said, "You are telling me something that feels very right. It stops me in my tracks. I didn't expect to have this conversation. I thought you would just say goodbye but you are telling me different. No one ever says no to me like that. This is very interesting Robert. Can I call you Robert or do you want to be called Doctor Waska?" The way Peggy said this made me feel like she was suddenly trying to dominate me or have one over on me, like a narcissistic takeover, via this alleged politeness. I also thought there was some genuine yearning for union with me. Trying to incorporate my need to retain my sense of identity as well as speak to her desire for intimacy, I interpreted, "No. I want to be called Dr. Waska. But, I think that in asking to call me Robert, you are showing me your wish to be close and need me. At the same time, you are announcing your termination. So, maybe leaving me and walking out on what we started together is like an abandonment that is taking place and you also want to stay and be close. Like you feel in conflict about our relationship that way." Peggy started crying and after a while, she said, sobbing, "I listened very closely to what you said and it brought me in touch with myself as a little girl, lonely and crying. Feeling abandoned." I added, "and wanting closeness and safety". She nodded and sobbed. She went on to associate to many childhood memories of feeling ignored and pushed aside, being left lonely. I commented that she had given me a taste of that when she was going to walk out on the relationship we had only started. As the session ended, she said,

"What you have brought up today has convinced me that I need to stay, at least for a while. I want to thank you for that."

Several weeks later, we had now spent some time examining how she felt very separate and ignored as a child and how she was trying as an adult to "reclaim herself". I had pointed out that this wish was not straightforward, but full of fear, conflict, and anger.

During one of the next sessions, Peggy came in and said, "I want to bring something up and see what you think. I have felt the sessions end abruptly because you say, 'we need to stop now' and then I have to spring up and go. Could you please tell me when we have about five minutes to go?" I said, "There are a few things for us to talk about with that. First, there is a clock over there that we can both see, so you could moniter the time if you need to. But, first, tell me about feeling the sessions end abruptly." Peggy replied, "Well, I just feel like there wasn't time to say anything, I had to bounce off the couch and go. In the past, other therapists have told me that we have time to gather ourselves and tie things together." I said, "So, you feel I abruptly bounce you out the door, abandoning you without a chance to separate with some warning." "Yes, that is what it feels like", she answered. I said, "I notice you have a watch on. So, maybe you want me to take care of you and do your work for you. It is easier for me to watch the time and tell you than you having to know we are running out of time?"

Peggy said, "Oh my gosh! Yes! I keep forgetting I have a watch. I haven't worn one in almost a year. I decided I wanted the freedom of not having to feel committed to anything. I just wanted some space from that constant feeling. It has been a mixed bag because I end up late for things, as you well know." I said, "Maybe that is another example of how you want to feel independent and do things your way, but there ends up a price to pay. You wanted to be separate and free by terminating from me but we talked about how you were paying a price for that too by walking out on something you had started. By wanting to be so free, sometimes you might end up feeling alone like that little crying girl you imagined from your childhood." She said, "I think I see what you mean. By trying so hard to not be on a leash, I end up lost and scared. It's not much better. I think this stuff has a lot to do with how I was treated as a child. In my family, there wasn't ever any time for me, just me. The family just moved along and I felt swept up in it, but ignored at the same time."

For the rest of the session, Peggy associated to many different situations in her past in which she had no sense of self and was just "along for the ride". Also, she talked about trying to reach out now, as an adult, to family and friends and establish a more meaningful relationship with those she felt distant from and only moderately close.

So, Peggy is still attending her once-a-week treatment and is well into establishing analytic contact in our meetings. It is unclear if she will be able to remain committed to a long-term psychoanalytic process or if she will ever be able to attend more frequently. But, in the time we have spent together, a fruitful analytic contact has emerged. This includes all the principles of psychoanalytic work: exploration and interpretation of the defenses, the transference, phantasies, and unconscious conflicts. As shown by the material, there is a way that Peggy fights this analytic contact, because it is *contact*. She pulls for us to spend our time in long discourses about financial difficulties, complaints about career options, and grievances over old boyfriends. When I try and link these items to the transference or deeper feelings and phantasies, there is a tug of war to keep us in something less than analytic. However, when I am able to maintain my stance as a psychoanalyst she is able to meet me most of the time in the middle and we create what I am calling analytic contact. This is what best describes the type of treatment she is involved in. It is psychoanalytic because there is analytic contact which has been established and maintained, explored, gradually understood, and used as the springboard for change.

While I do think there are differences between psychoanalysis, psychoanalytic psychotherapy, and supportive counseling, I believe these differences are more often the result of the transference, counter-transference, and unresolved enactments. Rangell (1996) states, "Analytic treatability is an individual judgment, dependent on the open interface of the patient intrapsychically, the affective and cognitive attitude of the analyst with that particular patient, and the analytic-therapeutic fit between the two" (p. 159). If the analyst makes a counter-transference judgment that a patient is too sick or has a defective ego, then the analyst will begin using advice, suggestion, and directive parenting as the mode of operation and stop pursuing deeper exploration, transference interpretation, and the study of defenses. This could be an enactment of the patient's fundamental phantasies and object relations that he or she has brought into the treatment setting.

So, the way the patient unconsciously interacts with the object of the analyst, the transference, is often the defining factor in what type of treatment emerges within the context of the analytic couple. Rangell (1996) notes that:

> supportive therapy aims to restore the functioning of the patient's ego to its premorbid state before its decompensation and the development of symptoms, while analytic therapy, from analytic psychotherapy to psychoanalysis, has as its goal an improvement of ego functioning to a higher level than prior to the onset of symptoms. An acquisition of an analytic skill, or at least an acquaintanceship that leads to an interest in this, can occur to a slight degree with minimal analytic sessions or exposure, to a considerable degree with long-standing and consistent

analytic psychotherapy, and to a maximum degree of which the patient is capable, with that analyst, in a psychoanalysis.

(p. 164)

I would add that the psychoanalyst must have a deep conviction that learning, change, and growth are vital to the human condition. In that light, we work with patients to help them understand their current psychological condition and ultimately add something to their life experience, not just merely bring them back to a symptom-free state. Unlike many other medical settings in which symptom resolution is the goal, we believe that by allowing the psychic apparatus, the ego, to grow and flourish, symptom relief will follow.

So, when I first meet with a patient, I am ready to assist them in a psychoanalytic journey of discovery and healing. They may decide, consciously and unconsciously, that this is too painful, troubling, or taxing a journey to take and their resultant transference and interpersonal stance will shift the treatment into a more supportive or even anti-analytic one. Nevertheless, the analyst must stand ready to be an analyst.[1]

The principal point of this chapter is that the trained psychoanalyst should attempt to establish analytic contact with all patients. By analytic contact, I mean that the analyst should always attempt to engage the patient in a mutual exploration of the patient's unconscious phantasies, transference patterns, state or style of object relations and defenses, and internal experience of themselves in the world. The psychoanalyst uses interpretation as the principal tool, with integration of the ego and resolution of psychic conflict as the goals of the treatment. In the process of reaching these goals, it is understood that symptoms, interpersonal behaviors, and external problems will be examined and hopefully settled or at least better understood. Again, I believe the trained psychoanalyst should attempt this analytic contact with all patients in all situations.

By trying to establish analytic contact with all patients, knowing we will only be successful with some, we set the stage to best understand what our patient's psychological needs really are. How the patient interacts with us within the envelope of analytic contact is the best therapeutic assessment tool for understanding and possibly bringing about the specific change that patient is seeking. Indeed, if the patient's interpersonal and intra-psychic reaction is to push the treatment into something less than analytic, this is important information in assessing their psychological struggles and shows us in what direction our interventions and interpretations should flow.

Note

1 This is somewhat parallel to a gifted golf instructor who has told me, "I am here to teach people how to play golf. I am here to show them how to play better,

more enjoyable golf. Some people show up and only want to talk about golf but never want to learn about their golf game. Others only want to learn how to hit the ball the greatest distance, I call them the 'size matters' crowd. They don't care about the more complex aspects of the game and the parts of the game that actually result in winning scores. With all these types of people, I try and engage them in the learning of golf. But, some people turn it into something else. I can try and turn that around and sometimes it works. Other times it doesn't work and it becomes a series of meetings in which the person tells me all about what the latest golf magazine says and nothing else happens. They leave with the same lousy swing they showed up with. It's a crazy world but what can you do!"

Chapter 2

Clinical reality and the concept of analytic contact

In examining the question of what makes a treatment "analytic", it is important to not become part of the timeless political debate that is only circular and often destructive to all parties. Rangell (1996) states "the specifically analytic is the direction toward the unconscious, the intra-psychic, and the scanning for conflictual states. These are the essential ... concerns of analysis. ... The sine qua non, which stamps a procedure or an explanation of behavior as analytic is its specific focus on the intra-psychic, unconscious, and conflictual" (pp. 143–4). This definition bypasses the tiring theoretical debate of "is it psychoanalysis or is it psychotherapy" and looks at what is occurring clinically.

Rangell is someone in the analytic field who has been involved for literally fifty years in the theoretical debate over the differences between psychoanalysis and psychoanalytic psychotherapy. Yet, he stands alone as one of the few who can step out of that debate to ask the bigger question, which is "what is analytic?" I am highlighting his ideas because he looks at what is important to the clinician practicing analytic work. Ultimately, all theory must answer to the clinical setting. What happens in the room with the patient should always be forward in the mind of those who debate these matters. Yet, the actual work with patients often seems to take a backseat in these discussions. Rangell (1996) notes that supportive therapy is a process in which the analyst acts as the patient's ego and attempts to restore it to the pre-morbid state. This is in contrast, he adds, to the analytic situation in which the analyst aims to develop or expand the patient's own self-analyzing function, bringing a greater depth to the personality and its capacities. I believe the achievement or failure of these two psychoanalytic goals is often the result of certain transference states and resulting counter-transference states.

In other words, the transference shapes the character of the treatment. Specifically, the patient's particular defenses, conflicts, phantasies, and method of relating to the object can end up defining the treatment, either limiting it or allowing it to be a path of change and growth. Steiner (1996) has reviewed the aims of psychoanalytic treatment and how the theories of conflict and later of projective identification have influenced the goals of psychoanalysis. While in agreement with his ideas, I wish to expand them to include the fact that the clinical dynamics of conflict and projective identification can in themselves end up defining the nature of the treatment.

In other words, if a patient is overusing projective identification as their primary mode of relating and dealing with the object, not only will the goal of analytic treatment be the exploration and modification of that pathological method of object relations but in some cases that dynamic could corrupt the treatment, resulting in more of a supportive or pseudo-psychodynamic situation than a traditional psychoanalysis. Hopefully, the analyst would be aware of this transference side-effect and use interpretation and analytic exploration to attempt to rebalance the treatment, promoting analytic contact. However, some transference dynamics are such that either the analyst is unaware of the pathological shifts or the analyst becomes part of an enactment that fosters the pathological shift and in that sense it becomes a two-party mechanism which corrupts the analytic treatment and redefines it into something other than a psychoanalytic therapy. In some cases, the patient's unconscious efforts to strip the treatment of any analytic contact are simply too intense to prevent.

So, the patient's phantasies, transference, and defenses all work together to shape, distort, enhance, or influence the therapeutic encounter into being a particular form of therapy. Likewise, the analyst's counter-transference can create various states of acting out, collusive enactments, and role responses that further distort the treatment into something less than analytic. Rangell (1996) states that

> An acquisition of an analytic skill, or at least an acquaintanceship that leads to an interest in this, can occur to a slight degree with minimal analytic sessions or exposure, to a considerable degree with long-standing and consistent analytic psychotherapy, and to a maximum degree of which the patient is capable, with that analyst, in a psychoanalysis.
>
> (p. 164)

I think he is masterful in summarizing the differences between the potential benefits of psychoanalytic treatment, at various degrees of frequency. However, what is missing is the confounding factor of no comparison with transference, counter-transference, and mutual enactment. If the analyst is flexible to the needs of the patient but still clear about offering the opportunity for analytic encounter by using interpretation, transference work, and exploration of defenses and phantasies, then the patient has the opportunity for psychic change and psychic growth, be it face to face, once a week, or multiple visits on the couch. However, the patient's intra-psychic and interpersonal interaction with the analyst will determine what the treatment ultimately becomes. If the transference is not recognized or properly analyzed, it can shape, refine, or corrupt the treatment in terms of its analytic quality and potential. An analytic exploration can, in some instances, be enriched in its analytic intensity by the transference and accompanying phantasies, but more often than not, the transference can shrink that exploration into more of a stagnant, supportive atmosphere or even a casual friend's mode of interacting.

If I, as a trained psychoanalyst, address only my patient's current external problems and psychiatric symptoms, attempting to restore the patient to whatever pre-problem state they were in before, I am advocating the use of supportive counseling. By doing so, I would not be offering the patient the opportunity to establish analytic contact, deeper exploration, and possible internal structural change along with problem resolution.

If I attempt analytic contact, by using the analytic method, I will of course still be examining and addressing the patient's current external problems and symptoms, but within a wider, deeper, and more comprehensive context. So, in this sense I would be offering the patient two ways of achieving growth, change, and conflict resolution. The patient may accept, via their transference, phantasy, and defense response, only the external problem-solving aspects of psychoanalytic treatment. But, we would still have had the potential and the opportunity for more. If nothing else, it might give the patient a lingering taste of what they might want to try later on in their lives. In other words, I think that due to transference–counter-transference issues, many analysts give up too soon on offering, establishing, and maintaining an atmosphere of analytic contact with patients. The recommendation of supportive counseling over psychoanalytic work is therefore often a collusion with unexplored transference climates in which analytic contact is avoided, attacked, and devalued by both parties.

In the moment-to-moment transference situation, the patient is either actively engaged with or actively disengaged from the psychoanalyst on many levels. This aliveness or deadness within the total transference situation (Joseph 1985) and the interpretation or non-interpretation of it is what can define a treatment as either analytic or non-analytic. The interpretation of the current state of the transference as well as the patient's phantasy experience of the object world (rather than interpretation of the past or external matters) is critical in general (Joseph 1989), but even more so when the patient's phantasies, transference stance, and defenses have begun to shift the treatment into something less than analytic. Certainly, the analyst's own counter-transference enactment of projective identification dynamics or personal conflict can escalate this problem. Overall, the resulting loss of analytic contact often occurs within the more interpersonal realm of the analytic relationship.

Feldman (1997) has stressed the idea of how a patient's projective identification process can organize or disorganize the analyst by pushing him into a pathological reenactment of certain object-relational patterns. I would add that these projective identification attacks include attempts to disable, distort, or destroy the analytic contact between patient and analyst, shifting the treatment into more of a supportive counseling situation. This often has multiple motives including control of the object, hiding out in the non-exploratory pseudo-parenting mode of supportive friendship, manipulation of who in phantasy is the authority or parent and who is the child, and finally the wish to merely evacuate conflict rather than own it and process it. Mourning is avoided and growth or change is aborted.

The psychoanalyst must contain, translate, and interpret these psychological maneuvers in order to restore analytic contact. Otherwise, pathological enactments will create a perversion of healing rather than a genuine opportunity for psychic change.

OUR CURRENT PATIENT POPULATION

The more difficult the patient, the more these conflicts around analytic contact occur. So, because most psychoanalysts in private practice see fairly disturbed individuals and couples, it is all the more important to examine the way in which patients try and convert, manipulate, or pervert analytic contact into something else. The atmosphere in which we offer the optimal chance for help, healing, and growth is attacked. The analyst must work to preserve the analytic space so that the patient can continue to have the best opportunity for change and self-understanding.

Gifford (2005) has noted that "in the U.S., at present, there seems to be three types of analysands: candidates in training, the very rich, and those individuals poor enough to qualify for institute analyses" (p. 403). I would add that those poor enough to apply for treatment at institutes are often deemed unanalyzable or too sick for treatment due to the overly rigid criteria of supervising analysts overseeing candidates who are looking for patients to fill the required hours to graduate. Once graduated and in private practice, the new analyst is limited to a very scarce number of people who seek out analysis on their own, simply due to a complete lack of knowledge that such treatment exists, lack of funds, and a general lack of respect, trust, and confidence on the part of the public toward the field.

The current patient who enters treatment with a psychoanalyst in private practice is often a borderline in functioning (Doidge, Simon, Gillies, et al. 1994). In fact, research (Leichsenring, Biskup, Kreishe, et al. 2005) shows that today's patient usually suffers from a combination of depression, anxiety disorders, mood disorders, and several personality disorders. This is far from the healthy neurotic so often characterized as the optimal patient for a so-called classical analysis. These research results are based on rigorous definitions that view psychoanalytic therapy to be a treatment designed to work through unconscious conflicts, transference, and resistance, not necessarily defined by frequency or use of couch. In addition, the 2005 research team stated that in terms of their investigation, "psychoanalytic therapy aims at modification of personality structures and developmental growth. Uncovering, interpretive, and insight aiming techniques are applied" (p. 436).

Rather than concentrating on frequency and other more political or organizational criteria, the researchers are examining the importance of clinical technique, interpretation, and structural change. I think this is the more modern shift toward honoring the importance of analytic contact, rather than debating matters far from the moment-to-moment clinical reality of psychoanalytic practice.

From a similar viewpoint, Gabbard (2004) defines long-term psychodynamic psychotherapy as "a therapy that involves careful attention to the therapist–patient interaction, with thoughtfully timed interpretations of transference and resistance embedded in a sophisticated appreciation of the therapist's contribution to the two-person field" (p. 2). This definition embodies the exact same elements most definitions of psychoanalysis include. Gabbard's view as well as the definition used by the above-mentioned Gottingen research project (Leichsenring et al. 2005) point to a refreshing and much-needed turn about in the field. There is a move away from the polarized, political debates that don't really look at what is happening in the consulting room. Now, more attention is being paid to the clinical situation. The definition of what should constitute psychoanalysis is being examined from the operating theater instead of the boardroom.

This shift is reflected on many fronts and includes a new look at the reality of psychoanalytic practice, not just an idealistic picture of what the field wishes for. In 2003, the president of the American Psychoanalytic Association (Fisher 2004a) noted the crisis in membership and lack of organizational stability. He pointed out the need for public outreach and a bridge to other professionals to insure the meaningful future of the field. In the same newsletter issue, Fox (2004) noted that psychoanalysts spend most of their professional time doing psychoanalytic psychotherapy.

The 2005 annual conference of the American Psychoanalytic Association featured a major panel on psychotherapy and psychoanalysis and an all-day workshop on psychotherapy technique as performed by a psychoanalyst. In doing so, these public forums are being more honest about the reality of psychoanalytic practice. Attending a workshop in 2004 by an internationally famous analyst presenting four cases in psychoanalysis, I was pleasantly surprised to hear that one case was seen face to face, one case was seen two to three times a week, and two cases terminated abruptly and rather early on. This is the reality of our work and it is refreshing to see some of the analytic community being honest about it rather than trying to deny it or pass it off as a form of inferior psychotherapy.

The couch, the item most of the public thinks of when they envision analysis, is also being shown some honesty. Sulkowicz (2004) states, speaking on behalf of the American Psychoanalytic Association, that "the psychoanalytic perspective and the analytic process, not the couch, are the important tools in analysis". He adds that many analysts "use the couch at times for dynamic psychotherapy, since analysts these days spend most of their time doing dynamic psychotherapy".

ESTABLISHING AND MAINTAINING ANALYTIC CONTACT: THE CLINICAL FOCUS

I will present several cases in this chapter to show how the transference and sometimes the counter-transference were responsible for shaping the work into either what I call psychoanalytic contact or in other cases something less analytic or even more akin to supportive counseling or advice giving. Certainly circumstantial and external environmental factors played a significant role in some of these cases, but ultimately, it was the transference, the phantasies, and the associated defensive structure of the patient combined with the analytic stance of the therapist that molded the treatment into something either more analytic or less analytic.

Case 2.1: A moment of contact, a base for the future

Joe was a rookie police officer who came to see me at the suggestion of his commanding officer. He was told he seemed angry, lacking concentration, and unmotivated. In fact, Joe had received several warnings about his "attitude" and was close to facing some sort of probation or even termination. As many patients do, he arrived at my office at the end of the line, without much between him and a full-blown crisis, both emotionally and interpersonally. Joe was in his early twenties, was over six feet tall, weighed two hundred pounds, and sported several tattoos. This all made him appear somewhat menacing. During the first session, I felt unsure and wondered about my safety, which gave me some provisional insight into his boss's comments, but I quickly felt more comfortable and trusting as we met and talked. The difficult situation for me from the start was that Joe's police health coverage would provide for five visits and then Joe would need to switch to a police psychologist for any other treatment. Joe told me he would never do this as it meant admitting how "fucked up" he felt and that would mean an immediate discharge from the police department. This type of impairment to the clinical situation is fairly common in private practice, where most patients are unable to pay out of pocket and depend on some sort of insurance coverage to receive services.

Most psychoanalytic literature doesn't bother with these sorts of cases because they are deemed non-analytic due to the extreme restrictions put upon frequency, duration, and third party confidentiality. Yet, there are many psychoanalysts providing good analytic help to these desperate individuals. I saw no reason to "not be analytic" with Joe. In fact, I relied on my psycho-analytic training to do my best to help him in some finite way. Here, I think we as a profession do ourselves and our patients a great disservice. Often, we view these patients as either untreatable or only worthy of some lesser or watered down therapy in which they need to be given suggestion and advice rather than respecting their own hidden resources. As for ourselves, on one hand we see ourselves as too skilled and trained to bother with such cases and on the other hand as unable to find a way to assist these sorts of patients. Either way, we tie our hands through political, theoretical, and group short-sightedness and neglect the patients who need us in their time of despair. The concept of analytic contact is helpful when considering these types of difficult cases. Analytic contact, if established, can provide valuable psychoanalytic assistance to these patients regardless of the often less than ideal setting or circumstance.

During the first session with Joe, I found out that he was very close to his mother and distant from his father. His parents had separated when Joe was fifteen. Joe said he has missed his mother terribly ever since he moved out of her home two years ago and tries to visit whenever he can, but his job prevents him from doing so very often. He told me he was having trouble sleeping because of chronic nightmares about the dead people he encoun-tered on the job. Joe worked in an extremely violent area of the city and was called out to the scene of many shoot-outs among gangs and drug dealers. It was routine for him to be called out to a scene in which someone was dead on the ground, either from gunshot wounds to the head, from being beaten to death, or as a result of being homeless. No doubt Joe was suffering from a form of ongoing stress and trauma. But, this didn't explain the bigger picture.

Joe said he often "got into trouble" and was prone to anger outbursts. Over the course of the first and second sessions, he explained how he had a history, dating back to high school and even earlier, of getting into fights and having a "flashpoint temper". He said, "I get drunk and dare people to fuck with me. Then, I beat the shit out of them for fun. But, the next day I don't feel so good about it." Indeed, Joe had a history of minor scraps with the law dating back to his teens and he had been issued warning by the police department for several near fights he had had with fellow officers in the past year. When I asked more about his drinking, it turned out that he had been getting drunk almost every day for the last few months, "trying to not think about the dead people". Also, towards the end of the second session, Joe said he felt "very disappointed with his life" and "wished he could either die or move back in with his mom". At the end of the hour, I told Joe, "I think you had better stop drinking immediately, so that you don't get into trouble at work and so we can try and sort out what is really going on. If you can't stop on your own, we will have to deal with that, but give it a try." Here, I was clearly giving him a suggestion. While not analytic *per se*, I was asking him to stop a behavior that was getting in the way of our gaining deeper under-standing of his psychological state. No doubt his drinking was a way to temporarily cope with intense anxiety. The immediate danger surrounding his drinking demanded that I deal with it as a crisis rather than the more exploratory method a non-crisis situation would have allowed. At the same time, I was aware of how I was taking over in a parental role, which might be a clue to Joe's overall transference and the resulting projective identification and counter-transference state we were in.

At the third session, Joe told me he had stopped drinking and "could tell the difference". I noted to myself the strong mother-like transference that probably enabled him to stop so quickly.[1] Joe discussed his history of anger for a while and puzzled over why he seemed drawn to picking fights at bars. At one point, I asked him about his angry feelings as a teen and what his ideas were about it. He said he had "no clue". I asked if there was any reason he might have been so angry growing up, such as troubles at home. Joe said, "no, nothing happening there. Mom had her moods, but no problems that I can think of." I asked him what he meant by "moods". Joe went on to tell me that his mother was "someone who was very unpredictable. She could seem normal one minute and then be yelling at you and threatening to kill you the next. She had a mean right hook. She would beat the shit out of me and then the next day would be nice as pie. So, I never knew what to expect. I had to watch out and be real careful. It was like something out of the movie Alien. She could change at any point. One day we would be at the park having a great time and that night she would split my lip open. So, it was a little bit unpredictable."

I asked Joe if he thought any of those experiences might have made him angry or moody himself. He said, "You mean like her fits might have influ-enced me? I never thought of that. Could that happen?" I said yes and added that perhaps he had both come to be like his mother and finally display anger toward her through his acting out as an adult. Joe said, "Well, I guess I might be doing what she did, sort of imitating her?" Here, he was demonstrating a moment of analytic contact, in which he was reflecting on himself and developing a moment of insight. I agreed with his idea and added that he might also be showing how angry he is at mom for being a frightening, unpredictable parent now by taking it out on other people. As we talked, it turned out mom was a heavy drinker as well and had been warned several times by the police to watch her behavior in local bars. Joe was genuinely amazed and interested in my interpretation that he could be both repeating his object's method of relating to him and reacting to that unpredictable object with rage. When he left the session, he seemed filled with a new clarity and was reflecting on his life in a new way. Even with such a chaotic and challenging case, analytic contact was achieved, however brief.

During the fourth session, Joe told me that "it was amazing to think that my childhood could be affecting me now and that I might be angry with my mother treating me that way. But, I see how I could be acting just like her." Then, Joe related a story about a party he went to over the weekend and how he noticed he was getting worked up, angry, and starting a fight, "just for the chance to be mean". But, then he stopped himself and calmed down. Joe said he "had no idea why he likes to be that way" but he was happy that he stopped himself before getting into another fight. Joe had stopped drinking to please me, creating the phantasy of approving good mother object. The management of his anger was much more self-directed, a good sign of his capacity for change. We talked some more about the obviously traumatic events in his childhood, such as his trying to be close to a mother who was often dangerous and violent. I suggested that was why he felt so in need of her to this day, that he was hoping to find the "good" mother to replace his memories of the "bad" mother. Joe said, "Well, she has mellowed out over the years so it is nicer to be with her now!"

Sadly, that was the last meeting with Joe. When he failed to show up for the fifth visit, I called and found out that he had shown up to work in an angry mood and become belligerent with his superior. When asked about his attitude, he told the officer of the day that he felt "out of control and ready to hurt someone or himself". He said he was sick of his job and wanted to quit and then became verbally abusive. This escalated into a fight and he was arrested and taken to a psychiatric facility for observation. I never heard back from Joe.

Many readers might think to themselves, did the "uncovering therapy" lead to his condition becoming worse and push him into a psychiatric crisis at work? I think there are three relevant answers to that idea. First, I think Joe was already on a quick spiral to mental crisis before I met him. He was on the verge of being fired from his job, arrested, and/or put into some type of psychiatric containment before I met him and I don't think I could have either slowed that path of self-destruction down or hastened it in the four visits we had. Secondly, there is a belief some have, based on Freud's topographic model, that supportive, repressive measures should be applied to the patient's unconscious conflicts to prevent them from emerging, with the idea that if these unconscious demons emerge they will overwhelm the weak ego. In this paradigm, suppressive therapy supposedly helps the person block, deny, and repress their troubling thoughts and feelings. Fortunately, psychoanalysis has come a long way from the hundred-year-old ideas that Freud himself moved beyond. The third way of answering the question is that, perhaps on an unconscious level, Joe knew that he only had one visit left and realized he needed much more intensive treatment than he could obtain from me, so by causing his superior to hospitalize him, he sought out and found the more long-term, intensive psychological help he needed.

I have presented this short encounter with Joe to illustrate a not so infrequent type of clinical encounter in which the psychoanalyst can provide a special type of assistance no other practitioner can. By focusing on the transference, the unconscious, and the defenses, I was able to foster a brief moment of analytic contact. This was a moment in which Joe had an insight into his life and into the internal mechanisms that shaped his current struggles. While not sustaining or curative, this was the result of my being a psychoanalyst and applying the analytic approach. This momentary analytic contact may be the start of something Joe can come back to later in his life, which would hopefully lead to the beginning of a new way of experiencing life. Or, maybe it will amount to nothing. Either way, he achieved a momentary glimpse into his inner world that he had never had before. This is the gift of psychoanalytic work. I don't think I could have offered anything else that would have benefited him more and I don't think any other psychological treatment would have produced any better results, given the restrictive circumstances. This was a case that was one of the many hard to reach patients clinicians face each day. These patients can seem to be failures for both doctor and patient. However, we should not write this type of patient off before ever attempting to engage them at a level which reaches for growth, change, and insight. The psychoanalytic approach offers the individual the chance to experience something unique and wonderful: themselves.

Case 2.2: A fight against analytic contact

Tom was a fifty-year-old man who worked at an art supplies company for many years as a manager. He was bored with his job, but took great joy in visiting museums and galleries and longed to go to school to study art as a profession. He adopted passive roles in his relationships, completely excluding his own feelings or thoughts from the equation, resulting in a lifeless one-way street in which he felt inferior and boring and the other person became bored or abusive. Tom felt stuck without a meaningful career and was painfully aware of a lifelong string of failed relationships with women. He felt unable to move ahead and completely hopeless about his future.

Tom had developed a mild form of rheumatoid arthritis while at his job and took disability leave. After six months of medical treatment, he was told by several specialists that while he still had some impairment, he was in remission and ready to return to work. Tom was unable to do so from emotional inertia. He was lethargic and pessimistic about his life and "had no clue what he wanted to do or what he could do with himself". So, we began meeting and discussing this lifelong state of non-progression.

For the first two years, we only met once every other week, with Tom using the analytic couch.[2] The surface reasoning about the frequency was his finances. While his insurance covered most of each visit, he had a co-payment that he felt was a strain, since he had now not worked in over a year. It was not until the second year of treatment that Tom was able to use my interpretive investigation to look into his reluctance to attend more often. In the third year of treatment, he began attending once a week and sometimes twice a week.

I wish to highlight several aspects of Tom's analytic treatment. There was a very particular way he tried, through the transference, to keep us from having successful or meaningful analytic contact.

When using the term "analytic contact", I mean the establishment of connection and communication regarding deeper, unconscious material and the exploration and interpretation of such material. This includes the mutual examination of dreams, phantasies, conflicts, wishes, and the defenses against them. It is the collaborative acknowledgement of something more important and complex, within the therapeutic relationship, than just the external symptoms or environmental problems that are being discussed. This analytic contact can occur even when the patient is engaged in resistant, combative modes of relating.

Tom attacked his own thinking, attempted to invalidate my interpretations, and tried to censor the reality of his dependence and involvement with me just like he attacked these matters in his own life and just like he felt these had been attacked in his childhood by his mother. His lack of engagement in his own life and lack of passion, love, or desire was evident in the transference quite regularly. I want to make the case that this lack of spirit came to be an element of projective identification and transference in which he, unconsciously, tried to strip the analytic contact from our relationship and leave it to be a shallow counseling at best, or even a useless meeting of two people without any mutual focus whatsoever.

Tom grew up as an only child with a rather passive father who was always tender and loving, but "seemed only a shadow to mother's bullying ways". Tom's father died of a heart attack when Tom was thirty years old. Tom still visits his elderly mother once a week, but usually leaves feeling angry and empty. He has told me that growing up and throughout his adult life, he has felt his mother "gives him no support at having a personal identity. In fact, she seems to make an effort to ignore any evidence that a personality might exist inside of me." This idea or haunting phantasy was a reoccurring presence within the analytic atmosphere, bringing a confusion, a stalemate, and a standoff to our mutual thinking and to the emergence of any analytic contact that might help reveal or enhance Tom's inner self and sense of personality. In fact, much of my interpretive work was around exploring the way Tom seemed to have both identified with his mother's lack of personality or identity and his way of rebelling against her selfish bullying by forming his own little non-world that was separate from her and all his own.

One day, during the fourth year of his analytic treatment, Tom came late to his session by fifteen minutes. There was a multi-car accident which had shut down the highway coming to my office. Tom began to talk in a rapid and rambling way about how much time he needed to leave next time to avoid that type of traffic problem and all the possible routes he could take next time if there was a similar problem. Tom went on about these details for several minutes in a very logistical and methodical manner. I thought about how he was putting so much energy into trying to avoid a collision and wondered if he was afraid of us colliding if he exposed his personality or identity. Also, I was aware of how much energy he was putting into exploring how he was late and kept away from the session, but never mentioned that all this was about our relationship being kept apart or postponed by the traffic. In other words, he talked about the trouble on the road to his destination, but never once mentioned the destination.

So, I interpreted that he was a long way away from me by being late and now was distant from me in the way he was talking and relating, or not relating. I suggested he was contemplating other routes to take to get closer to me but he wasn't sure about how it would go. Tom replied, "I think you are right. I was talking in a way that is like a ritual. I use rituals like that to control things, to keep my distance. I want the world to go my way before I am willing to make a move." I said, "You want to be in control before you take a chance in being yourself with me or anyone else." Tom agreed and went on to say he "white-washes his mind" with me and "erases any emotional content that could come up in the session". Then he was silent. After a few minutes, I said, "So one way of gaining emotional control is to void or erase your own identity, leaving a void between us." He said, "What? I am not sure what you just said. My mind is drifting, totally blank. I heard what you said but I only registered sounds. I don't know what those words even mean!" I replied, "So, you are illustrating what you just told me. You have erased your mind to cut off the connection with me. You are now in control of your own blank world, but very alone."

Tom associated to his mother and said, "She always made me read her mind. I felt like she held back and made me figure out what she was thinking. Now, when I confront her on that and urge her to be more independent and not rely on me to be her mind reader, she collapses and gets angry." I interpreted, "You white-wash your feelings and thoughts with me so we are only left with the logistics of your everyday problems, like your physical problems and money problems. Those are important, but we are prevented from ever looking at what is deeper. I have to read your mind to discover your true feelings, thoughts, and identity. So, that relationship to your mother seems to come alive in our relationship."

Here, I was interpreting the projective identification cycle in which Tom white-washed the analytic contact we built, repeating the shallow, discon- nected relationship he had suffered with his mother. This was one of the many ways his phantasies, defenses, and transference pushed the treatment back and forth from something more analytic to something less analytic. By monitoring my counter-transference and continuously applying the psycho- analytic method to our relationship, we maintained a rocky, slow, but fruitful psychoanalytic process.

Tom cluttered his mind with logic and intellectual distractions, as well as his more forceful mental erasing that he himself had noticed. These self- destructive internal processes erode the healthy, natural benefits of splitting, in which the mind creates option A or B. Then, with the trust of the object and a sound sense of self, the ego can create more complex variations and combinations of A and B, eventually creating C. This psychic development gradually generates a spectrum of self–object experience in which to interact in the world. It is the gradual healthy transition from useful paranoid-schizoid functioning to a normal depressive state: the shift from a dyadic lens to a more oedipal way of operating in the world.

Tom, on the other hand, tried to eliminate both A and B, leaving himself with no choices. He was a non-participant in his own life as a way to both control the object and to avoid conflict with the object.

As the fifth year of analytic treatment with Tom unfolds, he seems to allow more analytic contact, shaping the treatment into something more analytic and less externally focused. There are certainly times when he reduces and constricts the treatment, through his transference and defensive modes, into something less analytic. However, overall he is more active in his own life and chooses to participate more actively and analytically with me.

An example of these dynamics occurred on a day when he entered the room, lay down on the couch, and said, "Today I want to really talk! I want to actually talk instead of just going on about something without ever really grabbing it, looking at it, and genuinely talking about it. I normally just stay at home and either do nothing or watch television. But, this weekend I saw an advertisement for a play that looked interesting, a musical. I decided to go! I didn't even hesitate! I got in the car, went down there, bought a ticket, and went in. I had a damn good time!" Tom went on to tell me about the show and how he felt about it. It was all in a genuine way that conveyed his feelings to me. He brought us to life and the session was punctuated by emotion, interest, and connection. He shared with me, I listened, and we were held together by his experiences. He went on to discuss how he prevents himself from this sort of participating in life and how sad he felt to think back to all the wasted opportunities and crumbled relationships this pattern of mental constriction had cost him. Toward the end of the session, he cried over these losses.

The next session, Tom told me he felt "back, backwards, stuck in the mud again". He felt depressed and unmotivated to do anything to better his life. There were several meetings with physicians he had canceled, a part-time job application he neglected to fill out, and a message from a friend he didn't return. I interpreted that perhaps his taste of life in the last session and making a genuine connection with me had caused him to retreat back to this state of nothingness. Tom said, "Could it be that I am more interested in dying than allowing myself to live? It is horrifying to think that could be true, but that seems to be the case." I said, "This sad and frightening realization is what we are together to face and hopefully undo. You seem to have a certain loyalty to being dead, with your mother and with me." Tom replied, "I must have been killed before I was born", and then began sobbing.

I think the concept of analytic contact provides the answer to the organizational and academic debates, largely political and theoretical, over what constitutes "true" psychoanalysis. I think the profession has stagnated and sabotaged itself through circular infighting that is mostly territorial, organizational, and self-absorbed. The concept of analytic contact brings the focus of what is psychoanalytic back to a clinical investigation.

Recent research by Jones (1993, 1997) has taken this up and examined case material from a clinical and psychoanalytic perspective rather than issues of frequency, use of couch, training certification, and so forth. In a similar mode, I have used extensive case material in this chapter to illustrate the importance of establishing analytic contact with patients, regardless of frequency, diagnosis, or external circumstances. The study of the transference is viewed as essential in the concept of analytic contact because of certain patients' unconscious desire to shift, distort, or pervert the analytic work into something less than or different from analytic exploration.

While the goal of psychoanalytic work should be analytic contact and the analysis of the attacks on that contact, the analyst must resist the desire for a particular outcome. Many of our patients terminate abruptly or discontinue treatment with modest structural change. Caper (1992) addresses these issues in great detail when he states,

> The analyst can only help the patient to think about and experience himself impartially. We may hope that when this integration occurs, good internal objects will in the end predominate over bad ones. We may reassure ourselves by recalling past experiences in which this has indeed happened. But we have no way of guaranteeing it. An analyst, as Meltzer has observed, is like a gardener, weeding and watering the garden so each plant might develop to its full potential. But he does not convert a plane tree into a fir tree or vice-versa. This sobering view of analysis highlights its limits as a therapeutic modality. I believe that these limits are real, and that we should keep them constantly in the backs of our minds. Analysis, like all real objects, is less than we would like it to be.
>
> (p. 289)

Caper goes on to say,

> If, as I have assumed, the analyst's role is simply to help the patient experience neglected aspects of himself and his objects as fully and accurately as possible, then the analyst must face the fact that this does not in itself provide the patient with a corrective emotional experience, mitigate the severity of his superego, or guide him along the correct developmental path. The analyst's acknowledgement of this limitation – which is equivalent to acknowledging that he can help the patient to grow, but he cannot "grow" him – places a psychological burden on the analyst that is painful and frightening, but that he must take up over and over again at each step in the analysis, since it is part of a state of mind that the analyst must have to do analysis. It requires him to recognize that his ever-resurgent belief in his healing powers is a

countertransference reaction that defends him against his fear that destructiveness – either his own or the patient's – will predominate over loving impulses if the two are brought together and simply left to their own devices. The analyst's belief in these healing powers, in conjunction with the patient's transference fantasies of an object that will cure him omnipotently, forms a folie à deux between patient and analyst, a joint delusion that is a vehicle of "cure" in many types of psychotherapy, but is antithetical to the integrative goal of psychoanalysis.

(pp. 289–90)

I would add that all we can really do is try our best to establish analytic contact with patients and see what happens. Inevitably, the patient will try to break off this contact out of transference-based phantasies involving hurt or hurtful objects.

The ways a patient tries to move the treatment away from analytic contact to something less object-related, less relational, less affect-focused, and less self-reflective are numerous. Primitive fears of persecutory guilt, retaliatory objects, and phantasies of loss (Waska 2002) are prominent in many patients. Defensive stances that prevent, erase, or attack analytic contact include psychic retreats (Steiner 1993), "no entry defenses" (Williams 1997) in which the object is pushed away and avoided, the defensive aspects of the death instinct, greed, paranoid phantasies, and internal self-destructive bargains are all part of the clinical picture with patients who experience change as dangerous (Waska 2006). The conflicts around mourning and loss are frequently defended against by a retreat into depressive states (Steiner 2005). Rey (1994) has noted that any successful contact within the psycho-analytic situation involves not only psychic change and understanding, but a corresponding sense of loss, neglect, and disappointment which is avoided and defended against. I would add that this sense of loss and neglect is always present if the transference and phantasies are being explored.

In other words, every moment analytic contact is occurring is a moment of dread and despair for the patient, as he or she struggles with change and a new way of being with their objects. Therefore, successful analytic work always involves the patient's moment-to-moment retreat, attack, hiding, and attempt to shift the treatment into something less than analytic, some-thing less painful. Thus, the analyst must include in his or her interpreta-tions an understanding of this retreat and attack, while attempting to steer the treatment back to something more analytic, something that contains more patient–patient and patient–analyst contact. The support that we should give our patients is a subtle and sometimes not so subtle belief that we will help them survive this painful contact and stay with them till they get to the other side of this frightening process of change.

Harris (2005) notes that much of today's understanding of the inter-subjective process that takes place in the analytic relationship and the powerful effects that process has on the treatment is rooted in the past and present Kleinian tradition. The Kleinian approach to the careful examination of the pervasive, total transference situation creates a special method of listening to the emerging, developing relationship. Tuckett (2005) notes that the three lines of great impact Melanie Klein and the Kleinian tradition have had on psychoanalysis are the concept of psychic reality and conflict, the idea that the patient's past and their core conflicts can be best understood and resolved through analysis of the present relationship to the analyst, and the importance of always linking theory to clinical evidence. Analytic contact is the comprehensive, clinical amalgam of these three principles.

Notes

1 I chose to wait till later to bring that up. If I never brought it up, I think that would push the treatment more into the realm of a supportive/manipulative counseling. Transference elements are best brought to light in an analyst treatment, but timing is important in order to adequately address them.
2 My decision to ask him to use the couch was based on my general approach with all patients. I agree with Gibeault (2000) when he notes that the couch is the most conducive element for more intensive regression or what I think is better called a slowing down of the external and a turning toward the internal. The couch simply helps many patients catch a glimpse of their internal state a little quicker or easier than when sitting up. I tend to assess patients based on who I think will feel too disconnected from their need to control or own their object and thereby become too anxious or paranoid. I would estimate that three-quarters of all my patients use the couch and seem to benefit from it, regardless of how often they attend.

Chapter 3

The Kleinian interpretation: bringing theory into a clinical stance

Regarding the criteria for termination of an analysis, Klein (1950) wrote,

> have persecutory and depressive anxieties been sufficiently reduced ...
> has the patient's relation to the external world been sufficiently
> strengthened to enable him to deal satisfactorily with the situation of
> mourning arising at this point? By analyzing as fully as possible both
> the negative and positive transference, persecutory and depressive
> anxieties are diminished and the patient becomes increasingly able to
> synthesize the contrasting aspects of the primary objects, and the
> feelings towards them, thus establishing a more realistic and secure
> attitude to the internal and the external world. If these processes have
> been sufficiently experienced in the transference situation both the
> idealization of the analyst and the feelings of being persecuted by him
> are diminished.
>
> (p. 204)

In this rich paragraph, she outlines not only her criteria for termination,
but the essential elements of Kleinian practice as well. She places emphasis
on the exploration of paranoid and depressive anxieties, the internal and
external world, and the various manifestations of the life and death
instincts.

Rather than assessing whether a therapist is a "Freudian", "Kleinian",
or "Kohutian", and rather than assessing whether they are practicing
psychoanalysis or psychotherapy, I ask myself how that therapist clinically
applies the principles of Freud, Klein, or Kohut, and, in applying these
principles, whether they have been able to establish analytic contact with
their patient.

In my clinical work, I apply Melanie Klein's criteria in the effort to create
analytic contact in the therapeutic setting. In making use of Kleinian
theory, I place an emphasis on the patient's phantasy life, their depressive
and paranoid anxieties that seem most current in the session, the patient's
defensive posture, and the place of splitting and projective identification in

their internal and interpersonal life. I also focus on issues of separation, loss, envy, and the desire for knowledge and power.

Some ratio of love and aggression always colors these areas. Riviere (1991) elaborates on this in writing,

> Each of us tries to deal with and dispose of the destructive forces in himself, venting, diverting and fusing them in such a way as to obtain the maximum security he can in life – and pleasures to boot – an aim which we achieve by infinitely various, subtle and complicated adaptations. The different outcome in each individual is in the main the product of two varying factors: the strength of the love and hate tendencies ... and the influence of environment throughout life.
>
> (p. 169)

These three factors (love, hate, and the environment) are the ever-present ingredients in every transference. Therefore, these three elements and how they are technically handled will always shape the nature of the treatment and the degree of analytic contact that results.

Generally, I work at understanding the nature of the patient's phantasies and how projective identification is being used as a psychological vehicle. This includes interpreting projective identification as a defense, a creative, loving, or adaptive act, a communication, a method of reparation, or an aggressive act. Also, I have noticed times when patients make extensive use of projective identification to deal with loss. As Riviere (1991) has said, the individual struggles with ways to manage the destructive forces within themselves, defined by either paranoid-schizoid or depressive anxieties. The outcomes of these struggles are the uniquely individual phantasies and patterns of defense that we encounter in the clinical situation. Projective identification is a bedrock layer of these coping mechanisms and as such is often at the forefront of transference efforts to destabilize analytic contact. Therefore, the careful analysis of projective identification and its associated dynamics (such as splitting, introjection, and manic postures) is crucial to each analytic treatment. Riviere (1991) eloquently writes of this core mental operation. She states,

> it is probable that our need in babyhood to project our dangerous painful states of anger out of us into someone else and identify someone else with them, and ourselves only with our good states, is one of the main stimuli towards recognizing other people's existence at all. In other words, our whole interest in the outer world and other people is ultimately founded on our need of them; and we need them for two purposes. One is the obvious one of getting satisfactions from them, both for our self preservative and pleasure needs. The other purpose for

which we need them is to hate them, so that we may expel and discharge our own badness, with its dangers, out of ourselves on to them.

(p. 197)

Our patients constantly struggle with expressing or defending these ways of needing us to be their important internal and external objects.

In moment-to-moment analytic work, the analyst may need to take different stances in dealing therapeutically with repetitious projective identification and splitting mechanisms, especially in regards to maintaining analytic contact. Sometimes, clinical judgment requires that I contain the projection and interpret silently to myself. Most often, I contain the projections for some period, attempt to translate them to myself, and then interpret them. This sequence is only possible by noticing my counter-transference and the patient's verbal and non-verbal associations to the moment-to-moment interaction in our relationship. If possible, I interpret the patient's anxiety and their defenses against it as it relates to the transference. What is the patient wanting from me or not wanting from me and how are they showing me what are some of the questions I try to explore, first with myself and secondly with the patient. Given the confusing, rapid, and multiple layers of unconscious interaction that take place many times over in each clinical visit, these are all ideals we never obtain. However, they are helpful guidelines to strive for and they form a useful map to follow in the course of an analytic encounter.

Listening closely to a patient's level of depressive or paranoid tension provides a gauge of how and when they may need an interpretation to help work through their current mental problems. In making interpretations, I try to "pick my battles". Freud used many military metaphors to explain the common clinical experience one has with patients who feel and react as though they are in a perilous battle with you for power, justice, and freedom. In any given hour, a patient brings up so much material, connected to so many layers of different wishes and fears, that the analyst has to sort out what they will and will not address in that particular moment. The patient's multiple phantasies have common threads, but some are too disguised, unconscious, or defended to bring attention to in the moment.

Timing and evaluation of affect can be more important in determining when to interpret than the idea of simply locating and interpreting a resistance. The former is more experience near, and the latter is more the idea of pushing aside a block, to the "truth", in line with Freud's original topographic model of resistance analysis.

A psychotic patient told me how she felt persecuted and unloved by men. She said men who were 5'5 tall disgusted her. Contemplating the fact that I am 5'5, I chose to not make the obvious comment as she would have experienced it as a defensive attack. However, when she asked if I thought somebody at work had deliberately been mean to her, I said "I don't know." She said that I was against her and dangerous. I replied, "You worry that there are evil, dangerous parts of yourself. Right now you are putting those into me and that makes me look pretty scary. That makes you feel like you had better attack me first or run away for safety." She relaxed and talked about how she felt she was full of unknown feelings and scary thoughts. By analyzing this paranoid transference phantasy, I helped maintain and enrich the atmosphere of analytic contact.

When analyzing this patient's defenses, resistance, and transference, I tried to not rush in and make what looked like easy or obvious interpretations. I waited for a moment that seemed to be more of an interpersonal and intra-psychic match between us. This was the result of my becoming a part of the patient's phantasy, through projective identification. I was a willing participant, which naturally meant that I was temporarily less objective and prone to acting out with the patient. However, it also meant I was more apt to understand the patient's core affect and the specific details of their phantasies. This approach results in interpretations that take longer to get to, but are usually more accurate. I believe this is in line with Strachy's (1937) recommendation to interpret the transference as it occurs, so it is current and alive. He writes,

> the prime essential of a transference interpretation in my view is that the feeling or impulse interpreted should not merely be concerned with the analyst but that it should be in activity at the moment at which it is interpreted ... it will only be possible to understand the results of those procedures ... if we pay sufficient attention to the mechanisms of introjection and projection.
>
> (p. 141)

Many patients, whether paranoid-schizoid or depressive, utilize projective identification as a mainstay in their moment-to-moment coping. With some of these individuals, projective identification dynamics predominate their relationships and define the transference. Therefore, the analysis of projective identification is often the cornerstone in a treatment and makes the difference in stabilizing an otherwise precarious analytic contact.

Projective identification influences both patient and analyst to the point that regular acting out by both parties is unavoidable. Rather than trying to deny or prevent such excursions, it seems more helpful to anticipate them and understand their intrapsychic function. Accordingly, the analyst's interpretations of the patient's projective identification mechanisms can provide a working through for both patient and analyst; in other words, interpretations for both parties.

Many factors go into deciding how to interpret projective identification. Carefully examining how the patient is using the analyst, and how the patient is asking the analyst to use him, provide the analyst with clues that shape the interpretative process. I try to notice what roles the patient's phantasies and actions put us in. I ask myself questions like who is giving or taking what from whom, who is controlling what, what is omitted, and what types of conflicts are being set up. I imagine the patient as creating a play, with us as the principal characters. He will introduce external characters who will offer disguise and diversion from the principal players. This internal dialogue is helpful in balancing and re-stabilizing myself during regressive projective identification moments and gives me direction in how to interpret the emerging clinical material.

At times, a patient may be so paranoid or confused by excessive splitting and projective identification that interpretation provides a way of preventing further disintegration of the ego rather than immediately resolving the intense reliance on splitting and projective identification. With these types of patients, it is important that the interpretation be given within the current context of their paranoid delusions. A generalized interpretation that focuses on reality testing will escalate their anxieties and push them to erect even greater defenses. Therefore, it is better to immerse oneself into the patient's phantasy and interpret the anxieties within that phantasy. This process of just "sitting with it and in it" may take days, weeks, or sometimes months. Only later, may the patient be able to tolerate stepping back and taking more of a "big picture" look at themselves.

This process usually comes up with patients in the grips of severe paranoid or narcissistic delusions. If given a reality check, they feel the analyst is trying to force ideas into them, shame them, or dominate them in some other way. If the patient is struggling with more depressive anxieties, a reality check is less threatening because there is room for two opinions and two objects. The depressive patient may take it as an invitation for competition, but not a potential annihilation. In the paranoid-schizoid world, there is less differentiation between ego and object, which means the patient lives in a "me or them" world. A reality check may mean they have to give up their identity and submit to the will of the analyst or die. Ambivalence, reflection, and symbolism are not yet fully functioning aspects of the ego structure.

During periods of closeness to unconscious phantasy material, the analyst can experience difficulties. Technically, the analyst tries to avoid a premature interpretation of the patient's projection and attempts to contain the projections of unwanted hostility or overwhelming desire. This can trigger intense counter-transference feelings, manifesting in wanting to clarify details and confront the patient with reality. The analyst can act out by lecturing and educating the patient out of frustration. This is really an aggressive act of spitting back the unwanted mental garbage the patient has put into the analyst. At these times, it is often better to contain this emotional garbage until both analyst and patient are more balanced. When the analyst is feeling less reactive and not as overwhelmed with persecutory or depressive anxieties, then these intra-psychic and interpersonal dynamics can be discussed. Containing the patient's mental discharges is a situation of psychic timing. When and how to reintroduce the patient's projections is the essence of the interpretive art.

When can both parties handle the open struggle of dealing with raw, painful, hateful, and scary feelings and thoughts without becoming over-whelmed? The analyst regularly poses this question to himself to determine when and how to intervene.

A patient's phantasies, anxieties, and defenses often are related to issues with separation, loss, or attachment. These conflicts may remain at a more primitive, raw level or be disguised by either defensive or healthy matura-tion, showing up as the urge to compete and a fear of defeat. Control and power are complex conflicts that originate from more basic issues of autonomy and intimacy. The ego often employs projective identification to cope with both levels of psychic struggle.

Case material 3.1

Dan grew up in a home where he felt oppressed by both parents. He felt his father controlled the family with his angry, drunken moods and selfish, bratty behavior. Dan recalls his mother as always putting him into situations where she wanted favors, but she would find fault when he tried to please her. Life felt unfair to Dan and he thought that somehow he was cursed with bad luck. Everyone else had it better and he just waited around "for the other shoe to drop".

The more established Dan became in his psychoanalytic treatment, the more he expressed rage at how good others seemed to have it and at how hard he had it. He ignored my interpretations as meaningless bother or felt I was making intrusive assaults into his mind. He insisted that if he were to remain in treatment, I would have to "mind my business and stop making him furious". If I tried to be curious about how life always dealt him a bad hand, Dan felt I was blaming him for all of his pain.

After the first year or two, it became clear that Dan used projective identification in two ways. He would deposit his oral rage and angry desires for a perfect breast into the analyst and then feel picked on and manipulated. He would be the helpless little boy who was enslaved to a nasty, demanding master. When he felt this way, he would fight back and tell me how mean I was.

Other times, he would push very self-centered aspects of himself into his analyst. Then, he felt that no matter how hard he tried, he went unnoticed and forgotten. I was self-centered and could not be bothered with him. In other words, Dan felt he would lose me and his other objects because of the thin, fragile, and conditional bond we had. These two ways of using projective identification were internal methods of dealing with his excessive aggression and intense fears of loss. Depending on what conflict he was experiencing, Dan would project, introject, and identify with various aspects of these internal predicaments.

Technically, I took two different tracks based on his reactions, his anxiety, and the way he was uncertain about establishing analytic contact. When Dan seemed to be highly agitated and obsessively stuck in making sure I suffered the same way he suffered, I remained silent. I quietly interpreted to myself what was taking place and let him simmer down. After attacking me for a while, he often apologized and reflected on the concrete reasons he was feeling so stressed that day. I would then begin to suggest deeper motivations for his feelings about me. At other times when Dan seemed mostly over-whelmed with paranoid anxieties about loss and destruction, I would gently but persistently interpret the projective identification processes I have described above. This would alleviate his tension and sometimes led to associations about his fears and his rage.

Rosenfeld (1987) writes,

> the principal therapeutic function of a psychoanalyst is to help the patient put into words and conscious thoughts the unconscious feelings and wishful phantasies which preoccupy him. In this way the patient's repetitions of early object relations and the omnipotent defenses built up in the infantile period can be modified. Gradually, the patient can tolerate more feelings (and particularly the anxiety they provoke), recognize conflicts, and become able to think about them. As this becomes more possible the need for gross distortion of inner and outer functioning ... is reduced ... the primary means by which the analyst achieves these aims is by precise verbal interpretations of the patient's phantasies of the transference relationship, focusing on the most pressing unconscious anxiety experienced by the patient at any time.
>
> (p. 31)

Rosenfeld feels the patient's anxiety is the best lead to follow in making the interpretation. In addition, close examination of a patient's internal struggle with their objects determines how and when to intervene and interpret. I find it useful to think of the three areas in which a patient can concentrate their anxiety in any given moment. In their unconscious phantasies, patients can be focusing on either themselves, on the object, or on the relationship between self and object. Optimally, an interpretation will concentrate on all three angles, but the patient may be defensively stuck on one or the other. Therefore, a careful understanding of the transference, the patient's current anxieties, and the nature of projective identification processes all help to show where the analyst can help the most at that moment. One way to achieve this clinical assessment is to keep a constant watch on the condition of the analytic contact and what the patient seems to be trying to do with that contact at any given moment.

After making these types of clinical judgment about the patient's leading anxiety and the nature of their current phantasies, the analyst may feel it best to work with the patient's feelings and thoughts about themselves and their inner experience as opposed to the way they view their objects and their relationship to those objects. This is a similar idea to that of Ruth Riesenberg-Malcolm (1995). She writes of locating the interpretation according to the patient being in either the paranoid-schizoid or depressive position. The analyst must ascertain if the affect and phantasy are felt as a product of the ego and its conflicts or as generated from the object. I am looking at these issues as well as how the ego views the total relationship between the self and the object.

If I decide the patient's leading anxieties and phantasies are in the paranoid-schizoid position and they are worried about what is occurring within themselves, I might point out the patient's projective identification phantasy and feelings as originating from within. In doing so, I will make a comment in the direction of "you have projected your feelings or thoughts into me". This underscores their fears and desires while leaving their objects and their relationship to objects as a secondary focus. Depending on the patient and the current condition of analytic contact, I will use language such as "You passed on your feelings to me", "You put your thoughts onto me", or "You're wanting me to have your feelings". I have likened it to "passing me the hot potato" and I have said, "You want to show me your feelings so I know what you are going through." These are ways of matching the same interpretative message to different patients who think of things in different ways and a way to work with the immediate level of analytic contact available.

Other times, I decide, based on the nature of the projective identification dynamics occurring in the hour, to focus more on the patient's anxiety about their objects. Therefore, I will comment on the patient's phantasy of how their projections are shaping the object. I might say, "You see me as pretty weak right now", "You worry I am crushed by obligation", "I seem pretty powerful and sexy to you right now", or "You are not sure if I am up to the task". These are ways of showing the patient their view of the object without making them immediately aware of their projection. Analytic contact is intensely affected by the patient's current projective identification efforts.

Finally, I often interpret the patient's intra-psychic view of our relationship. This puts words to the patient's unconscious phantasy of themselves with an internal object in some type of soothing or uncomfortable connection. Often, it is a conflictual relationship that involves loving and aggressive feelings in opposition to each other. In other words, I verbally translate the current profile of our analytic contact.

I may say, "You view us as in quite a fight right now", "You don't picture us able to negotiate the problem", "You want us to be together forever", or "You notice a difference between our opinions and that worries you". The same type of interpretation can be given by commenting on the type of relation the patient believes we are in. I might say, "You are worried one of us is going to get dominated and the other will be cruel", or "You are hoping I will be the brave mother who rescues you, the little lost boy".

In explicating the patient's unconscious phantasy, the current state of anxiety must be addressed. Therefore, the ways of interpreting I have just outlined are usually best combined with a comment about the fears, worries, and excitement that go with the phantasy. Therefore, with one patient I said, "You picture me as a wise father who will care for you as a little boy. At first that feels so wonderful, but later you worry that I will push you around and not let you grow up. Perhaps that is why you seem to want to fight with me right now."

Case material 3.2

Dreams can contain projective identification elements that occur as the result of previous analytic hours. One patient's main struggle was with dependence and independence. She wanted to be close to me and feel cozy, but was mortified that she wasn't perfectly independent and self-sufficient. She would often tell me how it was ridiculous to imagine that there could be any feelings between a therapist and patient and if there were it would be "unhealthy and suspicious". Therefore, she used denial, splitting, and projective identification to ward off any degree of desire or neediness she felt toward me.

She told me a dream in which she was trying desperately to find my office to make it to her appointment. Somehow, she could not find the building. She became very angry and thought about giving up and charging me for her wasted time. This was her projection of anxiety and superego pressures into me. Also, she had shifted it from her neediness to my neediness. Then she found the office. Once she entered my office, thirty minutes late for her hour, I broke down sobbing. I told her I was so worried about her that I felt like dying. I was so relieved that she was OK and had made it to see me that I couldn't stop crying. By the end of the dream, she had lodged all of her desire and fear about losing her object into me. In the dream, I was the one who suffered the loss.

This patient was usually receptive to hearing my interpretations about her image of herself and her thoughts about her objects. However, she would routinely deny any reference to the idea of us in relationship.

Therefore, I interpreted that when she thought of being close to me it was difficult because it brought on feelings of being pressured and rushed as well as worries about burdening me. I said it was hard for her to imagine leaning on me when I looked so fragile and easily frightened. She responded by saying she worried about how much I could endure and how much of a parasite she might be. This shows that while she was more and more able to think about the link she wished for between us, it left her incredibly uneasy. She tried to keep us apart by focusing mostly on herself and then on me, but hardly ever on us together because of the scary consequences of making that link. This kept me safe and her free from guilt.

Case material 3.3

One psychotic patient, Hillary, told me a dream in which a fat peasant girl gave birth to Hillary's baby. Somehow, the baby needed to grow in and be born from someone besides herself. When my patient tried to feed her baby, poisonous pus came out of her breasts. The peasant woman turned into a wooden stick man who controlled my patient by spinning her around in a dance that kept her under his power. I interpreted that she used splitting to project the good baby part of herself into the peasant woman/analyst for safety. She was left alone to suffer with the poisonous milk she had inside her. She had become envious of the peasant girl and spoiled her with her feelings of envy. This created a persecutory attack by a controlling stick man/analyst. My patient felt these ideas were accurate and added that she was unable to feed herself or sustain herself, leading to a feeling of internal starvation. She said she was then a starving little baby who was poisoned and dying. Later in the hour, she told me of a friend who had told her what the dream might mean. Then my patient asked me for my interpretation. I said that she had taken in my earlier interpretation but it somehow withered away and did not fill her up anymore. She wanted me to feed her again but she may be feeling envious of my supply of food and that could turn me back into the manipulating stick man. Then, she felt less tense and was able to tell me more about her fears of being controlled by those she felt close to.

Case material 3.4

Another patient had been spending several weeks detailing the ways I was judging, controlling, and "trespassing" into his mind with interpretations. He would try to shut me out of his mind to escape and retaliate. I felt like a door was being slammed in my face during these moments. This had escalated to the point of his talking about terminating. The excessive projective identification processes he used left him feeling overwhelmed by persecutory part-objects. Feeling trapped, he began thinking of how to flee his tormentors. Obviously, analytic contact was fragile and difficult to maintain.

In this particular hour, he talked about feeling disrespected and controlled by his brother-in-law and betrayed and controlled by his own body. He has asthma. Then, he talked about how his antidepressant medications were bad because of the side-effects "they" gave him. He told me, at length, about the wonders of herbal medicines and the miracles of organic healing. Feeling irritated by his soapbox speech, I found myself arguing with him about how herbs are chemicals too. I noticed my tense mood and managed to lay off. He went on to tell me how his boss is incompetent and lazy and that he feels controlled by him. My patient said he could do a much better job.

I listened quietly. I studied the way my emotions had bristled and how I had acted out with him. With ideas gained by stepping back from our interactions, I was able to interpret that he projected controlling feeling into his boss, his analyst, his brother-in-law, and his medication. He tries to escape this persecution by finding fault and then becoming the controller. He turns the tables. Essentially, I told him he was so anxious about being controlled that he had to wage battle with me ahead of time, just in case. He was able to take this in and began to talk a bit about how disorganized life feels. He told me how he feels he must constantly watch for problems and that he knows he is controlling but he sees no other way to cope. This created an open space to begin talking more about these anxieties.

In this example, I had noticed myself acting out the role of an attacking and judging foe. Once I was able to manage my own anxieties, I could see how he had deposited those tensions into me and his other objects. His provocative tone and critical stance invited me to debate back with him. Eventually, he was able to listen to my interpretation when I was more analytically balanced. This, in turn, allowed him to enter into a state of increased analytic contact.

Case material 3.5

In my work with another patient, Charles, I learned over the years that it was best to wait and see what form the transference took in any particular moment. Otherwise, Charles quickly ushered me into various forms of acting out with him. At the beginning of this hour, he had been looking at my atlas in the waiting room. He walked into my office and asked to borrow "the book on the world". I asked for associations. He said he wished he could escape to those far-off wonderful places. Charles said he wanted to read up on these places but didn't have time to look at the book in my waiting room so he wondered if he could take it home with him. At this point I thought of saying something about how he wished to bring a part or aspect of me home with him and escape from another more dreaded part of me. I wasn't sure if this was totally accurate or if it would cause Charles to regress into the paranoid silence he so often sank into. I decided to just listen.

Charles went on to say how he felt rushed by life. "There is no time for me, I feel pushed around by everyone and everything", he snorted. Then, he started to tell me about how he was reading the story of *Moby Dick* for a class and how the character wanted to explore the world. After a while, he switched to telling me of how dominated he felt in class. There were several students who talked all the time and didn't seem to ever give him a chance. At that point, I felt like Charles was talking in such a distant way that I did not have a chance to communicate with him. I also thought of the themes in *Moby Dick*. Charles went on to tell me about how dominating and insensitive his mother had been recently. He said, "She punches me with words, never giving me respect or caring about my rights!"

I began to think of how Charles probably wanted to be close to me and take me home to study, but he wanted to do it on his own terms. I wouldn't have a say in how he becomes intimate with me. Then, I thought about the bloody struggles between Ahab and the great whale and how we might be pushing and shoving each other in some sort of struggle. Then, I reflected on Charles' relationship to his mother and his relationship to me. Finally, I continued to just listen.

After sorting through all these thoughts, I interpreted that he felt per-secuted by a dominating object who feels superior, while he feels upset and angry. He feels there is no way of showing his own true identity in the face of such a force. Here I decided to give a specific interpretation framed in a general manner, rather than a comment about our relationship. He said, "I guess so" in an angry and sad way. Then he started to cry. I then commented on the repetition of prey–predator conflicts within our relationship and his worry that we were getting pulled into the battlefield with all these other conflicted relationships. Charles responded by talking about his anger with his mother, his classmates, and his friends. I pointed out his leaving me out of the picture of all these persecuting objects. He told me I am in a favorable, or at least neutral, light in his mind for the time being. I said he wants to keep close to that aspect of me and take me home for safety. But, I added, he is worried that the good light that shines on us could easily turn into a dark, negative light. I said that while he feels in such conflict with all of his objects, he is trying hard to keep me out of the fight so he has someone to turn to.

While there were other possible approaches to this hour, I concentrated on the details of what he said and what those details evoked in my mind. Knowing that this patient easily drew us into different forms of acting out, I tried to be reflective instead of reactive. I felt he was struggling with a division between the warm and safe relationship he wanted with me and the dangerous, controlling relations he split off and projected into his external objects. Because of how paranoid and volatile this patient had been, I tried to warm up to him by first making more general interpretations and later making more transference-specific comments. Even when I brought in his phantasies about us, I remained a bit distant about interpreting his resistance to those interpretations. This was based on my experience of his regressing to an even more paranoid and obsessively defensive stance. Rather than a series of interpretations that stood out as an inclusive working-through process of conflict–interpretation–insight, my comments were more like layers of gentle observation that built up a gradual sense of mutual analytic investigation. With some patients it can feel like you swoop in and do the job and all is figured out one-two-three. With this patient, it was more of a cumulative process.

Klein (1950) writes,

> during an analysis the psycho-analyst often appears as an idealized figure. Idealization is used as a defense against persecutory anxiety and is its corollary. If the analyst allows excessive idealization to persist – that is to say, if he relies mostly on the positive transference – he may, it is sure, bring about some improvement. The same however, could be said of any successful psycho-therapy. It is only by analyzing the negative as well as the positive transference that anxiety is reduced at the root.
>
> (p. 47)

In line with Klein's ideas, I would eventually need to focus more inclusively on this patient's negative transference fears. The level of anxiety he feels regarding me as a potential member of the persecutory pack of evil agents in his life makes that difficult. At the moment I've described, he was more able to integrate interpretations about the positive transference than the negative. However, as Klein says, eventually both need to be fully addressed as much as both patient and analyst can tolerate.

Case material 3.6

The next patient, Boris, was an obsessional character, filled with fears of dominating and harming his objects. He would regress to paranoid-schizoid anxieties and defenses during moments when he was unable to see us as having one mind. The concept of our being two separate beings with our own identities was hard for him to hold without thinking that one of us was being controlled and the other becoming a powerful master. He also employed manic defenses to ward off this realization of shared space.

Boris was in his forties and had been going to school to become a therapist after being a nurse for many years. During one hour, he started asking many questions about becoming a therapist. He wanted to know about renting an office, billing patients, and so forth. After a while, he made a comment about how expensive my office must be to rent and that he would certainly do it differently. I inquired what he meant, noting the possible condescending quality to his remark. He assured me that he meant he could never afford to have an office like mine so he would have different accommodations. His negation of aggression was common. In fact, he devalued his own striving as a way to make peace with me and hide his own envy. If I attempt to explore it, he usually regresses to a paranoid state, feeling persecuted by me for his "ordinary and normal" feelings. This usually produces a therapeutic stalemate.

With this type of patient, I find it hard to go directly to the more aggressive phantasies, as it can trigger such an *impasse*. What seems to work better is to take the long way there by addressing the equally conflicted libidinal wishes and eventually link them to the more hostile feelings. Therefore, I chose to silently interpret to myself his desires to get inside me and possess my identity as a therapist. Also, I elected to be silent about his wish and fear of wanting to best me.

I first interpreted Boris' desire to be cared for by me as a loving wise mentor father (the projection of his ideal object). Next, I interpreted his feelings of hope and excitement as a little boy who, with father's help, could grow into a strong man who can be a potent and powerful therapist. I showed him how he became fearful that by being so vulnerable and dependent on me, I could turn into a dominating and manipulating therapist who would force him to be in my mold and never let him grow up.

Rather than telling him he wants to overpower me and dominate me, but feels scared of the consequences (all of which are true), it was more helpful to interpret the current projective identification process he was involved in. I interpreted his view of me, resulting from his projection of hostile and competitive urges. Not only is this technically most salient in the moment, but with this type of defensive patient it also helps avoid a regressive *impasse*.

Essentially, I did interpret his envy, which was being managed with these projective identification dynamics.

Boris then agreed with my interpretations and associated to material about his father. He told me how his father was very much like his vision of me. His father wanted everything to be his way and seemed to fear his children's autonomy and potency. After telling me about his frustrations with his father, he began undoing and negating much of what he had said and the value of what I had said. I chose not to comment on his devaluing. He continued to obsess about the different angles he felt existed on each topic we had discussed. Boris now seemed to be caught in his usual quandary of who is right and who is wrong. This one step foward and one step back, with a lot of sideways shuffling, is common with Boris.

Case material 3.7

The next patient, Joan, relied on splitting and projective identification to relate to me. Joan had recently left an abusive relationship with a man who was quite disturbed. They would get into shouting, pushing and shoving, and tormenting one another for days at a time. Joan's boyfriend was prone to violence and was clearly a replacement for her controlling, erratic mother. All of her friends had told her to steer clear of him, yet she persisted. After a close call with financial disaster and near violence, she managed to leave him. For months after, she told me "what was I thinking? I was crazy to have ever been with him!"

In this particular hour, Joan told me in a casual offhand manner that she was planning on going out dancing with him. She displayed no tension and said she thought it might be "fun and interesting" to see what he had been up to since they split up. This was all said in such a bland way that it was as if she was going to mail a letter. I noticed myself becoming irritated and flabbergasted that she was actually thinking of stepping foot near this person who had almost wrecked her life. I started to offer bits of "common sense" and tried to get her to see the naive, dangerous approach she was taking. Basically, I found myself giving her suggestions and advice and I was on the verge of manipulating her with my authority. Surprised and a bit embarrassed with myself, I tried to understand what was happening. It occurred to me that she was splitting parts of herself and projecting the wise parent, common-sense side of herself into me. I began to interpret this process to her.

My approach with Joan was in accordance with Klein's technical recommendations. Klein (1946) writes,

I have repeatedly found that advances in synthesis are brought about by interpretations of the specific causes for splitting. Such interpretations must deal in detail with the transference situation at that moment, including of course the connection with the past, and must contain a reference to the details of the anxiety situations which drive the ego to regress to schizoid mechanisms.

(p. 21)

In addition to integrating the splitting, the interpretative approach creates the potential for analytic contact and is the primary technical tool for repairing breaks in analytic contact.

Case material 3.8

One patient, Frances, was mired in obsessive phantasies about power, control, and righteousness. She used manic defenses to feel correct and better than her analyst. Any interpretations I made, she had already thought of. This was to prevent the breakdown of her omnipotence and to avoid the loss of her fragile, idealized object. We could have no differences. She was very anxious about my keeping secrets. Frances felt I might have knowledge about her or maybe a hypothesis about her problems that I didn't share with her. This was unacceptable because it showed we were separate and different entities. It also made her feel inferior and humiliated.

During one period in her analysis, she became convinced that I had an opinion about her condition that I wasn't sharing. She demanded to know. Her insistence to have the information she felt she "had a right to know" escalated over several hours. It began to take on a repetitious and paranoid quality. She would not rest until I handed over the secret. Frances felt I had a piece of her and she was ready to fight for it, to prevent a collapse of her integrity and feeling of power. After one rather grueling hour of her becoming highly agitated and demanding, I was left feeling cornered, controlled, and on the verge of being rejected. I was sure she would stop her treatment unless I gave in and "surrendered the goods". In the counter-transference, I had lost ground in my own analytic contact with this patient.

In between her hours, I found myself thinking and worrying about our relationship. It occurred to me that I was feeling as she often had when growing up. She had felt bullied and controlled by an alcoholic father and a manipulative mother. Frances had felt an obsessive need to confess all her shortcomings to her mother, feeling any aggressive or sexual urge made her dangerous and sinful. By confessing to her mother, she regained her feeling of being the same or better than her family. Omnipotence or loss and conflict were her choices. By studying my counter-transference and reflecting on my knowledge of Frances' background, I brought back some stability in my contribution to analytic contact.

When Frances arrived for the next hour, she refused to use the couch and demanded I tell her what I thought of her. She was highly anxious and agitated. She said she was on the verge of quitting. I took her seriously. Diagnostically, Frances was an obsessive neurotic. While she mostly organized her mental life within the depressive position, she easily regressed into paranoid-schizoid phantasies of persecution. Therefore, I felt it important to be very sure of what unconscious state she was in before making my interpretation.

If she was mostly managing her inner world from the paranoid-schizoid perspective, I felt it unwise to make a transference interpretation about her thoughts and feelings toward me. This almost always makes such a patient defensive and prone to a paranoid flight. In such a situation, I find it more clinically useful to interpret the ego's vision of the object. Rather than comment on the patient's unconscious libidinal and aggressive phantasies, I comment on how the patient unconsciously perceives me. If I had interpreted this patient's internal state, I would have said, "You feel angry and demanding that I give you everything." Instead, I was going to comment on the effect of her projection on me, her object. Therefore, I was ready to tell Frances that I felt confused and cornered, as if things would go sour if I didn't "come up with the goods". I was prepared to say that I would share my thoughts with her about how she was doing, but that I felt nervous about what exactly she needed. Everything suddenly seemed to have so much weight, as if everything could rise or fall based on what I said.

When I began to tell Frances I was willing to talk with her about her worries and to try to help her out with what she needed, she calmed down. She visibly regrouped and began to relate to me from much more of a depressive perspective. I was less of a dominating dictator in her eyes. By my acquiescing somewhat to her phantasy about our tug of war, she felt less griped by such severe anxieties. When I saw that she had reintegrated a bit, I decided to make more of a standard transference interpretation regarding projective identification. I said, "You want me to tell you what I think of you. You grew up with a father you wanted to be close to and get inside and understand. You wanted to look up to him and be close. You craved to know how he felt about you. Instead, you had a father who was angry and drunk most of the time. You felt blocked from knowing him and from knowing if he cared about you. Then he killed himself and you felt you would never be able to get inside him and know anything. Now, you are letting yourself be more vulnerable with me and are starting to want to know about me. You want to know how I feel about you, but you are worried I am blocking you as well. This makes you furious and sad and you want to try and push your way in. That conflict of wanting to be inside of me and feeling shut out is happening more and more lately. You are hoping I will see that and help you out."

This was a more oedipal-based interpretation that directly addressed her urges and fears. She listened intently and seemed to immediately relax. After a long silence, she began associating to memories of her childhood and her desires to be close to her father. Frances also told me she wanted to find out more about me but felt unsure if I would be nice to her or if I would be mean and withhold things from her. Based on my assessment of her intra-psychic structure, her unconscious phantasies and anxieties, and my own counter-transference, I was able to make sense out of her projective identification mechanisms and offer appropriate interpretations that fostered analytic contact.

Chapter 4

Projective identification, everyday life, and the analytic situation

Transference interpretations are statements the analyst makes about the way the patient perceives, relates to, and experiences the analyst. The analyst interprets the patient's deeper phantasies and fears about the analytic relationship as well as other objects in his or her internal and external life. Then, the analyst listens closely to the patient's response to locate evidence regarding the accuracy of the interpretation.

Interpretation is the analyst's main occupation in relation to the patient, whose main occupation is the attempt at free association. The patient provides the analyst with information via memories, phantasies, wishes, fears, and actions that the analyst translates into words that go beyond the patient's conscious awareness. In the treatment process, the patient eventually shifts their psychic relationship with the analyst to meet unconscious expectations and to relive old experiences. This establishes the transference neurosis, which interpretation is designed to explore, translate, and work through.

I am in agreement with these ideas. As illustrated by the last chapter, I think that the process of projective identification is often at the core of transference and this element must be interpreted in order for change to occur.

Projective identification involves a phantasy of splitting off unacceptable parts of the self and sending them into another object as a communicative, loving, protective, defensive, or aggressive maneuver. Inner anxiety and danger are externalized and then managed in the outer world before reinternalizing them in a more manageable manner. Along with danger and hostility, loving feelings are also projected into the object as expressions of caring. Therefore, projective identification can produce cyclical anxieties as well as an ongoing sense of soothing, safety, and support. So, understanding and interpreting these cycles is important to foster, maintain, and generate analytic contact with all patients, but especially our more difficult cases.

Projective identification has different meanings and various clinical consequences. Chronic and desperate attempts to locate aspects of the self in the object result in ego depletion and a weakened sense of identity. This is clinically significant and requires particular interpretations to restore the integrity of the ego.

Since projective identification manifests in different forms, it affects the analyst–patient relationship in various ways. The therapeutic unfolding of projective identification can be better understood by making a parallel with how this dynamic occurs in everyday life outside of the clinical setting. The point of doing this is to show the various levels of projective identification and how the analyst must find a way to interpret its meaning in each different occurrence.

This chapter will compare non-clinical and clinical situations in which projective identification is coloring the immediate relationship. The unique nature of analytic interpretation will be highlighted by starting from more chaotic and destructive instances of projective identification and moving to more organized and balanced ones. In doing so, it will be evident how analytic contact is affected, positively or negatively by projective identification and by the analyst's interpretive attempts to understand it.

PROJECTIVE IDENTIFICATION OUTSIDE OF THE CLINICAL SETTING

There is something about the private trust of a stranger, the idea of being able to give all your secrets to them for just a minute, whether it be to dump your emotional trash or to trust someone new to engage with you and your life story. There are times when people purposely seek out a complete stranger, whether it be for instant relief, to begin to modify or transform their internal world, or to continue to integrate uncomfortable states of mind. Sometimes, it is an aggressive exchange, sometimes it is touching, sometimes it is enlightening. It happens all the time, people weaving themselves into other people's lives for different reasons, but all with a similar need for a stranger. If you start looking around, you notice it happens everywhere.

Non-clinical situation

One day, sitting in the hot-tub at my health club, I witnessed a particular dynamic. A man in his forties was sitting next to a woman in her thirties. They did not know each other, but he began to chat with her. There were a few typical topics like the weather, how crowded the lap pool was, and the upcoming holidays. But, fairly quickly, he brought up some article in the morning paper that had mentioned parenting as part of the story. Then, he proceeded to tell this woman, who just listened patiently, about how he thought "Today's parents are way too permissive. They just let the kids get away with everything. The kids today are too spoiled. They need to be shown some discipline."

Within a few minutes, this man shifted from a casual conversation to an aggressive, tension-bound lecture that also had a hollow and desperate feel to it. His audience, the poor woman next to him in the tub, looked more and more pressured and cornered, maybe duplicating the feelings this man grew up with and now harbored inside of himself. She tried to act polite and nodded her head as he went about his one-way conversation. Now, he went from his overview of society's woes to something more personal. He said, "My mother wore the pants in the family. She was always right and we respected that! If we didn't respond to what she told us, she had a wooden spoon to remind us. I remember being chased around trying to avoid getting hit by that wooden spoon. Of course, it is not something I dwell on now! It certainly isn't something that left any lasting scars!" His emphatic tone and underscoring of how he was in no way affected now as an adult was of course revealing about how very much scarred he was to this day.

He went on, "We were taught discipline. Today's kids are spoiled. They whine and always want their way. They need to get shown some discipline. We knew exactly when mom was in a bad mood and we knew how to behave to not get her worked up. Nowadays, everyone blames their parents and says how dysfunctional it was and how they need to 'heal' from it. How stupid is that! I was taught how to behave and I don't need any healing from that!" At this point, the woman next to him looked like she was behaving as nicely as possible, pretending to listen and be interested, for fear of being hit with a wooden spoon!

This man was clearly still suffering from his upbringing and managed to dump some of that trauma into the stranger next to him. It probably served to provide him with some temporary relief and let him feel like the aggressor instead of the victim. But, ultimately, the fact that he had to, and I emphasize his lack of choice, spend his time worked up in a state about discipline, being hit, childhood memories, and parenting issues, instead of being able to relax in the hot-tub, showed how much he was still captured and tortured by his past and how much he needed to discharge, dump, and purge that inner poison onto others for a moment of false peace.

Non-clinical situation

Isabelle was a woman who was very similar to the man in the last example. She had the same type of impact on those around her. She came to the swim club almost everyday and we felt like her hostages. She was probably in her late fifties but her bitterness gave her an ancient, carved-in-stone look. For years, Isabelle made a trail over to the hot-tub. The tub was built to hold ten, but she seemed to take up most of that space with her negativity. It was truly amazing how many things she could complain about, but Isabelle did have her favorites. Most everything about the pool and the tub were never good enough. I felt like a prisoner in the "Three Little Bears" story: the water was too cold, the water was too hot, it had too much chlorine, it was too dirty, the children may have peed in it, and the jets weren't strong enough. It wasn't that she was always wrong about these things, but her droning on and on about it was worse than any amount of pee or chlorine.

Rather than single out one victim like the man in the last example, Isabelle shared her psychology with everyone within earshot. We all dealt with it in our own way. Some people listened attentively and took it as an opportunity to voice their own options and complaints. But, this approach was never too effective. Isabelle bulldozed over anything different than her agenda.

We all felt sorry for new, uninitiated visitors to the hot-tub. We saw them innocently strolling over for a relaxing soak. They appeared naive when she asked them, "Where are you from?" It didn't really matter what their answer was because after their first sentence Isabelle would use it as a springboard to dive into her own murky litany of personal difficulty. For example, one young man replied he was visiting from Texas. Isabelle used that to announce to us all that she had always hated the heat and humidity of the South and that she had never been to Texas before. We were supposed to be impressed that she felt this way and to make special note to never travel to Texas now that we had received her special review. A visiting couple replied that they were traveling across the country for the summer. This gave her the chance to announce that her sister hated to travel. Silently, we all thought, "So what!? What the hell does that have to do with anything and why the hell would we want or need to know that?!" But, because of the power she seemed to hold over us, we all tried to be polite and act interested.

At some point, no one could take it anymore. Isabelle's pronouncements prompted mass migrations from the tub to any and all directions. Some of the hot-tub detainees would opt for a swim, decide it was time to head home, or dash over to the weight room. Others, like myself, would stay in the tub, close our eyes, and try to retreat inwards. Pretending to be reaching for a meditative moment of relaxation was really a desperate attempt at building a wall between yourself and Isabelle's unfolding banter.

Over the years, we collected bits of information about her and who she was. She was a social worker but didn't like to take care of people. She said people could be "a real pain". It was things like this that made her look self-centered, yet sad and lost. We all wondered who this lady was, wading her way into our lives.

It was amazing how much power Isabelle held over all of us. When she wasn't there, we would chuckle about "getting a reprieve from the governor". When she was at the pool, we would roll our eyes and give each other the secret wink. She never made friends with any of us but she held us all close with her sad and sadistic ways.

At the end of the day, the men escaped with a bit of relief and dignity into their private locker room. I felt sorry for the women, exposed to a naked version of Isabelle with nowhere to hide. Apparently, the women's locker room was just one more place Isabelle held court. Isabelle was angry that the showers were too dirty, the water temperature fluctuated too much, there wasn't enough soap, and the lockers were too small. She was an artist at finding something wrong and making sure you knew about it.

Isabelle seemed to be one of those people who was so unhappy that she just had to make you share in that grim world. Rather than ever talk about her actual feelings, which I imagine were loneliness and depression, she made you listen to complaints about her environment. Nevertheless, most of us at the pool sensed a sadness about her. People who offered her kindness and reached out, ultimately regretted it. She was that person in every crowd that we, over time, both hate and feel sorry for. We respond to what they express on the surface, but we know there is something more meaningful, more lovable, underneath. But, it remains in the deep end, unreachable.

Clinical situation

Mr P was a middle-aged car salesman referred to me after he "was fired by his last therapist" and his psychiatrist told him that he would give him medications but didn't have the time to see him for psychotherapy. Mr P said, "My therapist told me we seemed to always disagree so that it was best to find someone else who would be a better match. I think he was just sick of me but wouldn't say so. He didn't have the balls. I think my psychiatrist doesn't want to bother with me. That is so typical. All you doctors are the same. You call yourself the helping profession. That is so not true. I haven't received a scrap of help from any one of you. It has proved to be a giant waste of time and money." I interpreted, "Without giving us a chance, you have decided we are not a good match. I wonder why you need to shut the door so quickly?" He responded, "I am giving you a chance by showing up today. But, I don't have a good feeling about this. I may choose to not be involved in therapy at all."

This was my unpleasant and sharp introduction to Mr P. I was met with some variation of this assault every session. It usually started out rather mild and then escalated into a non-stop verbal attack on my lack of talent, our lack of connection, and his general disgust of the entire field of psychology. Mr P came to see me for help with his depressive feelings about a stagnant career and a girlfriend who "doesn't ever come out and say it, but I don't think she has ever loved me and probably has never liked me either". So, very quickly, I noticed that there were several important people in his life whom Mr P felt did not like him but would not come out and say it. In that vein, I interpreted, "You seem sure that these important people in your life don't like you but won't tell you that. The way you are treating me and the way you relate to our work here makes me think you want to push me to not like you as well. You must feel both in control and very alienated to think I might not like you but can't speak the truth. In fact, I am willing to tell you that you seem to be trying to make me not like you. Perhaps it is safer to be this way than to build a connection?"

Here, I was interpreting his distancing from analytic contact and his particular attacks on our contact. Mr P replied, "We don't have a connection because you don't help me. You haven't told me what to do or how to change things. All we talk about is how I feel, which is useless. I feel angry and stuck in a dead-end job. What are you doing about that?" I interpreted, "You are illustrating what I was just saying. By being pushy and telling me to 'do something' to fix you, you are inviting me to say I don't like you because you are pushy. Maybe this whole thing of people not liking you is very important to understand. Does it ring any bells?" Mr P said, "People that are there to help you just disappoint you. That is what bell it rings. You are just one more disappointment. I can't believe I am paying for this crap." I said, "When you said people that are there to help you, what about your family? How did that go for you growing up?"

This comment was a turn away from the transference but for good reason. While Mr P never talked about his past or his family, the history I had been able to gather seemed remarkably important in understanding the trans-ference and the projective identification process he was so invested in. Growing up, Mr P was the only child of a father who was quite old by the time Mr P was born. Mr P's mother was a problem drinker, who kept in the background and was only available for "the basics", as Mr P put it. Not only did his father's age preclude him from being an involved and active father during Mr P's early development, but when Mr P was ten years old, his father was diagnosed with cancer. This led to fifteen years of treatments, bed rest, and a curtailment of everyday activities.

It was obvious, listening to Mr P's description of this, that growing up was a time when Mr P not only didn't have his father to nurture him, but the roles were actually reversed. He had to care for his father. I brought this up and wondered if Mr P might still have a great many feelings, such as anger, sadness, and grief, about it. He said, "I certainly missed out on a lot of things. When my classmates were going out to party, I was staying home to make sure my father's chemotherapy was going OK. There wasn't too much father–son time for me. I had to figure out things on my own." I asked him how that was and how he felt about it. Mr P said, "What on earth are we talking about that for? How is that going to change anything? You really aren't providing me with any assistance or answers to anything!" I said, "Maybe just like you felt your father didn't?" He said, "What the hell are you talking about? Maybe I had a hard time on occasion, but I was just dealing with what life brought me. Everyone has something to deal with. How is this discussion going to get me a better job? This is as worthless as I thought." I interpreted, "It looks like you were starting to feel something that was uncomfortable and then you started to put me down instead". He said, "Well, I don't see the point in discussing my past which has nothing to do with my present. I am here for you to do something to help me feel better. But, you aren't doing much at all. This is really a waste of time. I don't think it makes sense to keep coming. You are not giving me anything. Like all the therapists I have seen, you are a disappointment." Here, it seemed he psychologically needed to do his best to prevent analytic contact in favor of this basic persecutory phantasy.

Theoretically and conceptually, I heard this accusation of disappointment as Mr P was revealing his childhood feelings of anger, sadness, loss, and dis-appointment in his father. I thought he was probably carrying around those feelings and they had become part of a phantasy in which his objects refused to deliver the emotional nurturing and care that he demanded. Through the vehicle of projective identification, this was a phantasy of angry expectations, disappointing unavailability, and an unwillingness to see the care that was present since it was not the love he specifically desired. This object-relational sequence brought on the experience of terrible loss and a feeling of abandonment. Then, Mr P used abandonment, devaluation, and persecution as revenge upon the disappointing object. However, this sort of genetic con-ceptualization of the case would not be helpful unless the immediate trans-ference, phantasy state, and projective identification process were consistently interpreted.

Mr P became very predictable after the first couple of sessions. It was as if his goal was to establish a state of anti-analytic contact, a way to prove over and over again that he was never going to be fed or loved properly. Analytic contact would disturb that phantasy and make him face the humiliation, pain, loss, and fear he had about his objects.

Mr P would come in and immediately start telling me how "We just don't have any connection. There is nothing of value I have ever gotten from any therapist. You are all basically charlatans who claim to provide something but really do nothing. I don't think we have any sort of connection or understanding at all. For something like this to work, you would need to give me advice and assistance and be able to relate to me in a way that I would know you care and want to help me. That isn't there. I get so pissed off when I think of the time and money I have wasted seeing people like you and for what? I would be way better off going to the bar and bending the bartender's ear. So, what are you going to do for me today? Like I said last time, I don't think this is going to work. We don't match up, not a good match at all. You definitely don't seem like you want to help me. I think I might not come back. You are definitely not reaching me. You are cold and distant!" Here, he again was making sure we would not establish any meaningful analytic contact, through this forceful projective identification attack.

After this sort of assault, I would feel irritated and agitated, leading me to think, "of course the other therapist wanted to fire him!" But, I also felt sad and curious about this man's narrow psychological cage that he was trapped in and how he tried to get me to join him in that cage. Using some of these counter-transference thoughts, phantasies, and feelings, I would interpret, "You set the stage before I ever have a chance. By walking in and immediately telling me off for not reaching you, you are preventing me from reaching you. You are eliminating the very thing you want. It is as if you need to control both sides of our relationship and make sure that I am a certain way in your mind, without giving me the chance to be myself. I wonder if you need to control me and us this way because that makes the disappointment something you create instead of running the risk of letting our relationship unfold. Maybe it feels more dangerous to gamble on me caring and then maybe losing out?" This was an example of interpreting the counter-transference role responsiveness that Sandler (1976) has examined.

In response, Mr P said, "I am sorry if I am a big pain in your neck. I know I can be that way. I am trying to relax and talk with you. [He paused for a moment.] But, you are not really giving me what I want. This is the same kind of waste of time I have brought up before. Here we are again, talking about nothing and doing nothing to resolve my problems. I still am in a dead-end job that I hate and I haven't seen a scrap of advice coming from you. This really is worthless. I don't know how much longer I want to do this. It is a total waste of time."

Here, just for a moment, Mr P was able to reflect on himself a bit and his state of anxiety seemed to lessen. There was a glimpse of analytic contact. But, almost as quickly as he was able to think of me independently from his vision of a disappointing object that he felt enraged with, he switched back to experiencing that phantasy as real. This is typical of the stormy work encountered with the complex and difficult patients seen in a typical private psychoanalytic practice (Waska 2005). Today, nine months into his analytic treatment, Mr P remains much the same in terms of relating to me as this bad, disappointing object. However, the fact that he remains in treatment with me says something about his internal world. On one hand, he is staying as a way to repeat his fight with this devalued, unhelpful father figure, still feeling he will never get what he so desperately wants in the relationship. On the other hand, Mr P is perhaps able to take in some of my interpretations and begin to think more deeply about himself. This subtle background integration is evidenced by much less tension in his relationship to his girlfriend and more contentment at his job. He reports less friction with his boss and occasional feelings of accomplishment and success on the job. However, analytic contact is still a kidnap victim of his cold and despairing projective phantasies.

In the previous two examples of everyday, non-clinical life, both individuals' projective identification process controlled others and created an atmosphere of resentment and discomfort. But, no one ever said anything to either one of them. In psychoanalytic work, the analyst operates with the belief that it is not only important to point out such acting out and pathological ways of relating, but critical to interpret the deeper meanings and motives behind such behavior.

Non-clinical situation

Some people seek out strangers to try and mitigate, transform, and heal their inner conflict and sorrow. This is not a forceful shoving of unwanted pain into someone else like the last several examples. It is more of a sad sharing of something that is still very much alive and burdening the person, a sharing of something that is making it difficult to move ahead. The sharing touches the other person in a way that can be intense, but also inspiring to the human spirit.

One day after I was done swimming at the retirement community where my parents live, I went into the locker room to dry off and change. It wasn't particularly busy that day and I was the only one in the room. An old man came in to put his things in a locker and to go swimming. I said hello and I asked him if he lived at the community. He said yes. I told him I had played golf there that day and asked if he was a golfer. He said, "Yes, I played today. But, I don't get to play as often as I'd like. My wife doesn't play and she doesn't like me to play. We have only been married for a few years and I try to make her happy. But, we have had a lot of arguments lately. I miss my first wife." On one hand, this was similar to the first man in the hot-tub in that there was an unsolicited part of his life suddenly on the table. However, with this man in the locker room, he seemed to hold it out as an invitation. It felt like he was asking for my permission to proceed. I took up the offer by asking, "What happed to her?"

This man, a sad-looking, kindly sort of person in his eighties, began telling me what felt like an intimate love story he shared with those who were willing to listen. Again, willing is a key word compared to the agonized woman in the corner of the hot-tub who felt no choice in the matter. He told me, "We met in high school and we hit it off right away. We were married for fifty-two years. There wasn't a thing we didn't do together. It was rough when I shipped off to war. I fought in two of them. We knew we might never see each other again. But, we made it through so much because we were like this [he crossed two fingers together tightly]. Seven years ago, she got breast cancer and died. I have never felt so bad. I have faced the worst things you could imagine in the wars and seen things no one should have to. But, this was something I just couldn't bear. I miss her every day. I don't know how to live life without her. I can't talk about it with my new wife. I thought it would help if I got remarried and had someone to do things with. But, we fight a lot and she doesn't like to do the same things I do."

He was finished. There we were, alone together in the locker room. There was nothing I could say. I just said the obvious, "You love her and miss her." He nodded yes, slowly and sadly. He was a man with a broken heart, but he also was trying to manage, to maintain, and to keep going. I was left with a sense of awe, sadness, and respect for him, but no urgency or anxiety. He just wanted me to be a part of his tragedy. I left and went to meet my wife. When I told her the story, she wept. I think this man was looking for strangers along the way to share in his sorrow, but in a way that felt honoring, not forceful or aggressive. And, he didn't make me feel guilty when I said goodbye. I suspect I was one of many over the last seven years who had the sad privilege of hearing this story of love and loss.

CLINICAL COMPARISON

In the clinical setting, I believe the analytic goal is to create a new internal experience for the patient. We do this by interpreting the projective identification dynamics and the transference–counter-transference that occurs, the two phenomena often being one and the same. In doing so, we establish analytic contact. We deal with the unconscious, which is something not done in the everyday life examples I am presenting. Because some patients are attempting to discharge their troubles into us so as to not have to deal with it, they avoid exploration of their troubles. In other words, the analyst can be drawn into this avoidance and denial. In this type of counter-transference acting out, the analyst can shy away from the transference and any discussion of the analytic relationship. This avoidance dilutes or destroys analytic contact.

The following case material illustrates a case in which I consistently avoided exploring the transference and, instead, paired with the patient in focusing on the difficult external circumstances that were occurring. While very important to be addressed, the external circumstances served as a detour around the important transference and projective identification process that colored the treatment (Feldman 1992). Thus, I treated the patient just like a stranger in day-to-day life with whom I interacted, but offered no real psychological assistance for his core struggles. Clinically, I did not build analytic contact. In fact, by not addressing how it was missing in our relationship, I worked against establishing it.

One could say that it is good clinical work to help a patient through the external stress and trauma they are experiencing, but I believe as analysts we must do that and then some. We must assist with the external and interpersonal as much as possible, but that interaction should serve as a porthole to helping the patient with the real core source of their anguish. This means exploring and interpreting the unconscious, object-related world of phantasies, defense, and transference. When we do this we are entering into a state of analytic contact with our patient. When we do not work toward these goals, we are shying away from analytic contact and therefore shifting the relationship into something other than analytic. This could be a supportive friendship, a pathological reenactment, a perverse acting out, or parental advice. But, it is no longer an analytic exploration.

Case material

C, a young man in his late twenties, had to move in with his father. C's father was recovering from a major operation, due to complications from years of drinking, and needed daily care. The operation saved his life, but there would be very limited recovery. C's grandfather, on his father's side, had been living with C's father for the last ten years due to his own ailing health and poverty. C's father had been without C's mother for many years, after she had yet another affair and then divorced him.

C smoked marijuana every day and experimented with other drugs. He had a shaved head and a tattoo on one side of his head. He was dating a woman on and off, but the relationship was extremely rocky. He would become very clingy and distrustful, accusing her of cheating on him. They had frequent fights and would break up and then get back together. This seemed like an old pattern in which he dated unavailable or troubled women, judged them harshly, and then cheated on them just when he started to establish some degree of commitment.

In the analytic treatment, it appeared I was providing much-needed supportive listening for someone who was in a difficult life crisis. However, I believe this was only part of a more complex picture. It is difficult to convey, even by presenting verbatim notes of session, the way C related to me. He talked so fast and so much that he filled the relational space between us. I felt there was rarely any time or space for me to be a part of things, to contribute, or to have any value.

The following is the ninth and tenth session in a treatment that only lasted eighteen visits in total. His full dialogue would take up far too much space in the chapter, so I will only present the initial statements and the main points he conveyed.

Pt: My father is doing alright but still in the hospital. But, the hardest thing to deal with is my grandfather. He makes mean comments all the time, everything he says is cruel. He puts me down for anything I do and criticizes me for doing everything the wrong way. It is very difficult because I am trying to be nice for the sake of my father. But, I snapped at him. I am so tired.

A: [I am thinking C is taking the place of his father. He is now the punching bag.] Is that how your grandfather usually treats your father?

Pt: Yes. But, now he treats me that way too. My grandfather denies it, but he is very cruel. He told me I drive an ugly car and he said my job is menial! I can't believe how much he criticizes me! But, then he tells me he respects me and is proud of me. He tries to boss me around. What do you think of this? He won't change, so maybe I should accept his comments or not embrace them so much. Maybe I should just ignore what he says and not react to it so much.

A: [I felt I had two choices. I could address his way of wanting me to take over and tell him the best way of handling the situation or I could focus on his comment about "embracing" the criticism.] What makes you embrace his cruel remarks? [So, I elected to avoid the transference situation.]

Pt: I think it is that my father sacrificed his whole life for my grandfather. I
       guess I am really angry on behalf of my father.

A: Your father doesn't get angry on his own behalf.

Pt: He does get angry, but he doesn't know how to express it or what to do
       with it. He keeps it to himself. So, I think I will try and detach from my
       grandfather and his weird crap. I am so tired from all this drama. My
       father is doing really well. He is fine. My mind is fine with that. But, he
       does seem depressed. Isn't detaching the best way?

A: The way you are asking shows me you logically know it might help, but
       emotionally you feel like fighting with him. [Again, I avoided exploring the
       way C is wanting my help.]

Pt: Yes. You are right about that. I find myself thinking of nasty things to say
       to him or hoping awful things will happen to him. That is not good. I have
       tried to talk honestly with him and tell him how he hurts my feelings, but
       he doesn't get it.

A: Growing up, did you spend time with your grandfather?

Pt: Yes. I don't remember him being this way. Since I have grown up, I have
       noticed my grandfather's moods. He criticizes and tries to control
       everything now. My father isn't like that and I don't think I am like that.

A: You don't feel you are critical.

Pt: Right. And, my grandfather loves to correct you and make you feel
       wrong. It isn't outwardly aggressive, it is subtle. It is very hard, very hard.
       I have wondered why I am so insecure. But, now I see my father and he is
       kind of a wreck. He has no self-respect and no confidence. Anyway! I am
       just not going to respond to my grandfather anymore. I am very angry.

A: You must feel stressed about not knowing how long it will be till your
       father is better and how long you will be stuck with your grandfather.

Pt: Well, I am praying and meditating a lot. When my father is better, it will
       be easier. But, right now it is harder because my grandfather is even
       worse to my father than he is to me. My mother would probably help out
       if she was asked, but my father has really pushed her away over the years.
       Of course, my grandfather also picks on her so why would she want to
       come and visit or help out. I heard my mother may be bipolar and she
       still drinks. She is a real fuck-up. I see my father's anger in me. I get angry
       at my father for being such a victim. [Here, C is starting to reveal his
       more negative feelings toward his father and acknowledge how he sees
       both his parents as defective. He also mentions his own aggression.]

A: You said you see the anger inside yourself. What is that about?

Pt: I don't know. It is better now that I am on the medications. But, not too
       long ago I was so anxious. I hated my job and overall I was very unhappy.

I don't know why. Now, I am happy and I don't know why either. Maybe it is because I am doing something nice for my father. He never experienced somebody loving him. So, now he can get some of that. His last marriage was terrible. There were physical fights and chaos. It was about the same as with my mother. I want to show him that he counts. I know how helpful it is to have someone else to love me. I used to feel ugly and pathetic. One old girlfriend really helped me with that, even though I still struggle with it. I normally am getting high on pot every single day but since I've been here I haven't as much. But, I am going to try and get some real soon so I can escape all this crap. But, not every day. I will only do it when absolutely necessary.

A: The way you are feeling right now, you probably wish you could escape.

Pt: Oh yeah! And, my father can really bother me too. It is lots of petty small things but it gets to me. Anyway! I am trying to focus on the positive. So, on to the flip-side of things. I met with Sally and we seem to be doing well. That is really nice. I am trying to not call her a lot and just trust that she wants to see me. Our relationship feels free and right. I am not asking her how she feels about me or how committed she is. I am giving her space. I pushed too much in the past and she told me so. So, I promised to not ask too many questions, not grill her about things. I am trying to not control things.

A: What is it like without that control?

Pt: It is OK. Great! I don't feel needy, I am fine with myself. I like the chance to get to know myself. It is fine! I just trust it will all work out fine. And if it doesn't that will be fine too!

A: You are trying to feel OK about all these changes and troubles in your life, things you don't have a way of controlling. But, your feelings are starting to come out. You try and manage your anger and upset but it's leaking out.

Pt: Oh yeah! I am hoping if I am a good example in front of my father, he can maybe follow my example on how to better deal with your feelings. I have given him so much advice and he never did anything to change. But, now with his illness, I think he is willing to ask for help and maybe change.

Next session

Pt: Well, my father is back in the hospital. He suddenly started having all these complications. His liver is not processing the toxins enough and he has maybe got some kind of infection from the operation. He is really weak. He has tubes going into his stomach and one in his nose. His system isn't responding to the antibiotics and his liver is having some kind of reaction. He is in horrible pain. They are giving him lots of pain medication from an IV tube. I am stuck with my grandfather. I yelled at him.

A: What happened?

Pt: I told him I was sick of him picking on my father. I didn't really yell or anything, but what I said was honest. I feel bad. I really freaked out. There was so much tension. My father tried to tell him what I meant, but he just does not get it. There is nothing to do but forgive my grandfather and try and heal the relationship. But, I hate him! [Crying] I can't stand him! I am so angry.

A: You feel really bad for your father.

Pt: I tried to tell my grandfather that my father would be happy if some of his friends could come around and visit. I also said it has been hard on my father to have to take care of my grandfather in the past. He just can't do it anymore. My grandfather offered to move out and go into an assisted care facility, which I think is a great idea. It would make things so much easier on my father. My father said no. My father's loving nature is his greatest downfall. He tries to be nice and suffers for it. My father doesn't have a lot of time left to enjoy himself and cater to his own needs. He deserves that chance. My grandfather doesn't see that.

A: Are you angry with your father for being self-destructive? His drinking led to this whole situation.

Pt: He is so sick. I can't be angry with him now.

A: You say you can't be angry now. Were you angry with him in the past?

Pt: Well, yes. When I was in highschool, he had a wonderful job offer to work for a racetrack out of state. He loved racing and anything about cars. I remember how he lit up for the first time that I can recall. But, I didn't want to move away from my friends, so he decided to not take the job. It would have been more money than he had made before and would have been good for the whole family, but he turned it down because of me. I feel bad that I was such a spoiled brat and ruined that opportunity but I also feel angry that he didn't stand up to that spoiled brat. As a result, my father's career went into the toilet. I see that as the same thing as him spending years married to my abusive mother, just taking her crap over and over and never standing up. She was drunk, violent, had affairs, and was mean to me. A few times she totally trashed the house. She was so out of control.

A: You are angry that he put up with all that. You are focusing on the impact of all that on him, but you were obviously impacted by all that chaos. Maybe, that is harder to think of?

Pt: Maybe. I don't know. There is my whole avoidance of relationships and how I have never been able to get close and stay with anyone for very long. I don't trust anyone. But, I have realized all that and forgiven my mother. But, my father is a different story.

A: You feel he could do things to change and improve, but won't.

Pt: Yes. He could encourage my grandfather to move into an assisted care place, that would help his life out, make it better.

A: It must be frightening to see your father go back into the hospital and take such a serious turn.

Pt: Well, he isn't on the edge of death yet. I think he is fine, just a setback. But, it is hard to see him this way. I don't want to have to see the things I am seeing.

A: You seem to try and be optimistic about things that must feel so terrible. [I am gently confronting the manic theme.]

Pt: Well, what is wrong with that? Otherwise, I don't know what to do! Like how my father freaked out under the influence of the morphine and started fighting the nurses. My grandfather is sure he is dying. So, I just try and go with the facts. Things usually work out.

A: It sounds like you feel you have to be the stable one.

Pt: Absolutely. Everyone is losing it.

A: When do you get a chance to lose it?

Pt: I talk with you. But, I don't feel upset.

A: Maybe, smoking lots of pot is a way of trying to maintain stability, not losing it. [Here, I avoid exploring his mention of our relationship.]

Pt: Maybe, yes. I think that is right. I try and overcompensate. Before the antidepressant medications I was crying all the time. I was totally out of it. So, what should I do, some sort of exercise?

A: You are avoiding the difficult and painful work we are doing together right now. The thought of exercise and medications takes you away from the anxiety and pain we are dealing with.

Pt: I see. Yes. I fear if I get weak, I will stay weak forever. I don't trust my home environment. I worry I will collapse. I try and stay strong at all times. I don't want my father to see me being sad. He is so guilt-ridden that he would blame himself. But, I can't see smoking less pot now, not now.

A: It is a safe haven right now, a way to not feel weak and hopeless. [I avoid exploration of the safe haven our relationship might be.]

Pt: Definitely.

I think I provided a temporary level of support for this patient, but was never able to reach the deeper internal object world he was operating from. His manic, arm's-length approach to the relationship kept us in a very limited emotional space that he controlled. The anxiety that fueled this stance was also very difficult to interpret. After eighteen visits, he was unable to continue since he could no longer pay. He was making no money as he had quit his job when he moved into his father's home. This, in part, seemed to be a way of hoping to finally be taken care of by his father. C also refused to explore his marijuana smoking and, since he smoked every day, was often high on the drug when he came to his sessions. This addiction clearly limited his ability to fully function in life and it provided a defensive shelter from having to deal with his internal and external problems. So, while I offered C a psychoanalytic framework, his projective identification dynamic, his manic stance, and my counter-transference issues all made it impossible to gain much of a momentum. I was unable to find a way to effectively bridge these difficulties, so the treatment was not only brief but not very fruitful.

C did thank me for my time and told me I had helped him to get through a real crisis in his life. He said he wanted to return in the future if he could afford it.

A year later, C mailed me a postcard, saying he was still taking care of his father. He said he was "having a tough time, but hanging in there". This was a frustrating case for me, one I wished I could have done more with and been able to establish a better analytic connection to. Yet, I try to understand and accept that there will be many more such cases where the setting and circumstances are meager and I can only do my best to be an analyst, listening closely and interpreting what I find. With C, I listened closely, but not closely enough to notice my collaboration in the avoidance of the transference.

C was a case in which I acted as a container for his troubled state of grief (Hasui and Kitamuca 2004). C's complicated grief experience intensified his paranoid-schizoid (Klein 1946) conflicts and feelings of persecution. At the same time, by way of C's projective identification process, I acted out a supportive yet non-confrontive role, the same sort of compromised state the patient felt to be in with his father and grandfather: helpless, used, ignored, and unable to do much to change it. This prevented much true analytic contact and in my acting out of his projected phantasy, I failed to try and explore or interpret much of what was going on unconsciously. Thus, I led us away from analytic contact and into other realms of discourse and relating.

In the end, this case was very similar to everyday life in that a person brought me into their projective identification sphere and I went along for the ride. As an analyst, my task was to notice this and attempt to intervene by means of interpretation. Unfortunately, I merely maintained our relationship within the same climate as the patient's other relationships so he was not able to make a significant internal change. At best, I believe I helped him cope with a very difficult external circumstance but did not offer him help with his overarching unconscious method of relating to himself and his object. So, one could say we found a certain type of contact, but it was not analytic contact.

CLINICAL COMPARISON

This is an example of case material from an analytic treatment with a different patient with whom I did interpret the transference instead of letting external issues and defensive maneuvers become the bedrock of the treatment. We were able to find a state of analytic contact in which deeper matters were worked with and transference issues were analyzed. At the same time, this was a very rocky treatment with a constant adversarial atmosphere that corrupted the flow and stability of our analytic contact.

Mr A came in and told me that he noticed some changes in my waiting room. He realized the large table that was usually covered in magazines was gone, as well as a smaller end table. I had removed them to open up the formerly cluttered area. Mr A didn't notice the three new pictures on the wall or the new end table and lamp. He said, "Wow! Your waiting room looks so lonely, so dark and empty. Surely you are going to be putting some more furniture in there? It just seems so sad and lonely right now." I replied, "Actually, that is the new look. We took out some of the older, bigger pieces to open up the room. But, I am interested in how you describe it, with such emotional terms. Is it possible that you are feeling a bit lonely or sad today?"

Mr A shot back, "That is exactly the kind of bullshit I can't stand about you. You take anything I say and immediately twist it into something else. Why can't you ever take anything I say and just respect it for what it is?" Mr A went on like this for a while, which was quite typical. I responded by saying I was trying to understand him better but that seemed to be something he recoiled at. I pointed out that it was also something he really wanted, so he was left feeling conflicted and anxious. Mr A responded, "Of course I want you to understand me, but you never do. I want you to really get me, to have some insight and compassion about where I am really coming from. But, you never do."

I responded, "The situation with the waiting room and my question about your feelings get right to that point. You are very urgent about me understanding you, but whenever I make a move in that direction, you are quick to shut me down and say it doesn't count. So, in that way I am helpless and can't win. I fail you either way." Mr A said, "Well, it is nice that you try and I am not telling you it doesn't count at all. But, I do want you to understand me and to stop picking on me about useless crap." I interpreted, "Maybe you want me to be exact in caring for you because then you feel in control. But, if you just let me bring up possibilities and show that I am interested in you, it feels like you are vulnerable and giving over control to me, so you stop it as soon as you can." Mr A said, "I guess that could be. I am willing to give that some thought. But, I still think the whole waiting room thing is bullshit."

This sort of power struggle and tug of war over compassion and control is an ongoing issue with this patient. Overall, Mr A is making progress in this area. But, it is painful and slow. He made an initial comment about the waiting room that in everyday life would have been left alone. When I interpreted his comment, it opened up the difficult and negative transference feelings and phantasies he struggled with and gave us an opportunity to work analytically on these unconscious pockets of dread and rage.

Mr A's seemingly ordinary comment masked deeper phantasies and projective identification dynamics that were part of the transference. This included a strong desire and at times aggressive demand for an ideally understanding object that would make it all better, followed by the vision of a withholding, persecutory object that refuses to care or understand. This left Mr A with the conviction that he must be in constant control of that object to prevent its betrayal and surprise attacks. This control, however, prevents the object from ever becoming a reliable, supportive, or understanding presence on its own.

CLINICAL COMPARISON

Mr B came into the session and told me how he was walking down the street earlier in the day and heavy rains were coming down and for a few minutes the rain turned to hail. He said it "was so cold and icy for that moment, it was really something. So cold." I made a comment about the recent period of intense winter weather and then said, "Should we talk about the cold and ice in your heart tonight?" This interpretation came from many years of working with him and knowing something about his general psychological stance and experience of life.

Mr B said, "Sometimes I forget you are an analyst because you sound like a poet. You say things that match exactly where I am at." He went on to tell me how he is "shut off and frozen closed from love" and how he felt hopeless at ever being accepted by someone. I interpreted that "It is a two-way weather system, in which you feel out in the cold, but you are also the one who is cold to others because you have decided ahead of time they don't like you."

So, very quickly, we were able to move into this patient's core phantasies about his objects and about himself. Analytic contact was easily reached, emerging from my interpretation of his weather comment. This is something that would have gone unnoticed and without comment in everyday life. But, in the analytic situation, it was something I thought was a vehicle for his unconscious projective identification dynamics. This dynamic process left him feeling surrounded by his own cold and icy attitudes about others and then he felt trapped and frozen over by them.

I made interpretations to both Mr A and Mr B from a very similar technical approach. But, since they are very different individuals with a different set of phantasies, defenses, and transference experience, they received my interpretations differently. Mr A tends to see me in a per-secutory, adversarial manner so he took my comment that way. Mr B tends to see me as a soothing, understanding object. So, he took my comment in that manner. By exploring that phenomenon and searching, mutually, for the unconscious phantasies that created those feelings, we were working within a state of analytic contact. That contact is never constant, it is fluid. Especially with Mr A, we could barely hold onto those moments. So, the treatment could be defined as more analytic at one moment and less at another, but hopefully the analyst is always working to bring the analytic couple back into a working state of analytic contact.

CLINICAL COMPARISON

Mr C was a young man who came into his session and immediately asked, "How are you?" I said, "I am good, thanks." He went over to the analytic couch and as he laid down, he asked, "So, how have you been?" I answered, "OK". In everyday life, this sort of dialogue goes on all the time, but as an analyst, I am listening between the lines. After the first question about my well-being, I wondered to myself what might Mr C be concerned about. After the second question, I definitely thought Mr C was in the grips of some kind of phantasy about my well-being. This was not strange, because he worried about most of the people in his life, hoping they were happy and pleased with him. After a moment, Mr C said, "Do you always work on the weekends?" I asked what he meant. "Well, you called me Sunday to confirm the earlier meeting today. I was so surprised that you were working. You must not get much rest!" Exploring his thoughts about this led to many important details about a transference phantasy, based on projective identification. Mr C has led most of his life feeling he needs to protect, support, please, and mend his objects. He feels in need of care and love but sees that is unacceptable so he projects that into his objects and then feels obligated to nurse them along. This leaves him very tired, overwhelmed, and angry. This is how he pictured me.

I said, "So, you are worried about me being this overworked, exhausted guy who works weekends and never gets a moment to himself. You want to rescue me from that because you worry that I am not happy." He said, "Yes. It is true I feel so bad for you. I feel guilty being here and taking up your time." I interpreted, "So, it is difficult for you to lean on me and depend on me for help with your tired, angry feelings." He said, "Oh yes! I don't want to be needy or pesky. That is something I have always avoided." I replied, "You want me to be rested from my weekend so I will be able to come in and take good care of you. But, that feels selfish so you turn it around to making sure I am OK."

So, by investigating seemingly normal comments at the beginning of the session, much came to light about Mr C's core phantasies and transference, which were then interpreted and worked with. My investigation brought us into a fluid, productive exploration of the transference. This is the embodiment of analytic contact. Seemingly unimportant external or interpersonal issues were valued and explored rather than ignored or treated as not containing deeper meaning. As a result, we began working on unconscious phantasies and particular views of self and object. This work created room for internal change. Analytic contact is the moment of interpretive connection with the patient's self–object world and the efforts at finding that connection as well as maintaining and cultivating that moment.

Non-clinical situation

Sometimes, people need a stranger to help them continue to integrate certain experiences. While the example of the man in the locker room who lost his wife was of someone trying to transform his internal pain by sharing it with me, it was clear that he was still stuck in it. He was spinning his wheels within an emotional ditch, but trying to move forward. Others have managed to move forward, but need to continue to affirm themselves and their choices. They need a stranger to hear that things are better, but the residue of the past still remains.

Our next-door neighbors are an example of this. They are both in their seventies. When we visit with them, it is common for them to eventually mention how they met. They both had been married for more than twenty years. They had been friends and had gone to parties and activities as two couples. Then, their partners died of cancer. They often say how they were "all that was left of the foursome" and then hit it off, dated, and married. When they tell this story, it is clear that they are still, on some emotional level, dealing with their respective losses and possibly the guilt they have as the survivors who banded together to continue on. Yet, it is much less charged than the man in the locker room. It is as if they need to periodically tidy up that area of their life by sharing it or touch base with someone about it to make sure it is OK. There is a flow about it that shows they are not stuck in it, but just need to honor it.

Another couple that we met at the retirement community were friendly and nice to chat with. During the course of our talking, they asked us how long we had been married. When we asked them the same question back, the man responded, "Oh, roughly seventy-five years!" They both laughed and then he continued, "She was married twenty years, I was married twenty-three years, and we've been married for almost thirty years!" They went on to joke about it for a while and then turned to other topics. They were in balance with their past and with their dead spouses, but needed to find a way to routinely realign its emotional stamp. Joking about it seemed to work. They were not necessarily resolved with it nor had they forgotten about it. They needed to bring it to a stranger's attention, as a way to continue integrating and unifying their life experience.

My experience of hearing about it was pleasant, funny, and made us think more deeply about these two people. Much like our neighbors, they seemed to need a stranger to share in a part of their lives that still had meaning and still had to be revisited periodically. By sharing it and tending to it in this way, they continued to bring clarity and balance to that part of themselves. They could continue on with their lives, while fostering a sense of peace in their heart and mind.

Everyone needs a stranger to talk to, just for different reasons.

CLINICAL COMPARISON

Mrs A came into treatment to "get help with the ongoing stress" of her husband's liver disease. He was diagnosed with hepatitis a few years before I met Mrs A and he had gradually become more tired and sickly. He was undergoing various medical treatments and was on a waiting list for a transplant, but had been told he could die before a transplant became available. They had been married for twenty years. Their relationship was close and they were happy with each other. At the same time, from the way Mrs A described the relationship, I sensed there were occasional tensions that never really were addressed or resolved.

Mrs A began coming regularly to her sessions and basically reporting what had transpired over the last week. I saw her once or twice a week, depending on our schedules. Mostly, the frequency was a result of Mrs A telling me it was "enough" and not wanting to explore it much further. The majority of what she told me was the details of her husband's medical condition, how he was doing that week, what doctor visits they went to, and what problems they were having with medications, side-effects, and insurance claims. Mr C was retired at this point so he stayed home most of the time, feeling too tired to go out. Mrs A worked as a secretary and part of her talks with me were about the difficulties of getting out of work so she could take her husband to his many medical appointments.

Over time, she also told me a general history of her family and her husband's family. Like the story of everyday life in which the married couple were conveying their history and using humor to share some probable sadness or anxiety, Mrs A seemed to want to come in and share her story of what life was like with a very ill and possibly terminal spouse. I think that would be fine in and of itself. This is a need many people have and when this need is met, the person is able to soldier on with their stressful life. Indeed, there are many schools of counseling and psychotherapy that see this as the principal goal of treatment. And, some psychoanalytic schools believe this is the therapeutic aim as well. In my Kleinian approach, I think this can certainly be part of a full analytic treatment, but should be only a part of it. As an analyst, it is my job to see if there are deeper areas to also address that might make the person's difficult station in life a bit more tolerable. I seek to find analytic contact.

In the case of Mrs A, this meant listening between the lines. For the first six months, and certainly still in the current treatment, we would talk about the ups and downs of daily life dealing with a very sick husband. It was mostly about external events and how she dealt with the nuts and bolts of caring for him.

But, bit by bit, I interpreted that she "was hesitant to reveal her deeper feelings and struggles to me". This was based on my counter-transference feelings of our having talks that were just a little bit too tidy, nice, or predictable. Mrs A said, "I try and keep them to myself." I replied, "I have to sort of read between the lines. Along with all the important matters we talk about, I think you are reluctant to share with me some of your stronger emotions. Maybe these are feelings you are more uncertain or conflicted about."

Again, this type of interpretation was based on my counter-transference feelings of being kept at a distance, her very modest and brief comments about her stronger emotions, and a sense of everything being a little too neat and packaged. It was almost as if we were following a script on the normal aspects of a life transition, or Grief 101. So, I was looking for some way to build analytic contact. It required patience and close, focused listening. Gradually, I found a spot where she was willing to meet me in an analytic manner.

Responding to my interpretation, Mrs A said, "I do have a lot of intense feelings at times, but I end up feeling uncomfortable and guilty." I said, "So, you might think I will judge you or not understand." She said, "Yes. And, what does it say about me if I don't just focus on my husband?" I replied, "It means you are human, but feeling uncomfortable with it."

Over time, with my exploration and interpretations, Mrs A was able to expand her stories to include deeper feelings of anger, resentment, loss, and sadness. The change in her marriage and the loss of what she enjoyed so much about it left her with great anxiety, depression, and anger. More and more, she was able to face this. As a result, she was able to care for her husband in a more honest manner, talk with him more openly, and start to look at her own life in a new way. While her treatment is far from over, as a result of the analysis of her transference, phantasies, and defenses, she is leading a much more productive and satisfying life. While it was helpful for me to just listen to her difficult circumstances, I believe I was able to offer much more meaningful help when we established analytic contact. Again, this was not a permanent state, but the more moments of this mutual, deeper, exploratory state we could create, the more chance she had to fully explore and work on her feelings and phantasies.

This case was quite different than the one in which "C" was dealing with his father's illness and I never made any interpretations and not much of an effort to create analytic contact. With both cases, the external reality of illness with C's father and Mrs A's husband was vital to discuss, follow, and work with. But, with both cases, it was also used as a defense or shield against other feelings, phantasies, and transference issues. The difference in the two cases was that while I was unable to separate myself from the projective identification enactments enough to make interpretations to C, I was able to do so with Mrs A. As a result, analytic contact occurred in one case and not the other.

Part II

Caution and reluctance concerning psychological engagement

Chapter 5

Reality, phantasy, and the fragile nature of analytic contact

Many authors have explored the idea of phantasy and the theoretical contributions are too enormous to detail. Laplanche and Pontalis (1973) provide several definitions of the concept:

> [phantasy is an] – imaginary scene, in which the subject is a protagonist, representing an unconscious wish in a manner that is distorted by defensive processes ... it is not an object that the subject imagines and aims at, so to speak, but rather a sequence in which the subject has his own part to play and in which permutations of roles and attributions are possible ... phantasy is also the locus of defensive operations ... themselves inseparably bound up with the primary function of phantasy ... what is prohibited is always present in the actual formulations of the wish.
>
> (p. 318)

Arlow (1985) states it in this manner:

> In the course of treatment one can observe how the symptoms of the patient's illness, how his life history and his love relations, his character structure and his artistic creations may all represent in different ways derivative manifestations of the persistent unconscious fantasy activity, of the "fantasized reality" that governs the individual's life.
>
> (p. 534)

Hinshelwood (1991) states, "Phantasy is the mental expression of the instinctual impulses and also of defense mechanisms against instinctual impulses." Finally and most closely linked to the focus of my paper, H. Segal (1974) has written that:

> phantasy forming is a function of the ego. The view of phantasy as a mental expression of instincts through the medium of the ego assumes a higher degree of ego organization than is usually postulated by Freud.

It assumes that the ego from birth is capable of forming, and indeed is driven by instincts and anxiety to form primitive object-relationships in phantasy and reality. ... reality experiences immediately influence and are influenced by unconscious phantasy. Phantasy is not merely an escape from reality, but a constant and unavoidable accompaniment of real experiences, constantly interacting with them. ... If unconscious phantasy is constantly influencing and altering the perception or interpretation of reality, the converse also holds true: reality impinges on unconscious phantasy.

(pp. 13–14)

The last part of Segal's idea, regarding the reciprocal nature of how reality and phantasy impact each other, will be explored in this chapter. In the process, it will be apparent how analytic contact is affected by phantasy and reality.

Understanding the specific manner in which new experience is received and perceived, consciously and unconsciously, provides a crisp window into the inner life of the patient and their particular interface between reality and various intra-psychic phantasy states. The psychoanalytic process involves the understanding of the patient's mind in all of its ramifications. The process of how the Self relates to itself and to its objects, via phantasy, is a constant focus of the analytic process. The better the analyst understands this process, the better opportunities they have to either forge analytic contact or repair fragmented or crumbled states of analytic contact.

What is the Self? The infant begins life with various neurological states of flux, psychological and physical tensions, somatic and cognitive experiences, and multiple complex interfaces with environmental stimuli. Melanie Klein has been a pioneer in establishing how from the very start the infantile organism seeks out the object and the phantasy of the object in order to bring about a subjective sense of organization, discharge, and understanding. At first, this is in more primitive ways and later it is conducted with more sophisticated expression and intent. These potentials of mind and body are innate and, in combination, make up the emerging substrates of the Self. The developing and never static nature of the Self exists in part as the combination of the psychological and biological needs and functions of the human organism, which include somatic states, core affects, mental wishes, and fears of both a predatory and a persecutory nature. These are all united with the varied integrative and perceptual and psychic components of the Ego, such as self and object representations, and compromise formations. These organizing functions of the human organism in addition to the subjective experience of one's self as a person and a body, the experience of being both passive and active, and the sense of being both an individual and a part of a whole are all fundamentally shaped, organized, and translated by unconscious phantasy to produce what is understood as the Self. This end product of phantasy formation remains the central fulcrum from which all future experiences revolve in some manner or form.

Therefore, I conceptualize phantasy as, from the birth of the organism, the foremost fundamental organizing, binding, and translating energy within the psychic system. In this context, it must be remembered that phantasy states allow for the inner aspects of self and object representations to move and shift in order to defend, battle, and/or adapt to the inner motions of the often opposing and conflictual elements of other constellations of self and object representations. Phantasy allows for inner movement, mutation, and transformation within the matrix of the self- and the object-representational systems and provides the fuel for this internal motion. In other words, the introjected relationship between the infant and the mother does not remain static, it continues on with a life of its own, constantly being reissued, reshaped, and recreated by both internal and external reality. As such, phantasy states make up transference which in turn dictates the degree of analytic contact available at any given moment. Understanding a patient's phantasy state and the influence of reality upon that state is important in helping to cultivate or sustain analytic contact.

I will illustrate these points by presenting my patients' archaic phantasy states provoked and amplified by the relocation of my office, an environmental change. Reality impacted their psyche and visa versa. After giving all of my patients four weeks' notice that I would be moving next door to a new office, I immediately noticed marked transference reactions. These reactions were accompanied by specific phantasies that crystallized upon the actual relocation. I believe this to be the result of the unique impact reality and phantasy tend to have upon one another and the way the combination shapes analytic contact. For some patients, reality seems to loosen their transference phantasies and for some patients reality seems to fixate transference patterns. One reason for this is defensive. Reality, or at least the illusion of reality, is safer than phantasy for some individuals and for others phantasy is safer than the experience of reality.

The cases presented in this chapter are from a period of time in my practice in which I saw many very disturbed borderline and psychotic patients. I choose to present these cases to make the point of how analytic contact is difficult to reach with many patients, but possible even if under difficult transference conditions. In addition, these cases illustrate how even very disturbed patients can withstand the increased anxiety and deepening phantasy state reality change can bring. We must be hopeful in searching for analytic contact and positive in our efforts to maintain it, even if conditions temporarily erode it. Sometimes, analytic contact is completely lost due to our mistakes or due to outside influences. However, we must always persist in reaching for even a moment of analytic contact from which to understand and help a patient. The nature of phantasy is a bedrock component to our work and shapes the level of analytic contact possible during any given clinical moment.

For two years, I had been renting an office space in which I shared a waiting room with one other therapist. I decided to relocate next door, approximately twenty feet away, to a similar office space where I would be the sole practitioner. In the new location, there was one large private office, one large waiting room, a kitchen area, and a bathroom. The floor plan was a mirror image of the old one. I chose to relocate for convenience, the pleasure of having my "own space", and the fact that I didn't particularly enjoy the person with whom I had shared the old office. I will present the initial responses or lack of responses of different patients to this new setting and the impact upon our analytic contact. Their reactions offer a unique view into the intra-psychic mindscape that they usually dwelt in and maneuvered from, as well as a view of the impact of reality factors upon their phantasy material. It was a reinforcement and validation of the theoretical concept of phantasy as a central organizing factor in the mind which has an inseparable relationship with external reality. Analytic contact was unaffected in some cases and negatively affected in others.

Some of my patients simply noticed the new office setting, looked around a bit, made a comment or two, and then settled in to resume business as usual. With this group of patients, the majority of the feedback consisted of either comments about how much bigger the space felt and how comfortable everything was or comments about how the floor plan of my office was now reversed and that it was a bit difficult to get used to. These types of superficial or screen comments persisted for a few weeks. On the other hand, there were other patients who had a much more jagged and direct set of responses very immediately. With these patients, the analytic contact we had established became much more unstable.

Mr A looked around the new office very slowly and intently. After a period of time that felt to me like hours, he looked at me blankly. There was no comment. He had taken it in, adjusted himself to it, and looked at me to begin. This data-gathering and robot-like approach to change was very much the way he usually related to life, warding off any hint of affect he might have. This was part of a phantasy in which he protected himself from what he called the "dangerous exposure" that would occur if he allowed his feelings to be known. So, the energy Mr A put into fighting off our very meager analytic contact was maintained and even increased with this new reality that posed a new psychological threat.

The next patient was a Mr B. His reaction was similar to one of mine in that he was glad to be rid of the therapist whom I had shared the last suite with. When I saw Mr B, he often engaged in a very loud, unusual, and piercing laughter that persisted for several minutes. We had begun to understand this as part of an anxious effort to control his environment and his objects. When he made this loud noise, the therapist next door would pound on the wall for the noise to stop. I had spoken to the therapist about this and had gotten nowhere. While I had previously asked the patient to quiet down a bit, this was mostly an unfortunate situation in which the other therapist had absolutely no room for any occasional disturbances. At times, his patients would also become loud or obnoxious to the point of intruding upon my work. But, this therapist was unable to discuss it as a mutual concern that could be worked with. The patient and I had mutually agreed that this therapist was selfish and insensitive.

I noted a sort of mutual hate that grew out of this situation, a hate that seemed to bond us together. This was a particular analytic contact that was strong and not necessarily explored or fully analyzed. However, these transference and counter-transference issues were a regular focus over the course of the treatment. In the setting of my new office, Mr B told me he felt a great freedom in being away from the other therapist. It was as though there now was a mutual state of glee as we mutually celebrated the freedom to express ourselves as we pleased. We were able to explore this as symbolic of a freedom that he never had at home with his family and in part symbolic of finally having someone on his side. In other words, he had phantasies of always being alone, not having anyone on his side, and not being able to freely express himself without some sort of punishment. These phantasies shaped the degree of analytic contact we were able to have, restricting our contact much of the time. This mutual acting out of our feelings about the move followed by analytic exploration of that acting out helped to improve the analytic contact. It seemed to pave the way toward a new freedom in working through his transference fears, his resentments with his family, and his self-imposed restrictions in life.

Mr B had grown up in a very oppressive, violent family where it was quite dangerous to express himself. As a part of the more stable analytic contact, he was more able and willing to explore his transference and phantasies. In this process we gradually came to see the piercing laughter as part of a projective identification dynamic that set the stage for him to be treated as he was in childhood and my office partner banging on the wall was a reenactment of his early experiences within his family. I was, in my old office, the ineffectual mother who could do nothing to help protect him from the abusive father. Later, in my new office, I was part of what he called "the escape phantasy" where he could rid himself of the noisy father and have an understanding mother all to himself.

Several patients commented that they hoped I would tell them where I was moving to. Upon exploration, they revealed phantasies of coming to their sessions, finding me gone, and not knowing where I had moved to. As we unraveled the transference meanings of this phantasy, the various strands of anxiety concerning abandonment, the fears of separation, and the terror of betrayal came to consciousness. These were patients who had enormous problems regarding phantasies of desiring attachment and dependency followed by terrors of being annihilated as the result of such connections. The nature of the analytic contact with this group was very fragile, yet they were able to explore and express much of their transference struggles. The reality of the move seemed to simply maintain the already precarious status quo of analytic contact. It was the type of contact in which they were willing to tolerate or endure being with someone they felt would easily throw them away, but only for so long. So, through projective identification, my experience of analytic contact was also one of "when will they leave me, when will it all come falling down?" I consider this state to still constitute what I am terming analytic contact because patient and analyst are still in the process of acknowledging, exploring, and working on these unconscious phantasies. However, the phantasy state is so intense and overarching that the patients often flee treatment early on or abort rather abruptly. The fact that a major reality change such as my office move didn't trigger that is testimony to this group of patients' hope, dependence, and ability to hang in there despite the adversity of their negative convictions regarding their objects.

Mrs K had marked negative transference phantasies both before and after I moved. She was convinced that I was moving because I wanted to get rid of her and that since "I was moving up in the world", I would "leave her behind". Feeling that I did not care about her well-being, she hated me moving. Overall, she felt very unimportant and generally slighted and rejected by me. This made it appear quite easy to make transference inter-pretations as to her various fears and wishes; unfortunately, with this particular patient, making interpretations was like trying to spread frozen butter over a delicate piece of bread. In other words, we had very little workable analytic contact. Once I had moved into the new office, she told me that she "definitely hated the new environment, she hated everything about it". She shredded each part of my new office into small piles with her criticism. A new light fixture had a rather bright bulb in it and instead of commenting on the brightness, she told me how ugly and offensive it was and how much it damaged her eyes. "You want to burn my eyes out", she yelled. Agreeing with her realistic observation as to the brightness, I picked out a dimmer bulb for the fixture. In the transference, I was also agreeing that I did want to burn out her eyes and would now try to undo my attack by changing the bulb.

When she noticed the change, she said she was sick and tired of my techniques to "break her down". When Mrs K used this phrase, as she often did, she meant that I must be trying to psychologically trick her, play mental games with her, and generally test her somehow for "secret reasons". Mrs K added that the change in the bulb would be welcomed by all and therefore it must be a trick on my part to get people to like me. I asked her why she thought I would work so hard and secretly to have people like me, and if she might be describing her own efforts and hopes for me to like her. She said, "I want to trust you and like you, but you seem to always be so mean to me." Here, we had a foothold on analytic contact and we continued exploring her transference phantasies that were stirred up by the change in reality, my office move. With Mrs K, her initial wave of persecutory phantasies made analytic contact very uncertain. But, when I hung in there, tolerated her attacks, and continued to make interpretations, we regained analytic contact and could explore her deeper fears and angry urges.

Two female patients made comments to the effect that they would like to move in permanently. "I love it, can I just move right in?" was the way one patient put it. The other woman said, "Let us always stay here, we can just sit around and talk all day long and never leave." I commented that she curiously left out what would occur at nightfall.

One patient has not shown up for appointments since I moved. I had a feeling that the move was, in phantasy, a perceived reenactment of the complete and total abandonment which she had felt in her early years, causing her to flee from me in fear of annihilation. A sort of "I will get him before he gets me" type of situation may have occurred. She has never returned my calls. Analytic contact was always difficult to find with this patient and easily crushed in the end.

Another patient, M, had a very immediate reaction the first time she came into the new office. She told me that she had realized it before, but now that she saw this new office she had proof that I was merely out to make money. She said that I was robbing people and seeking only my own pleasure and the new office furniture was proof of this idea. This woman's transference was usually a state of fluctuation between the projection of a rejecting internal object and the projection of a rewarding or exciting object. I gently reminded M that I actually was seeing her for a reduced fee and that I could not make a profit from her if I wanted to, given that she is not even paying my lowest fee. I also made a genetic interpretation concerning her feeling ripped off and taken advantage of by me, as similar to her experience in her family where she felt worthless and was "only alive to be taken advantage of" as she put it.

In that moment of accusation, analytic contact was not available. Her phantasies stood in the way of reaching any working analytic contact. But, after she calmed down, we gradually were able to see this way of relating as a way of protecting her from the fears she had of my not having any interest, care, or love for her. This would be an example of a clarification of reality, followed by a genetic interpretation, paving the way to the more here-and-now transference phantasy material.

One patient, who is usually very timid, was fearful and shy about the idea of a new office. She had a hard time coming into the waiting room and was very afraid that she was disturbing me. So, I had to coax her into the room, assuring her that she was welcome and was certainly not disturbing me.

This woman had an enduring childhood phantasy in which she was always causing trouble and disturbing people. The level of analytic contact possible with this patient has also depended on my willingness to occasionally reassure her or coax her out of hiding.

These cases show how easily patients' primary phantasy configurations came alive in the context of an environmental change. While many of my examples are with quite regressed patients, I believe that relatively innocuous environmental change triggering archaic phantasies which in turn shapes the degree of analytic contact that is possible in that moment is applicable to more neurotic patients as well.

One patient who had been the subject of his father's sadistic emotional attacks for years, wherein his own identity seemed to be stolen from him over and over, remarked that the door to my waiting room was unlocked. I told him, "Yes, it is open for you to come in and sit down until I come out for you." He replied "Any kleptomaniac that was walking by could come in and clean you out." This is a man who feels the world is impinging upon him and that people usually have evil motives, frequently taking advantage of each other, taking away emotional bits and pieces as they wish. His phantasies regarding his internal father were often of a sadistic and psychotic nature and these as well as his own wishes were always very warded off and usually projected outwards as greed, lust, and violence coming from threatening strangers. I asked him if there was anything he had his eye on in the waiting room. This started what proved to be a fruitful session about his own interests and his anxieties about his desires, which led to his hiding and projecting them. So, again, this was a patient whose persecutory world made analytic contact very difficult to maintain. However, by patiently and consistently investigating his fears and phantasies, I was able to create islands of analytic contact in which we could touch on and work on these frightening states of mind.

One patient who is loyal to placating, rescuing, and caretaking others at any cost was walking around outside, waiting for me to open the door to my new office. It was her first time in it and I was running five minutes late. I noticed that she was pacing around furiously. Not until late into the session was she able to say that indeed she was furious that I was late but felt it was not "proper" to show her anger because it was "my day", meaning my first day in my new office and she didn't want to "spoil it". Instead, she praised me for the new office setting and held off expressing her rage. I pointed out that this was a very common theme in her life, wherein she sacrificed herself for the sake of others through some sort of rationalization which in the long run created a pathological relationship with me very similar to the one she had with her mother. She was sure I was celebrating and basking in my own glory and didn't want to be bothered with the needs of anyone else. Indeed, we eventually discussed the fear and excitement concerning her "first day" in my new office that was being projected into myself and then defended against. We explored how distant we were from each other in this particular phantasy, leaving her alone and unable to reach me for help or closeness. So, with this patient, the change in reality momentarily left her with phantasies of alienation and rejection, but fairly quickly, with my interpretative investigation, led to increased analytic contact and a further working through of unconscious patterns.

Some patients did not appear to realize the office change. No comment was made and they did not even look around at anything. Months, and now years, later they still have not given any indication that they are consciously aware of the change. I speculate that this is a remarkable demonstration of the complete encapsulation that they have constructed within parts of their psyche for a state of paradoxical protection. These are patients who appear to be deadened and often have phantasies about the need to remain buried safely behind a protective shield from the over-whelming and destructive qualities of the world at large and intimacy with the analyst in particular. Analytic contact is extremely difficult with these individuals and the sudden change in reality only seemed to stiffen this resistance.

Chapter 6

The analyst as translator: speaking the unspoken

Melanie Klein based her interpretive technique on the transference. She consistently linked the here-and-now of the patient/analyst pair, the patient's internal phantasy life, and the external reality of past and present. Rather than rely on suggestion, reassurances, or authority, she stayed with the transference theme within the clinical situation.

Klein believed, as do her followers, that both the positive and negative transference must be analyzed. She thought the entire personality, the full spectrum of emotions and thoughts, is important to understand. Klein thought that regardless of diagnostic issues, proper analysis of the patient's anxieties and troubling phantasies promoted growth and strengthened the ego. I would add that this analysis of anxiety and phantasy is what provides the optimal opportunity for sustained analytic contact.

Klein felt that the infant is faced with two developmental levels of experience. She called these positions and felt we all are constantly moving back and forth between them. The paranoid-schizoid position (Klein 1946) is the earliest state of more primitive anxiety and idealization. The infantile ego is faced with desires for knowledge, satisfaction, and gratification. At the same time, aggressive drives aim to do away with these needs in oneself and others. These conflicts between the life and death instincts are difficult for the mind to deal with, so certain defense mechanisms are used. Splitting, projective identification, denial, and idealization are common ways of coping. Love and hate, good and bad, are artificially separated. The ego and the object are split into good and evil. All mental activity begins to revolve around this internal situation.

Later, with positive internal and external experiences, the ego starts to integrate. This new depressive position (Klein 1935) ushers in a time where ambivalence is possible. Finally, the self and the object are felt to be not all good or all bad, but a mixture of both. Separation, difference, and imperfection can all be tolerated. Mourning is the new developmental task as the ego feels capable of hurting its objects. With whole-object functioning, reparation, guilt, and forgiveness are possible. If one loves and hates the same person, ambivalence is achieved and complex internal and interpersonal negotiations are necessary, instead of a black-and-white world. The paranoid-schizoid position is mainly a pre-oedipal two-person experience and the depressive position is home to more complex two-party interaction as well as three-person oedipal conflicts.

Melanie Klein put clinical life into Freud's ideas about unconscious conflict. To her, these were not biological urges in mechanistic conflict over sexual gratification. Klein felt the mind was full of dramatic phantasies, with different aspects of the personality in union or in battle with different aspects of important persons. She called these unconscious representations of loved and hated persons "objects", to make it clear they were internal images, not actual people. Klein showed, through her analysis of children and adults, that there is an internal theater full of ghosts of ourselves and others that are in constant relationship to each other. These unconscious relationships are played out in the transference and throughout daily life. Therefore, how the patient relates to his boss, his wife, his children, his co-workers, and his therapist all give clues to the conflicts, anxieties, and defenses in the unconscious. Just as Freud pointed out, Klein felt these phantasies were a shifting, dynamic record of actual external events, heavily distorted by the wishes, fears, and conflicts of the ego.

In 1946, Melanie Klein introduced the term "projective identification". Segal (1974) examined the different motivations and goals within this mental dynamic. Segal states:

> Projective identification has manifold aims: it may be directed toward the ideal object to avoid separation, or it may be directed toward the bad object to gain control of the source of danger. Various parts of the self may be projected, with various aims: bad parts of the self may be projected in order to get rid of them as well as to attack and destroy the object, good parts may be projected to avoid separation or to keep them safe from bad things inside or to improve the external object through a kind of primitive projective reparation.
>
> (pp. 27–8)

Projective identification is an intra-psychic event, in which aspects of the ego interact with aspects of the internal and external object. Evidence of this interaction and the specific nature of its dynamics become clearer through close clinical examination. These include the patient's free associations, the analyst's counter-transference, the interpersonal dynamics between analyst and patient, acting out of the clinical situation by either analyst or patient, and symptom formation. Once the analyst becomes aware of the projective identification mechanism, he may decide to make an interpretation. This interpretation will be shaped by the specific nature of the projective process and exactly how he came to be aware of it. In other words, while projective identification is a complicated matter that is difficult to immediately and fully understand, it presents many guideposts for the clinician. There is usually a combination of projective identification situations occurring at all times. The analyst must try to tease out certain portions of them in any given clinical moment and attempt to explore and interpret them within the context of the transference and the patient's unconscious phantasy states.

THE ANALYST AS TRANSLATOR

In the Kleinian tradition, the interpretive process aims at modifying anxiety. This anxiety is the result of particular object-relational phantasies that the analyst invariably becomes drawn into by either the patient's interpersonal or verbal use of the analyst (O'Shaughnessy 1983). By interpreting this involvement and the patient's unconscious desires and defenses behind that relational invitation, both patient and analyst create new knowledge about the patient's inner life and learn about previously unknown aspects of the patient's internal world (Hinshelwood 2004). This in turn creates new opportunities, choices, and potential for change. This sequence, when successful, defines a balanced, sustainable, and fertile atmosphere of analytic contact.

The reach for and the relationship with a new understanding object, first in the image of the analyst and later as an internalized part of the ego, makes anxiety tolerable and understandable. However, the analyst interpretations that aim to modify and explore the patient's anxiety inevitably give rise to that very anxiety and then a resurgence of pathological defenses aimed at re-stabilizing the former psychic equilibrium (Meyer 2004). Projective identification is often the principal defensive attempt to fight off the analyst's interpretive efforts. So, the interpretation of projective identification phantasies, often the core transference element, is crucial to sustained analytic contact.

Many patients, including the one's highlighted in this chapter, make a strong effort to fill the time and space with the analyst with stories about current external difficulties. Often, these problems are discussed in a way that makes them sound hopeless and destined to remain so for all time. It is an invitation for both analyst and patient to ignore their significance, as if they are an understood, unchangeable disaster that must be accepted as simply one's plight in life and somehow adjusted to. This is a projective identification strategy of avoidance. It is avoidance of exploration, confrontation, or change. This constitutes an active, unconscious stance against the principles of analytic contact. The analyst must see these types of standoffs as an important method of communication that needs to be understood and interpreted. Segal (1967) states, "all communications are seen as communications about the patients phantasies as a well as current external life – this is equivalent to saying that all communications contain something relevant to the transference situation. In Kleinian technique, the inter-pretation of the transference is often more central than in classical technique."

This emphasis on the interpretation of the transference is often made more difficult and confusing because of the patient's excessive use of projective identification. While understanding the nature of the patient's internal objects is critical, the exploration of them through dreams, stories of external drama, and the historical details a patient provides can be colored by projective identification so it becomes a mutual avoidance of the transference and the object relations being played out in the room. The alternative is for the analyst to realize he is being put in the position of being the translator of the patient's unwanted, unacceptable, unspoken feelings and thoughts. Feldman (1992) reminds us that regardless of the lack of or wealth of information from dreams, history, and the external facts provided by the patient, the purest evidence of the patient's internal object world comes out of the analysis of the transference.

Successfully interpreting a patient's desire for a personal spokesperson

M was a forty-year-old woman who came to see me in a state of frustration and despair. She had been dating a man for several years who was on occasion verbally abusive and emotionally manipulative, but mostly just neglectful and selfish. He had two affairs over the years, which M found out about. He blamed her for not providing him with enough sex. M loved him and wanted to eventually marry, but could not picture a secure future with him. He had been laid off his job for drinking a year prior to M seeking me out, and he still had no job prospects.

M worked as a retail sales clerk in a dress shop and had been there for eight years. It was the type of job she had stayed in since graduating college with a dual degree in Arts and in English. She, way back as a teen, had dreamed of painting and writing for a career. But, soon after graduating, did nothing to pursue that desire and fell into a receptionist job that a friend had recommended. M hated her current job and told me she couldn't imagine being more bored.

In the beginning of her analysis, M strongly believed the best thing to do in life was to avoid more pain. She felt her distress and despair was as good as she would ever have it, as good as she should ever have it, and as good as she could ever have it. In the transference, she kept to the facts rather than risk sharing her emotional truth. Expressing your needs was the same as com-plaining and asking for trouble. Slowly over the years, we were able to explore these anti-growth phantasies and found out more about her feelings of being greedy. M was sure she always was overstaying her welcome and asking for too much. This resulted in her asking me in various ways for permission to do what felt like indulging her greed.

M was not operating from a purely paranoid state. She exhibited many depressive qualities and tried to relate in a whole-object manner at times. However, there was something incomplete about these efforts. Trying to not offend or hurt me was part of a phantasy of my losing my grip on the shred of tolerance I had and then completely rejecting her. There was a lack of reciprocal thinking on her part. It was more of a steady monitoring of my temper and mood with her in the background.

I saw M for six years, using the analytic approach. This meant frequent visits, the analytic couch, analysis of the transference, and the exploration of defenses and unconscious phantasies. By actively using these ways of engaging the patients, I fostered an analytic contact with M. During M's treatment, many issues emerged and much was worked through. The core theme that presented itself rather immediately and remained central to our analytic journey was M's reluctance, fear, and outright aversion to taking in, building, or finding a bigger, stronger, more pleasurable life.

This anti-growth, pleasure-avoidant, independence-shunning stance first took the form of her censoring the negative feelings she had toward the objects that either hurt her or denied her love and pleasure. This initial struggle gave way to M's not feeling safe to risk broadening her life and also manifested in the transference as hiding her desires and feelings from me. So, in the beginning of the treatment, M would tell me stories of what her day or weekend was like in a very straightforward manner, with only the facts and sterile details.

My counter-transference feelings were very important to monitor and analyze during these periods. I would listen to her stories and find myself feeling irritated, angry, or protective of her. In her stories, I heard variations of her being used, ignored, or unappreciated and then I would feel like coming to her aid. I understood this to be part of a projective identification process in which M would give me pieces of her experience to hold, detoxify, or champion. These were aspects of herself and feelings that she did not want to deal with. Many of the projected feelings I was encountering had to do with early, primitive states of loss (Waska 2002) that had origins in her infantile experience of neglect with her parents.

Sometimes, I would be taken over by my counter-transference experiences and act out these projective identification dynamics (Waska 2004). During those moments, I lost my interpretive footing and let go of the analytic contact we had established. Those moments became part of something less analytic and more repetitive of a pathological object-relational cycle. I would listen to a story about her new boyfriend and end up thinking to myself, "What a selfish guy. He didn't even bother to return her calls. How rude!" Then, I might say something like, "I bet you felt like giving him a piece of your mind about that", or "What stopped you from confronting him on that?" Some of my comments sounded relatively benign on the surface. They seemed aimed at eliciting more discussion on the matter or interpreting her resistance to standing up for herself. Over time, what I noticed was that my comments were really a combination of a reaction to feeling deprived or neglected by her silence on the matters at hand, an aggressive push from me to get her to show some feeling or response to the people who seemed to victimize her (I was bullying her for not responding to the people who bullied her), and I was becoming the spokesman for all her silent protests.

Slowly, I came to better understand these reactions as components of a counter-projective identification (Grinberg 1979). As I noticed this intra-psychic and interpersonal phenomenon more clearly, I was able to interpret it with the aim of integrating these scattered aspects of M's inner world. Analytic contact was gradually restored.

I interpreted that she seemed to have a difficult time sharing many of her more negative or angry thoughts and feelings with me. By holding back and keeping these private, she gave me an idea of how isolated she might feel sometimes. This comment prompted M to recall feeling very isolated and neglected when she was a child. She told me she had many angry feelings about being left alone and ignored, but she thought that voicing them would only make her parents more neglectful or even angry and abusive.

I interpreted that we sometimes were in a situation where I was like the angry parent she feared. I was essentially attacking her by saying, "What is wrong with you? Why can't you stand up for yourself?" Exploring this inter-personal and intra-psychic aspect of the projective identification in the transference led to more important associations. M told me about how her sister would often criticize and bully her for "not having any common sense and never doing what needed doing." M recalled many times when growing up in which her sister responded to M's timid nature by lecturing, yelling, or telling her what to do and when to do it. We gained a good deal of ground by discussing how this happened on occasion in our relationship.

Unconsciously, M wanted me to be the spokesman for her feelings and ideas. In the first few years of the analytic work, this meant I held all of what she felt to be negative, angry, and confrontive. So, my interpretations were usually aimed at exploring how and why she felt she needed to hide those feelings in me. We worked on how she felt it was rude, unacceptable, risky, and even dangerous to own those types of urges. M told me that voicing "those sorts of things could make me look like a selfish bitch."

Imaging herself as selfish, aggressive, or troublesome created a fear of being shunned, ignored, or abandoned. She cried a great deal when sharing these phantasies. Given the clarity of the transference, we were more able to explore her vision of her objects. M felt I was someone who would only accept, tolerate, or love her if her personality were tailor-made to my likes. Her image of me was strict and demanding, wanting her to be an agreeable little girl who didn't make trouble. This, of course, made it impossible for her to embrace life, showing all of herself. Bit by bit, we worked through this victim stance in her phantasy world to the point where she could own her own refusal of the good object, the accepting analyst, because it was a risk she couldn't control. Keeping the good object at bay allowed her to know, control, and predict her world, sad and stuck as it was. Making changes in this arena was slow and choppy, but deeply rewarding and hopeful to M. Analytic contact defined the relationship at that time in the treatment, producing change, knowledge, and growth even in the midst of her resistance and arm's-length defensive mode.

Later in the psychoanalytic treatment, M's arm's-length approach shifted from avoiding expressing what she felt to be negative or selfish to a general, softer reluctance to let in pleasure, success, or growth. Once again, M used projective identification to enlist me as her spokesman, this time for the parts of her that were ready to thrive and reach out for the good object and a vision of an accepting world. As M's spokesman for pleasure, I found myself voicing her wishes in numerous ways. She would say something like, "On the way to work, I stopped off at this new bakery. I got myself a coffee. On the way out, I noticed they had quite a selection of freshly baked donuts, scones, and muffins." The way she said it made it obvious to me that she was really wanting to order something delicious to go with her coffee. I would be caught up in the feeling without giving it much thought and I would say something like, "I bet you wanted to take a few with you to work!" She would hesitate, but agree and maybe elaborate a bit. This was all part of a projective identi-fication process, involving both interpersonal dynamics and intra-psychic phantasies, in which she managed to get me to hold and live out her desires for fun, pleasure, or growth.

Over time, I came to understand this more, started interpreting it more, and began acting out the projective elements less. I would say, "I think you are reluctant to acknowledge how much you want from our relationship or from life. It is hard to show me that you want more pleasure, more fun, and more fulfilling relationships with men. You get me to be your cheerleader for these things. But, I think it is important to understand why you can't voice those hopes and wishes yourself." M would tell me, "When I first started seeing you, I wasn't even aware that I had these feelings, these ideas for things to be better. But now, I do find myself thinking that my boyfriend could treat me nicer, my parents could be more loving, or that I deserve a raise at work. So, I now think these things but I don't tell you. I don't want to seem too selfish or pushy. It feels like I would be asking for too much." I interpreted, "So you would rather stop yourself short than to tell me and risk that I would find you selfish and greedy." M agreed and said, "I think it is easier to just dream of those things than to put it out there and have them backfire."

So, at that point in the analytic work, M no longer feared her aggressive and negative feelings, but she hid her desires for more and for better. Her view of the object and the world was essentially the same, but now more flexible. Before, the object in M's internal world was hostile and angry if she expressed any conflict or autonomy, due to how she disowned her own controlling, aggressive side. Now that this splitting pathology had been worked through and considerably reduced and more manageable, her needs and desires became evident. However, these phantasies provoked the same type of retaliatory object relations as before, due to the same type of projective mechanisms.

Therefore, I made interpretations, much in the same manner as before, that explored these areas of stagnation and resistance. I pointed out, usually in the moments it was taking place in the transference, how she was enlisting me to be her spokesman for an improved life, a more enjoyable day, and a more rewarding, bountiful existence. I said, "You want me to be a good, accepting parent, willing to hear and understand your hopes and dreams. You want my support, but you are still frightened that you want too much. You worry I will be angry, see you as greedy, and slap you down." M responded, "Exactly. And, if you don't put me down, you might still choose to cut me off, have nothing to do with me. Wow, I can't believe how strong those feelings are!"

Over the years, M changed her view of me, due to a shift in how she felt about her needs and wishes. Tied to this change, was a conflict over her sense of entitlement to more love, respect, and enjoyment from her objects. The way this would manifest was in her looking to me for permission to proceed with first having the desire for more and then acting on that urge. When M put me in the role of spokesman, she could then feel safe and wait till I gave her permission to have those thoughts and feelings by the signal that I was thinking and talking about them. If I was talking about improving her life, then it must be OK for her to entertain those feelings as well. During one session, I interpreted, "You use me as your translator. You have me say what you feel and think so you don't have to face the danger." She replied, "You are not just my translator. I take in what you translate and listen very closely. But, you also give me permission to feel!" Then, M broke down sobbing.

As a result of our analytic work, M was more and more able to speak to these forbidden hopes, without being overcome by fear of rejection or retaliation. So, M gradually became her own spokesperson. The next step of this new freedom was difficult. It became more acceptable to think about these forbidden wishes, but to actually do something to obtain them was very frightening. So, M now felt she needed permission to take action to achieve these goals of self-improvement, whatever they might be.

A major vehicle for this part of the transference working-through process was when M decided to change careers. It was a real success that she allowed herself to think about wanting a better career and realizing how unhappy she had been for so long. Brainstorming about what she would really like to do and what type of job or career seemed most exciting was a major step in not just giving herself permission to thrive, but realizing she didn't need permission in the first place. It was OK to want more and to grow. It didn't need justification.

However, when M had to make phone calls and go on job interviews, many of the same fears returned. She projected her own stringent, rigid phantasies into me and into her potential new bosses. Was she really cut out for it, would they see right through her, would they kick her out of the interview, was she taking up too much of my time boring me about details of her job hunt, and was she just setting herself up for an embarrassing fall and failure? It wasn't that the object was deliberately attacking her, but it was responding to her outrageous requests. Gradually, we worked through these phantasies. M faced her internal demons and took actions to reach her new goals. Due to this hard work, M landed a new job at a company dealing with something that had always been an interest to her.

At the end of her analysis, M felt "like a whole person, able to own my heart and mind and actually pursue who I am and what I am about!" She was now engaged to a man who treated her with respect and love. While she still felt timid and unsure at times, M was proud of her new job and felt fulfilled by her work. The world seemed more accepting and giving, because M allowed herself to be more accepting, giving, and loving. She could now be herself without repercussions. Indeed, M realized that being herself actually brought about more support, interest, and devotion from her objects. She had become a good, balanced, and accepting object for herself.

Reading between the lines

A is a forty-year-old woman with three children, all on their way out of the home, headed for college or already in college. She is married to a mechanic who is an alcoholic. He drinks every day, but usually only gets drunk two or three times a month. He feels A is just complaining about his drinking and doesn't see it as a real problem, except on the day of a drinking binge.

Initially, I saw them as a couple. After three visits together, he decided it was "a waste of time. We don't have any problems that we can't work out ourselves". A was obviously very worried about her marriage and the quality of her own life, so I suggested she continue on her own, with the under-standing that perhaps her husband would return at some point. We began to explore how helpless her husband's drinking made her feel. This line of investigation brought out many sad stories about her upbringing, in which her father's drinking was part of an extremely abusive background. As an example, when her father thought that she had possibly stolen some candy from the neighborhood store, he hit her so hard that two teeth came loose. I made many interpretations concerning how she must have had to come up with creative maneuvers to avoid the physical and emotional pain of her life. I also suggested that these psychological defenses were still being used and instead of protecting her they may actually be creating the same feelings in her today. In other words, I interpreted that there was some level of repetition going on between her and her objects.

The more we talked, the more examples of this emerged. It turned out that she worked for a boss who approached her sexually. A felt uncomfortable with it, but usually thought she had better just find a way to distract him rather than confront him. This abusive relationship had gone on for many years.

Over a period of several years, A made great progress in her analytic treatment. As a result of exploring her deeper unconscious phantasies, fears, and transference feelings, she was able to gradually shift many of her lifelong patterns. She became more assertive, more expressive of herself both at home and at her job, and she took steps to change her career. For most of her life, she had dreamed of becoming a policewoman. We traced this desire to her want for order and justice in her early family experience and the idea that right could conquer wrong. Also, it was a position of power and auth-ority that demanded respect, something she never felt she deserved. So, with her busy schedule, she began to take classes and prepare herself to one day take the necessary tests to see if she could qualify for the police force.

This progress was fragile and A could sabotage it quite easily. One session, A came in and laid on the couch for several minutes without saying a word. Then, she started crying. "I almost didn't come in. I though very seriously of not ever coming in again. I wanted to figure things out myself", she said. I replied, "Something must feel very tough for you right now, almost too tough to be able to share it with me." A told me that her husband had gotten very drunk and crashed the car into the garage when trying to park it. During that session and the next one, we explored how she blamed herself for this terrible incident. I interpreted, "If you feel you are too blame, of course you won't want to come in and tell me about it. I would think you are a failure. You must think I see you as doing nothing to stop his drinking." A said, "That makes me think immediately of my mother. She never did anything to stop my father's violence, his temper, or his drinking." This line of thought led to A's telling me she was furious at her husband sometimes and has thought of leaving him. Then, she discussed her fears of him leaving her. I pointed out that when she felt her anger and had thoughts of leaving him, she seemed to retaliate and punish herself by turning the tables and imagining herself being abandoned instead. Then, A associated to phantasies of confronting her husband's drinking and how that would "create a lot of trouble. I don't like to cause trouble. I feel like I am a bad person for creating grief or picking on someone. I should just keep it to myself." I interpreted, "I think you didn't want to come in today because you thought that telling me how you really feel about things is causing trouble. You don't want to be bad and cause trouble for me, putting your needs on me." A replied, "Yes. That is exactly right. I see what you mean. It's like I am the cause. I am complaining too much and somehow I could prevent these problems, so why am I complaining about them."

Here, I was exploring her phantasies and transference state, both of which were based on projective identification. Her phantasies, based on projective identification, corrupted our analytic contact as she pictured herself as a useless failure and me as someone who would have no understanding and easily reject her. This was a phantasy that felt real and her anxiety prevented her from reflecting on this as anything except reality. Therefore, my interpretative stance was crucial to maintain analytic contact, otherwise I would be confirming her phantasies by my silence.

A felt her objects (father, husband, boss, and others) were throwing their problems and distorted needs onto her, causing her trouble. She wanted to confront them and stand up for herself but she envisioned that she would be putting her needs and problems on them in an angry, attacking way and we would feel as angry and disapproving as she does in turn. Therefore, most of the time she chose to do nothing, an identification with her passive mother. Part of my interpretations at that moment were aimed at showing her the either/or way of thinking she was trapped in, as a result of pathological splitting. I interpreted, "You feel that the only options for you are to be a doormat like your mother or an angry, aggressive person like your father. Maybe there is a third option, a third choice, something different than a carbon copy of your parents." Here, I was pointing out that rather than being trapped in the father–mother aspect of the oedipal triangle, she could access herself and be separate and different than them.

The next session, A came in and said, "What you said last time made a real difference. I thought about it a lot. When you said I could have a third option, it was like a revelation. I had never thought of it like that before. It seemed like a burden came off of me or something, like a new freedom I've discovered. You made me think!" After talking about her job and how that was going better and some details about her car being in the shop, she settled in to telling me what felt like comfortable stories about her husband's alcoholic behaviors, her challenges with police academy classes, and the ups and downs of being a parent. I noticed how comfortable it all seemed and how I felt pulled into just being an audience member, relaxing and listening to a nice, interesting story. One factor I did notice, that seemed to stick out, was how she kept telling her husband what he was doing wrong. He drank too much, he neglected the children, he didn't empty the garbage, and so on. I interpreted, "You only tell him what he does wrong. And, you only tell me about the bad things going on. I think it is way more frightening to tell your husband and myself what you want, what you need. In other words, it might be easy to hide behind what you don't like, so you never have to share what you wish for. Your needs and hopes don't get much air time here." A said, "My husband says all I ever do is bitch. I think that is kind of what you are saying. If I didn't bitch so much, I might have to say what I do want. I don't know. That feels scary, confrontational, weird. Like I don't have the right."

Later in the session, A was telling me about the different police schools she had been researching and the pros and cons of each one. It all sounded very educational and factual and her reasons for preferring one over another sounded rational. However, I was left with the feeling that A was missing from the story. I interpreted, "By the way you are describing these different programs and from what I know about you already, I think you have strong feelings about the school you want to apply for. But, I think you are trying to hide your excitement and desire from me, so as to make sure I don't get angry or judgmental. You make all the schools sound nice and interesting without putting your own opinion in the mix. Somewhere inside you there is a little girl who wants to share her excitement and choices with me, but you are muffling her, keeping her silent to keep the peace with me." A said, "I can't lie. You are right. It just feels selfish to come right out and tell you what

I think. But, it is true. I would really like to go to the 'x' academy. It may be too costly and the hours might not work out, but if it were up to me, that is what I would choose." I added, "But, it is up to you." A said, "I don't want to be shot down, so I play dumb." Here, she was actively gaining knowledge about herself, insight that gave her the power to change. That moment of working together (my interpretations, my self-analysis into my counter-transference reactions, her reflections, her awareness of her resistances, her allowing herself to creatively associate to her feelings and thoughts, and her acceptance of where she has been, where she is, and where she needs to go) is the essence of analytic contact.

Chapter 7

The patient's push to be parented void of growth and change

INTERPRETING THE WISH FOR PERMISSION

B was a middle-aged woman in treatment for depression. She would usually spend her sessions talking about her mother and her ambivalent feelings toward her mother. B's parents divorced when B was twelve. When B was twenty, her father died of a heart attack. B felt her mother was always coming to B to rescue her, reassure her, and parent her. B told me, "I feel like I am the mother and she is the kid. That is not right!"

Over time, B's stories about how bad her mother was and how difficult she made B's life had a particular effect on me. I noticed myself feeling irritated with her mother, wanting to tell her, "Hey, treat your daughter better. She needs you to be a mother, not such a needy loser!" And, I felt the urge to tell B that she "would be all right" and that it was OK to go ahead and be angry at mom. My phantasy was to tell B, "No little girl should have to put up with that kind of situation!" I thought a lot about these counter-transference feelings and came to think that B was projecting her wishes for a limit-setting, accepting, and strong father onto me, someone who would stand up to mom on B's behalf.

I used these ideas to translate this projective identification process by interpreting several points. I said, "I think you have been looking to me as a father figure who could tell you it's OK to be upset and that you are not a bad girl for feeling these nasty things toward your mother. You want me to step in the middle for you and sort it out for you. Also, when you feel guilty for not liking your mother in all these ways, you look to me as a father who can reassure you that mom will survive your attacks, she is strong enough to withstand them." B told me that she did feel guilty because of her strong feelings and wondered if I just thought she was a selfish, angry person. B said she also hoped I would "somehow understand her and help her through these terrible feelings". Later, I interpreted that "You must feel you can trust me to hold up to your strong feelings without being hurt or offended. You must believe I won't retaliate." B said, "I do for the most part and that is a really important feeling. I feel safe here. There is just a little part of me that does worry what you think, but it isn't as strong as how I feel with my mother."

It would have been quite easy for me to merely listen to B's stories and let her go on and on about her mother. To some minor degree, just talking about it over and over may have provided her with some relief and tension reduction. However, the fundamental issues would remain. This would be the absence of analytic contact.

I could have acted out her wishes by actually giving her permission to be angry with her mother. This could have been an explicit statement like, "You should be angry with her given all the bad things she has done!" or it could have been more subtle in the form of a silent approval of her anger by way of no comment.

Instead, the analytic method is defined as making the attempt to bring the unspoken, the unthought, and the unfelt to light. The patient's desire to not think, feel, or speak is often actualized through the vehicle of projective identification, which comes to be the foundation of the transference. Therefore, I attempted to interpret these hidden aspects of B's inner life, translating her feelings, desires, and struggles. In totality, these measures equal analytic contact.

The fact that she wanted me to be her translator and placed me in that position was important to notice and explore as well. However, she tried to make me be a particular type of parent-translator, which allowed her to take a particular stance as a child who hides, denies, and discharges her feelings and thoughts into the object.

Another way B's desire for me to be the translator manifested was in B's stories about her husband. She would relay different stories about minor fights and disagreements that had occurred and how frustrated she was about them. It was again like listening to a story that I could just nod my head to or somehow show my allegiance to her feelings by agreeing that her husband was a nasty man. However, when I stood back and thought about the feelings she was engendering in me and the way she was utilizing me in the transference, I realized that B was again asking me to either be a passive person just standing by like an ineffective, absent father, or be a strong translator, an idealized strong father, for her true feelings. So, I interpreted that she was reluctant to share with me the full extent of her feelings toward her husband, her own contribution to the fights, and the true way she was feeling in those moments. I said that she seemed to first hide those truths from herself, then from her husband, and then from me. In B's treatment, successful analytic contact came from my ongoing interpretation of her desires for me to be her emotional spokesperson.

As a result of the desire to disown her own feelings and thoughts, B invited me to translate those censored phantasies and states of mind for her, so that she could vicariously claim ownership of them. If I interpreted/translated these unwanted elements for B, she felt she had permission to then express herself more openly. This felt safer because she was merely carrying my message. She could take credit for it but felt immune from being blamed for it. B said, "I see what you mean. I think I sugar-coat things for you or only tell you the surface details so we don't have to talk about what is really going on. But, when you help me see what it is that I am hiding, I feel better and more hopeful, more confident." I added, "So, seeing me as a strong father who can intervene and help you understand yourself leaves you feeling more confident and strong yourself. If we can better understand how you need me to be that father for you, you can do that for yourself as well." Here, I was continuing to analyze the transference, clarifying that she was using me as a strong, available father but unless she internalized that function and mourned the loss of this idealized father, she would be unable to cope and take care of herself.

THE FEAR OF SUCCESS

C was a middle-aged man who came to see me about "feeling stuck in his career". As we proceeded with the analytic treatment, it turned out C was unhappy in many other areas besides his job. His friendships, his love life, and his overall ability to engage and enjoy life all were severely hampered.

After five years in analytic therapy, on the couch, C was doing much better in many ways. He was working at a better job, he was working more at his potential in that he was demonstrating leadership skills at work and stepping up to challenges in daily life instead of hiding from them and dreading them. He was now married with two children and allowed himself to feel great joy from being a father. His marriage was stable and happy. Overall, C was a different man than the one I met five years prior.

However, the central theme that we had gradually uncovered in the first year of analysis still remained, but to a much smaller degree. C felt a great amount of anxiety over any situation in which he would achieve, enjoy, or show off. He fought off any sign of pleasure or growth, not wanting to admit or accept his own phallic power or desire to enjoy life. Therefore, he sought to neutralize his potential and hide any growth or joy.

Through the dynamics of projective identification, C put us in a relationship where I needed to encourage him to try things and take risks, thereby giving him my parental permission. I was to show my power by brainstorming and coming up with ways for him to progress in life and take new steps in life. This situation occurred many times over the years. The interpersonal aspects of this projective identification process were quite obvious, but I would nevertheless be pulled into it. He was a very likeable man and I did want to see him succeed in life. So, when he would come in and tell me, "Well, nothing to report", I would know from our history together to say, "You mean nothing positive, fun, or successful to report, because you don't want to admit that side of yourself or let me see you as an independent, strong man on your own." He would agree and tell me of some current conflict he faced which would be either a situation in which he needed to be decisive, confrontive, or expressive but he was too scared to carry through, or, he would relate a situation in which he wished to break new ground, individuate from someone or something, or creatively put together a new chapter in his life, be it job, career, hobby, or friendship.

Two transference/counter-transference situations emerged in these moments. First, I would be placed in a debate or standoff with C, with me being put in the position of spokesperson for growth and change. He would have the pessimistic and risk-adverse side of the fight. This standoff could bog down to a grind and then there was silence. Analytic contact was thin and tenuous.

The second transference/counter-transference situation would then occur. I would feel compelled to come up with suggestions, ideas, or to brainstorm some new creative possibilities. C often liked my ideas but would say he could never make them happen because he was too anxious to take the stance to see them through. Now, analytic contact was becoming more and more distant. Thankfully, I would become aware of my participation in this parenting process right about then by noticing how distant we were from any real analytic work. I would interpret this parenting situation and explore his thoughts and feelings about it. C would tell me how it felt good to be parented, but he knew he would need to "parent himself to make it really work". He said this in a way that was genuine and alive with both reluctance, fear, sadness, and hope. Associating to the idea of parenting and parents, C reflected on his father and said, "He seemed so very restricted in life by his own inner demons. I don't want to repeat that."

During the course of his now six-year analytic treatment, these types of internal conflicts with progress and growth have appeared within the transference many times over. These inner struggles would emerge within the interpersonal aspects of our relationship. For example, about one month after I had moved my office, he asked if he could use the bathroom at the end of the session. In my old office, I had my own waiting room and private bathroom. In the new office, I shared the waiting room with another office and the public bathroom was a part of the entire building and separate from my office suite. When I saw C for the next appointment, I brought up that he had a strange look on his face last time, after I told him that the bathroom was located outside of my office area. C said, "I didn't want to tell you. But, I didn't end up using the outside one." I asked why. "Well, I felt more comfortable when it was in your office, a part of the office." I said, "So, you wanted to be in the safety of my area, with me, not outside of my circle." Here was an example of my interpreting the projective identification process that made up the transference situation. Analytic contact is often made up of projection–identification–transference–counter-transfernence–

interpretation–association/reaction–secondary interpretation. At times, there can be a breakdown in some aspect of this sequence which creates a stagnation or collapse of analytic contact.

As Mitchel (1995) points out, the intra-psychic phantasies that create the need to use projective identification become part of the interpersonal interaction between patient and analyst. So, C's sense of dependency, neediness, and desire to have me as his instead of having to expand his own life was enacted with the phantasy of the close safeness of my old office, where he felt a part of me, and his reluctance to leave that warmth and go into what he experienced as a cold, forbidding, world of my new office, where he would be forced to grow up and face scary situations and people. I made that very interpretation and C replied, "Yes. I felt good being able to use the bathroom in your old office, but last time it felt like I was going out into the wilderness to use this one." So, we talked for a while about his sense of protection "under my wing" and his sense of discomfort and even anxiety about having to be more on his own, out in the "wilderness". Here, C was able to tolerate his anxiety and desire to control me enough to work with my interpretation and together we forged a moment of successful analytic contact.

Another time this same sort of dependence on me and wish for special parenting rather than separation and growth came out was when he had to be treated for a sprained ankle. His physical therapist, on a follow-up visit a couple of months after the sprain, told him he was "fine" and to "quit complaining". C said he was shocked to hear this and was also concerned because he was still having significant trouble with his ankle. But, he said he merely nodded to the physical therapist and went home. Certainly, one way to see this material is that C is possibly feeling that I am dismissive or insensitive. But, that didn't seem to be the case in that particular moment. I suspected C was acting needy and was pushing the therapist to be more parenting to him and the therapist may have reacted negatively to that.

What seemed to be very alive in the transference at that moment was a pull on me to step in as a supportive, protective parent and stand up for him against this bully therapist. I made this interpretation and C said, "Well, that would be great if you could do that for me." I said, "You say that half joking and half serious. I think you have a hard time feeling safe by yourself and want me to step in for you to do the hard work, the scary stuff. Sometimes, I think you are even stubborn about it and don't want to be a grown up and try to get me to do the thinking and talking instead." C replied, "You are right about that. Until recently, I never noticed that. When I see myself doing it, I feel frustrated. I shouldn't do that, I should be more adult about it. But, it is tempting to have you or someone else do it. No risk, no sweat. I usually freeze up if I try something new. So, it is easier to do nothing."

C made a great deal of progress as time went on, but even his progress was used in the transference as part of his reluctance to be on his own, creating a sense of self. C told me that moving ahead with his life felt "like I was signing up for a lot of obligation and pressure". After a work situation that had haunted him for quite some time, he reported how he had "really made an impression on everyone at the last meeting" and how his boss told him he was "shaping up to be his right-hand man". C said this made him very nervous because now he had to come up with all sorts of big shot deals and ways to "wow" the stockholders. I interpreted how he downplayed and even attacked his new accomplishment and instead of sharing it proudly with me, he played it safe by talking about it as an obligation. I also mentioned that he might be scared that he made a big impression on me at the last meeting we had. C said, "Yes. If I tell you how good things are going, then you will expect that much more from me. I don't want to let you down and I don't want you to be expecting so much more out of me." I said, "You have a lot of demands you put on yourself and then you picture me as demanding too. You want me to be an overly supportive parent for you who does all the thinking and doing, but you have a hard time just letting me be a proud parent, listening to your achievements. I think your high expectations and control get in the way of having me be the loving parent you want." C said, "Wow! I never thought of it like that. I push you away. I see what you mean. Even though I like the idea of you being in my corner, I can't really picture you simply being happy for me, without demanding that I do more, accomplish more, or be more." I said, "So, you have this wish for me to be a caring parent who takes care of you in every way, but your own sense of control and demand makes me into a harsh parent who is never pleased." Here, I was interpreting his projective identification phantasy in which his own exacting hunger and need turns his object into a demanding taskmaster. So, for this case, establishing and maintaining analytic contact not only meant the usual psychoanalytic techniques of interpretation and analysis of transference and defenses, but a specific focus on this patient's phantasy of being parented as his ultimate goal.

In researching Melanie Klein's unpublished papers, Spillius (2004) points out that Klein focused most of her interpretations on the patient's anxieties and the defenses against it as combined dynamics. This is what I tried to do with the patients presented in this chapter, especially trying to link the transference anxieties with the defenses against them. Not only is this an important technique for all patients, but when a patient is trying to mold the therapeutic relationship into this specific type of parent–child scenario, it is even more critical to draw attention to this and begin to explore and understand it rather than to let it be acted out for so long a period that it begins to become the reality of the treatment. In other words, the focused interpretation of this parent–child phantasy is what gives stability and value to the analytic contact already in place by means of analytic exploration of transference, conflict, and defense.

Many of my interpretations with C were centered around his projective identification efforts to see me, use me, and enlist me as a special parent who would do his painful and frightening emotional work for him. This was not just a projective identification pull to have me reassure him in difficult moments, which he did attempt many times over, but also a strong effort to have me tell him what to think and what to do, which would in effect remove him from responsibility and from the perceived danger of that responsibility.

If C did do something to change and move forward, it would be with my stamp of approval, my permission. In this way, he could claim no part in it, so no blame or guilt could befall him. Steiner (1984) has commented on this way that patients try to recruit the analyst to act out with them. Britton (1998) has explored the way unwanted aspects of the patient's psychology are pushed into the analyst through what he terms attributive projective identification. Both the desire for the object to take over the ego's struggles and the efforts to locate these struggles outside of oneself are usually the outcome of an intra-psychic phantasy that creates great anxiety combined with some current, external, problematic situation. This was emphasized by Melanie Klein (Spillius 2004) when she stated that a patient's deepest anxieties are always related in some way to current reality and our interpretations must make that link. This was certainly represented in many of the cases in the chapter regarding my office move. In exploring the current reality–current anxiety link in any case, the patient's deeper phantasies will become clearer to both patient and analyst. This clarity and understanding of the internal world is a component of the transformative power of analytic contact.

Carey (2002) discusses the need for containment as well as the rigorous and consistent interpretation of the transference as a way to ensure containment, in treatment settings restricted to low-frequency meetings. In addition to this important technique, I have found that patients who need and wish that the analyst become the parent will keep the frequency of meetings low as a way to pressure the analyst into bestowing more suggestions and parental advice. Also, the cases in this chapter and of similar patients are individuals who avoid the self-reflection and self-parenting inherent in more frequent visits. In the case material, it was the acting out of the patient's psychic reality that became the critical element of the transference that needed to be interpreted. Specifically, the desire to be overly parented and have the analyst do for the patient what the patient doesn't want to face was a projective identification dynamic that colored the analytic relationship and therefore needed to be interpreted consistently and rigorously. Finally, the containment that Carey (2002) mentions is perverted by this projective dynamic so that the containment is pushed from a temporary intervention to an ongoing, permanent circumstance or corrupted from a contained mental experience that can be examined into an acted out situation that is very difficult to examine, process, or experience.

Feldman (1993) points out that the patient often tangles external with internal object relationships as a defense and the analyst can become tempted to deal only with that external reality. Only by noticing the imprint of external relationships on the analytic relationship can the analyst begin to properly interpret it and begin to unravel and understand the underlying phantasies.

Some patients, who try and turn the analytic relationship into a parent–child situation with the analyst/parent doing all the work, are functioning at a more primitive paranoid-schizoid (Klein 1946) level. Developmentally, this is an intra-psychic state conceived of by Melanie Klein in which anxieties of a primitive nature threaten the immature ego and lead to the mobilization of primitive defenses. Splitting, idealization, and projective identification create an internal landscape made up of idealized good objects and persecuting bad ones. The infantile ego projects all its love toward the good object and all its hatred against the bad one. As a consequence of these projections, the leading anxiety is paranoid, and the preoccupation is with survival of the self. Fluctuating between feeling in union with an idealized parent who will take care of all their thinking, feeling, and doing or feeling persecuted and forced by the bad parent-analyst to face reality, grow up, and endure the hardships of life, these difficult patients see analytic progress as a threat, an insult, and an irritation. Making change and fostering growth produces phantasies of attack, abandonment, and sadistic guilt regarding their separation from the object. These patients utilize intense levels of projective identification to place their unwanted desires, dreams, and fears into the analyst (Grinberg 1977), making counter-transference acting out quite common and working through fairly difficult.

With depressive patients (Klein 1935), the issues are similar, but also quite different. The depressive position is a developmental, intra-psychic state conceived of by Melanie Klein in which the ego can tolerate the experience of whole objects and the mixture of good and bad feelings directed at them. The mix of love and hate toward the object brings out a particular sadness which Klein called depressive anxiety. The healthy, maturing ego comes to be able to tolerate this anxiety and the accompanying sense of guilt and loss. These developmental changes result from an increased capacity to integrate self–object experiences and lead to a shift in primary concern from the survival of the self to a concern for the object upon which the individual depends. Destructive impulses generate feelings of loss and guilt. Reparative desires as well as the ability to forgive become possible in the depressive position.

The depressive patient is more able to recognize the analyst as a whole person with his or her own life, own needs, and own identity. Thus, the ego discovers its own helpless dependency, separateness, and aloneness. If there is enough internalized good object experiences, the ego is able to survive this new awareness and slowly sustain itself. This psychological growth also allows for a more balanced view of the self and object, with love and hate possible in the same relational sphere (Segal 1974). These higher functioning patients struggle with phantasies of their growth, success, and change being equated with harm, friction, and betrayal. Guilt is overwhelming and leads the ego to cling to the object, possess it, and rigidly maintain the current object relationship within whatever climate it is in. Bringing things to a halt is safer than the uncharted waters ahead. Growth is seen as dangerous to the object and therefore a threat to both parties (Waska 2004, 2005).

Attempts to save or repair the object relationship can become centered around reduction of change. The depressive phantasy becomes one of trying to prevent change or hide progress so as to protect and restore the object. Theoretically, this can be understood as the defensive dynamic of the death instinct, creating a significant transference standoff. In addition, Klein (1921) has brought attention to the instinctual need for knowledge which she thought has its origins in the infant's desire for the insides of the mother's body and ownership of the breast, milk, mother's love, and later, knowledge of the oedipal couple's activities. The aggressive urge behind this quest for knowledge can leave the ego convinced of the object's injury, anger, or collapse.

All these factors were part of C's treatment at one point or another. He wanted to know more, learn more, do more, and be more. But, he unconsciously thought I would be upset or disturbed by this and that his quest for knowledge and growth was a threat to our relationship. This was exemplified several times by his saying, "Well, I guess if I get better, that is the end of us."

C's phantasy that his growth would "be the end of us" colored the transference in many ways. After the positive work meeting, C told me his boss had a special meeting with him. C told me, "Everything I could have hoped for came true." C said he was shocked at the rewards his boss gave him and the appreciation his boss and the board of the company expressed for his continued good work. At one point, I asked C what exactly were these rewards, since he was talking around it but not coming out and saying it. C began to tell me, but then detoured into a lengthy, intellectual, and obsessional dialogue about his job and the different situations in his department. I interpreted that he was anxious about sharing, showing off, or boasting to me about his success, so he was covering it over with intellectual gibberish. C said, "Yes. I look for the long way around the subject, the direct way makes me uneasy. I don't want you to think I am out of line, thinking too highly of myself, like I need to be put back in line." I replied, "You think I can't handle your growth, your joy. I might be uncomfortable or envious and put you back in line." C nodded yes. I said, "So, this is a very specific kind of relationship you push us into. On one hand, you want to be a passive kid who doesn't know what to do and then I can be the strong, wise parent who saves the day. But, you must think I need that role because when you grow up and prosper, you picture me getting upset and angry." C said, "It's like we can't be equals."

This same type of depressive, oedipal transference phantasy in which one of us had to be dominant and one had to be passive came to light when C's car was stolen and the insurance company gave him a check to buy a new car. Over a period of several weeks, it came out that he wanted a fancy sports car, but felt extremely conflicted about it. At first, he said he didn't want people to see him as a snob, only interested in fancy toys. We explored this in terms of his trying to control the object's perception of him and wanting to make sure he was seen as a good, sensible boy who followed the rules. I interpreted this as a way to control me and the parent-object, pretending to be a good little boy, when really wanting something personal and fun. I also said I noticed how he was just telling me the facts, but making sure to not include much about his personal interest in the sports car or anything about it that might reveal his excitement and anticipation for something he truly wanted, just for himself. C said, "I keep that information from you to protect you, I think. If I tell you how much I want it and how I will get it, you might be hurt somehow. It might even make you sad, like it is something you would like too, but never will be able to have." I said, "So, you picture leaving me in the dust, upset that you are able to have what I can't. By hiding your successes and your interests from me, you can take care of me and not hurt me." C said, "That is right. But, it is also a way to protect myself. If you get too sad, you might end up angry or resentful of me and I don't want that either." Here, C was feeling a more paranoid phantasy of my hurt causing resentment, leading to my taking revenge. So, the fear of hurting me was mixed with a more persecutory fear as well. Often, this is the case. In states of fragile object relations, the ego can easily be overwhelmed by the image of a hurt, injured, or even dying object that then shifts into a revengeful, attacking, betrayer (Waska 2002).

I told C that he must have to work very hard and sacrifice much of himself to always be hiding his true feelings, his aspirations, his dreams, his desire in life. He said, "I let myself think of that stuff some of the time, but you are right. I have to keep a very tight lid on it and not share it, and often I don't even realize that side of myself exists." Segal (2001) points out how the essence of psychoanalysis is the search for personal truth, with insight being the tool for therapeutic change. For C, to search for his own personal truth and to dare to share that truth with me was a threat for him. It meant putting us both at risk for harm, judgment, and loss. Segal goes on to speak about how falling into the trap of becoming the supportive parent for the patient means widening the patient's internal split between good and bad, rather than helping them to find the truth of reality. This is a moment when psychoanalytic work shifts into supportive counseling, in which there is a collusion between patients involved in this sort of "do my dirty work for me" projective dynamic and therapists who are acting out this supportive, "I will take care of you and show you the way" type of counter-transference reaction to that projective identification system.

All patients show an internal conflict between wanting to master reality versus wanting to run from reality and hide in their phantasies. The patients I am highlighting in this chapter are especially reluctant to face, master, and own reality and try very hard to enlist the analyst to do that for them. When I say "for them", I mean in a manner that the patient really disowns any displeasure, anxiety, or fear associated with their own inner world. The analyst's desire and need to help others becomes hijacked in service of a one-sided treatment in which the patient provides the map or the clues and leaves the analyst to find the buried treasure all on his own. Therefore, these patients need to be closely monitored and their interpersonal as well as intra-psychic relations in the transference situation must be examined for signs of this handing off of unwanted emotional baggage. Otherwise, analytic contact can be lost and the treatment shifts into more of a pathological recycling of archaic object relations. Interpretations about this behavior should be consistent, direct, and address the specific unwanted psychological element that is being given over and projected into the analyst.

COUNTER-TRANSFERENCE AND THE DESIRE TO PARENT THE PATIENT

S was a woman in her early thirties who came to see me for help with depression as well as a chronic sense of anxiety that seemed to intensify whenever she would try to express herself to those close to her. S was white and lived with her boyfriend who was black. They had been together for five years and S called it a "turbulent and complicated" relationship. Over time, I understood this to mean S was scared about the frequent arguments and disagreements they had, but felt even more scared about expressing herself to him.

Over the course of two years of analytic work, S made significant progress in many areas. She had worked on her conflicted feelings toward her mother, who was an alcoholic throughout much of S's childhood and left S feeling intimidated, wanting to please her to ward off the threat of trouble. S's father was a placid, passive man who tried his best to stay out of the way, offering little in the way of a buffer or pillar of strength for S to go to in her times of need. During the analytic work, we had sorted out many ways that S had formerly sabotaged herself at work, alienated herself from friends, and generally avoided a sense of personal power, pleasure, or identity. Now, she was much less disabled by depression and the chronic anxiety she suffered when first entering treatment. However, there were still a few core conflicts that plagued S and colored the transference.

There were ways S would behave that elicited certain feelings in me which were part of a projective identification process. Specifically, S would interact with me in a particular manner that seemed designed to pull me into being a certain type of parental figure. At times, this was a pull for a permissive, supportive, and encouraging father figure, one that she wished for but never had. Other times, it was more of a pull for a punitive, moody, demanding, or judgmental parent, much like the drunken mother S remembered.

At the start of one session, S sheepishly said she had forgotten to bring her checkbook to pay me. S said, "I am sorry, I hope it is OK?" From what she said and the tone in which she said it, I interpreted that S left me with only two specific choices. Either it was not OK and she was in trouble or it has to be OK whether I like it or not. In other words, I pointed out that S was being manipulative and forcing me either to be a punishing or forgiving parental object. I said that she seemed anxious about just letting me be myself and seeing what emerged. Yes, I could be angry so she needed to control for that. But, I wondered if it might be even more uncomfortable for her to let me naturally be OK with it. It felt to me, in the counter-transference, that she did not allow me the opportunity to show my flexibility or understanding. She had to prevent that. So, my interpretations were giving voice to S's fears, manipulations, defenses, and phantasies. This was not so much her wanting me to be a spokesperson for her unconscious mind as it was a more traditional analysis of the transference.

During the course of several months, S told me many stories about how her black boyfriend would engage S in very charged discussions about race and the unfair treatment of blacks. He told S, "All whites are arrogant and controlling of minorities and whites are not willing to look at how prejudiced and one-dimensional they are." He would bring up topics about race in which he polarized blacks and whites and always made out whites to be the oppressing, cruel, overlords. S reacted to these inflammatory remarks by doing her best to be politically correct and respectful of all opinions. She agreed with him and "admitted" that she was "part of the problem". He would ask her to go to racial awareness rallies and conferences on slavery and the oppression of the black race. S told me these stories as factual events that went on in the relationship. The most she would express about it emotionally was that it made her "nervous" when he was so worked up about these matters.

I noticed myself feeling a certain way in the counter-transference. At first, I felt sorry for S because it sounded like she was always getting bullied. Then, I began to feel like putting my two cents into the conversation and pointing out how one-sided and prejudiced her boyfriend sounded. I felt quite worked up at times, fairly righteous and even indignant. Part of guarding and maintaining analytic contact with S was noting my counter-transference feelings of wanting to step outside the envelope of analytic contact. By not letting myself act out these wishes and instead reflecting on them for some time, it occurred to me that perhaps my desire to put my two cents into the conversation was really S's desire to put her two cents into the discussion with her boyfriend, but she was enlisting me to carry that desire for her. In other words, through projective identification, she was putting her identity, her opinions, her aggression, and her outrage into me.

For a few months, we pursued this line of investigation. On one hand, this was very productive. S was able to talk about her fears of expression, such as "being rude and arrogant, like a bully", and "selfish and out of line with what is right". So, we were able to slowly understand how she would present herself in a modest, polite, agreeable way so as to enlist me to hold her more raw, and uncensored feelings. I was the one who told it like it was, on her behalf. We explored how this was the manner in which she used me, a manipulative way to have her way without risk, but also a way in which she got me to be on her side and stand up for her in a pseudo-protective parent sort of way. All this was positive and productive. However, it was a little too neat and tidy.

Over time, I grew to see another side of all this. I slowly realized that while I was interpreting the projection of her more raw desires and strong opinions, along with her placid, accommodating defenses against them, I was colluding in creating a split between nice ways of relating and more aggressive, "tell it like it is" ways of relating. It was becoming a repression versus catharsis type of analysis. This led me to see that while we were indeed making progress, this sort of progress was also a shield against the harder struggle of accepting things for their totality. The middle of the road, reality of life was missing. Analytic contact had become partly corrupted.

S's boyfriend had many good points to make. At the same time, he was quite caustic in his presentation. There were ways of bringing together the good and the bad that S and I were avoiding. I interpreted these ideas to S and she agreed. She said, "That middle ground is more messy, scary, and not as easy to control. Either/or is more manageable." I said, "Yes, but you lose out on all the flavors in-between."

Even though S agreed with me about these matters, it was a difficult and uncomfortable journey for her. To put things together, to work toward integrating her feelings about herself and her feelings toward her objects, left her anxious and unsure. Therefore, she would often rely on the old method of "either/or is more manageable". Because of that more regressive, defensive stance, I found myself becoming S's mouthpiece for the middle ground. Often, she enlisted me to give voice to the more balanced view of things. This was a difficult period in the analysis. S felt a great deal of guilt when she faced these more layered, holistic views of her objects. She was overwhelmed by the range of her feelings at times and therefore phantasies about her objects being overwhelmed as well. Therefore, this guilt was often experienced as unbearable (Safá-Gerard 1998) and she had to look to me to hold it and bear it. By holding it, I mean that she looked to me to not only talk about it, but endure the feelings that went with it. Therefore, when I made interpretations about her avoidance of an inclusive spectrum of thoughts and feelings, S might acknowledge it, but in an intellectual manner. So, I would need to follow up with an interpretation about how she was wanting me to feel for her and be the voice of her thoughts and feelings. I pointed out that she seemed to want me to be a special sort of parent who did the dirty work for her and felt the intolerable or dangerous feelings for her as well. Then, she would be safe, in control, and powerful behind the scenes. And, she could rest assured that her objects were neither endangered nor enraged. But, if they were, it wasn't her fault since she had passed on her expressive side to me. Over time, we made significant strides in this area. S became more open and direct with me about her view of the world and the people in her life. In the transference, she was less apt to idealize me. Also, she was less worried about my retaliating and/or abandoning her if she revealed her full range of emotions toward me.

As we worked on these deep and difficult areas of her psychology, S came to think about her family more. S said, "I now realize that as a kid, I had to see my mother as this perfect person who does no wrong. I made her into an ideal figure because otherwise I had to face the overwhelming reality that I had this drunken, inferior mom. I think I also try to always keep a safe balance with you and everyone else so I don't ever have to see the reality of who you are. If you are this perfect person, there is no reason for me to have bad feelings. If I treat you like you are perfect and right all the time, then I don't have to face my feelings either. Sometimes, I feel like a worthless, drunken mother and have to find ways of getting people to like me. Other times, I feel like I had better keep the peace because people seem unpredictable and unsafe, so I just go along for the ride. If I tell my boyfriend I disagree with him on some of his beliefs, I am not sure what is worse. He might crumble and be really hurt, which I certainly don't want. Or, he might get angry and yell at me. In the confusion of all that kind of thinking, I just end up feeling like being a chameleon and agreeing to everything is the best way of all." This was a remarkable insight. S was starting to understand herself and beginning to own up to the way she was coping with her fears and phantasies. This helped her begin to have more of a choice in her life and be able to relate to her objects in a more honest and whole manner. So, part of working toward analytic contact with S was the specific interpretive focus on her phantasies of parental rescue and me as her parent who could do her dirty work. Her desire for parenting stood in the way of analytic contact, for she knew on a deep level that working through her difficulties meant growing up and having to give up that phantasy. In turn, we both needed to be aware of and mutually explore the pain, fear, and anger that went along with giving up those desires. Maintaining analytic contact often means constantly acknowledging the efforts to dismantle that contact and the associated anxieties.

Part III

Drugs, mutilation, and psychic fragmentation: is analytic contact still possible?

Chapter 8

Addictions

Patients who come into psychoanalytic treatment while using drugs, drinking excessively, relating in repetitive, abusive patterns, or involved in destructive sexual behaviors need to be assessed in a certain manner. Particular questions must be answered. Do they need detox? Does the legal system need to intervene? Do they need to be encouraged to join a 12-step group of some sort? Do they need an inpatient or outpatient treatment program? Are psychiatric medications indicated? Is a medical checkup necessary? Are they in danger of killing themselves or harming others?

Once all these areas are sorted out, the psychoanalyst must ask, what are the deeper issues at play? In this chapter, I will present two cases in which the psychoanalytic focus was on the internal conflicts and object-relational pathology behind the addictive behaviors. One case was more successful than the other. By not only acknowledging and working with the external symptom of drug addiction, but making sure to try and establish analytic contact whenever possible, the patients were given a comprehensive treatment. Rather than judging the treatment on diagnosis, frequency, or use of couch, the attempt to reach some level of analytic contact is what best defines these cases as analytic and helpful to the individual.

In general, the field of psychology and medicine sees addictions as a mix of external, physiological, and behavioral problems that need to be dealt with by behavioral, cognitive, or medication approaches. Yet, psycho-analytic treatment is often a far better choice, in that it seeks to find the root of the behavior, so the individual can regain a better balance in their life and learn to deal with what caused them to be so self-destructive in the first place. This is different from simply eliminating the drug, drink, or action by some external injunction. Certainly, the issues of medical care, detox, and support groups need to be considered. But, those would only be the beginning of a full and proper treatment of addiction.

The psychoanalytic literature is rather sparse on the subject of addiction. In a broad sense, I think this is due to an unfair and largely incorrect bias against addicts and the phenomenon of addiction. Far from hopeless cases that only benefit from medication or behavioral therapies, many addicts may profit from the analytic method.

Dodes (1996) sees addictions as part of pathological compromise formations involving compulsive patterns that revolve around intra-psychic conflicts. Dodes (1990) also cites the elements of narcissistic rage and the attempt to regain a sense of power as important in understanding addiction. As such, Dodes believes addictions are well within the realm of analytic treatment. Johnson (1999) reviewed the psychoanalytic view of addiction and found it divided into theories of biological cause, incapacity to tolerate affect, and object substitution. Volkan (1994) concludes that addicts have suffered early object loss and are within a range of severe neurotic to borderline pathology. He advocates the psychoanalytic model as helpful, especially if the transference relationship is focused on. Rosenfeld (1960) discussed the link between manic defenses and addiction. The addict uses the drug as an idyllic state or special object that can ward off anxiety and persecutory phantasies. Rosenfeld thought the addict had regressed from the depressive position into the paranoid-schizoid position. Specifically, when discussing the addict's ego prior to this regression, he states, "he has partially reached the depressive position" (p. 467).

In the two cases presented in this chapter, there was a particular transference pattern and phantasy profile that emerged. These two patients had different types of addictive problems, but similar psychological issues. Typical of many difficult patients, these two patients were troubled by a dread of abandonment and persecution from a narcissistic object as well as the phantasy of harming or disturbing their object (Waska 2003, 2005). While this object-relational phantasy was the predominant mental experience for them as adults, they revealed backgrounds in which these stressful and often traumatic images and feelings were part of everyday family life. As with most if not all patients, there is a critical intersection of external and internal, past and present.

With many addicts who enter into analytic treatment, one gradually finds that the patient has identified with a narcissistic object and now feels entitled and superior in some ways, but inferior, fearful, and ashamed in other ways. Acting out is not only part of the addictive process, but becomes part of the transference dynamic as well. I propose this acting out to be unavoidable and even quite necessary to the analytic process. However, in some cases, it becomes too consuming and poisons the treatment. The analyst must struggle to work with this acting out and to prevent it from choking off the evolution of analytic contact. If patiently and consistently worked with, acting out can often be a helpful bridge into insight and growth. But, if left to spread, acting out replaces analytic contact as the primary relational field.

Mertin Gill (1979) has pointed out the critical importance of the patient's use of transference as a path either to learning and change or for resistance and defense. Regarding how this matter should be treated clinically, Gill states:

> first distinguish clearly between two types of interpretation of the transference. The one is an interpretation of resistance to the awareness of transference. The other is an interpretation of resistance to the resolution of transference.
>
> (p. 264)

In many successful analytic treatments, it is the analysis of this type of acting out and resistance that fosters a genuine working through. Betty Joseph (1983, 1985, 1988, 1992, 2000) has made many important contributions in this area. The dynamic of mutual enactments is common, including acting out from the analyst. In other words, there is a parallel between the interpretive process and the acting out of pathology. In the following cases, the acting out was of an addictive nature and often involved sadomasochistic relating with the object. I think one could argue that addictions are always sadomasochistic in some manner. Control and dominance of the attacking and abandoning object are central to these patients' internal struggle.

Case material 8.1

Jane and Joe came to see me because Jane had been smoking pot and binge drinking for ten years and it was destroying their relationship. They came together at my suggestion, because when Joe called requesting help, I inquired as to how motivated Jane was to change. Frequently, addicts will enter treatment because of legal problems, divorce situations, and other external forces. Therefore, I try to assess how much they want to seek help and look at how I can bolster that desire to change. Based on Jane's questionable desire to stop her addictive behavior, I asked Joe to attend with her. I have found that in many situations, not just addictions, the partner acts as a buffer, support, container, and encouragement to the addict and helps to prevent the rapid projection of badness, judgment, and persecution onto the analyst. Without the partner present, the addict will often abort the treatment rather quickly. Also, the partner often plays a significant role in the entire addictive cycle. Without their willingness to explore their own troubles and ways of contributing to the addict's problems, the addict may not be able to sustain their own shift in behavior or emotional growth.

Theoretically, one could posit this situation to not be in the realm of psychoanalytic treatment: addictions, severe pathology, couples work, acting out, lack of frequency, and so forth. However, analytic contact is a clinical concept, not one dependent on rigid external criteria such as one individual, neurotic patient on the couch, attending four or five times a week without any severe acting out. Analytic contact is the establishment of a working focus on unconscious conflicts, transference, and phantasies that provides an opportunity or potential for lasting change and growth. To determine if a treatment is psychoanalytic or not, one is clinically better off asking if analytic contact is being attempted and whether analytic contact has been established. In other words, is the analyst working as an analyst and is the patient able or willing to be receptive to that way of exploring and relating? The answer to both those factors defines the subsequent avoidance of, the resistance to, the attack upon, or successful emergence of analytic contact.

So, I began meeting with Joe and Jane. Because of insurance coverage restrictions, the couple's financial state, and their mutual reluctance to make financial sacrifices for their treatment, we were limited to meeting once or twice a week. These external factors are almost always used as elements in the patient's internal, defensive standoff with the analyst. Most treatments are shaped by external factors but the patient's involvement with those factors is important to consider.

Over their eight-year relationship, Jane had shaped the course of the relationship by her desire to stay home and get high. In addition to smoking large amounts of pot every day and sitting around "spacing out" and watching television, she would drink herself unconscious almost every weekend. Joe would sometimes be able to talk her out of smoking so much and they would go out for a walk, a movie, or dinner. But, usually they ended up sitting around the house. Joe found solace in reading or exploring the internet. They lived next door to Jane's mother. Jane's mother and father divorced when Jane was five years old because her father was an alcoholic and cheated on his wife.

So, after a few sessions, certain facts emerged. I had the sense that Jane's drug addiction and drinking problem was psychological in nature. I wasn't clear why or what the dynamics were, but I thought there was a connection between her family issues, her marriage to Joe, and her own internal struggles. She did not appear to be a candidate for detox or any outpatient program. She told me she was against 12-step programs and would not try one. I didn't see any reason for a medication evaluation. As I mentioned, she did not seem willing to attend therapy by herself and I assumed some of her troubles lay in her relationship with Joe, so I recommended they both begin to see me on a regular basis.

I made certain transference interpretations early on. I asked Jane if she honestly thought she had a drug or alcohol problem. She thought a bit and answered yes. Given that she only showed up at my office because of Joe's prodding, I interpreted that she seemed to need someone else to tell her what she needed (Joe) and she seemed to need others (Joe and myself) to look after her. These were comments based on her helpless presentation and her need to have Joe be the guiding force in finding treatment. Based on these ideas, I also suggested that it must be painful for her to look at herself and what is going on with her life. It might be easier to feel that I or Joe was pushing her to get better than to look at how she was really feeling. Here, I was exploring the possibility that projective identification was the primary object-relational vehicle in Jane's psychology (Waska 2004).

Jane said I was correct and that she had been feeling "pretty depressed and troubled lately". She said she didn't know about what. I said we could find out, together. So, I made some comments early on to point out how she seemed to need others to contain her troubles and become her caretaker. I also suggested that she may be controlling others in some ways, since she made Joe and herself housebound and essentially dictated what they do together. And, I interpreted that her addiction might be a way to protect her from painful feelings of some sort. Finally, I asked Jane if she was willing to begin cutting down on her intake of drugs and look at what emotional states were underneath. She said, "I will try. I will give it a go." So, my interpretations were aimed at her possible need to control her objects, her difficulty with affect, and her wish to be cared for. These elements were in alignment with the psychoanalytic literature reviewed earlier in the chapter.

Over time, I gathered information about Jane's past and slowly got to know more about Joe. Jane's father had been a drinker and a gambler and left the family when Jane was ten years old. Jane's mother raised her and was prone to be quite critical and contrary. To this day, she influences Jane's life a great deal. In fact, she bought the house next door to the family home and let Jane live there for a modest monthly fee, but requires her to always run errands and frequently reminds Jane of her generosity by way of guilt-inducing remarks. She uses the house and other financial gifts as a way to keep Jane on a tight leash.

Also, Jane developed a friendship with a boy her age during her teens. Almost fifteen years later, they take walks together and stay in touch by phone. This man has been her supplier of pot the whole time. Joe is naturally jealous that Jane seems to have a good level of communication with this man but none with him. There is no sense that anything sexual takes place. It is more of an intimate sharing of the past and what they are going through in their current lives. When not working at fairly menial jobs, Jane stays at home getting high, watching television, or chatting with her friend. She is not social otherwise and has few friends.

Over the course of several sessions, I interpreted that Jane may feel a deep conflict about her past and about her current internal state. I interpreted that she may want to share herself with her husband Joe and with me her analyst, much like she seemed able to with her pot dealer friend. And, she probably wished she could have that closeness with her long-gone father. But, she seemed to want to withhold and make us suffer as well. This comment was based on the withholding way she spoke in the sessions, much like a passive, withholding teenager. Part of this was because she initially attended her sessions high on pot, but mostly it was an emotional withdrawal and withholding from me. I had to patiently ask her to share her thoughts and feelings and she would ration out her comments. Was this anything to do with her depressed and angry feelings about her father and her current relationship with her mother? Jane said, "Maybe. I have never given that much thought. But, it could be. I think all of that could have gone better." Then, bit by bit, Jane made comments about how "it didn't seem fair" that her father was an alcoholic and that he left her. She also said she thought her mother's controlling ways "could have driven anyone to drink". I said, "You mean your father as well as you?" Jane said, "Oh! I didn't think of that!", laughing nervously.

I also interpreted that her bond with this other man, the pot dealer, might represent the hoped-for closeness with her father and the pot smoking might represent a way to carry on that magical wish for connection with father. I was considerably active with this patient, at least initially. This is often necessary with some very stuck or stubborn individuals for a period of time. However, the analyst must be careful as this can turn into an acting out of transference/counter-transference feelings of withholding, frustration, rejection, despair, need, rebelliousness, and phantasies of parental omnipotence (Feldman 1992; Goldberg & Grusky 2004; Bell 2001; Joseph 2001; Schafer 2003).

I told Jane her pot smoking might also represent a way to resist mother's controlling ways and rebel against her. Finally I interpreted that the drugs and the drinking may protect Jane against the sadness and loneliness she has over her broken family. Jane nodded, "I think some of that is right." I asked her what parts felt right and after a bit of reflection, she said, "maybe all of it". When she said this, Jane was sad and thoughtful. It was as if she suddenly emerged from a shroud.

At this point in the treatment, Jane had been able to reduce her pot smoking to half. I believe this was because she was willing to think about herself more and willing to engage with some of her previously warded-off feelings. We had found a certain level of analytic contact, the result of psychoanalytic exploration of transference, defenses, and conflict. This created the possibility for some change with her internal objects. She was not exactly participating in the analytic treatment in a very active sense, but she was willing to slowly allow and experience new ways of feeling and thinking. This reduced her anxiety in general, which was very important because she told me the main reason she smoked pot was to "relax and get rid of the tension". When I asked what she meant, she was vague. I interpreted that the smoking might be a way to avoid the tension, anxiety, and sorrow she felt around her family. Also, I interpreted that being high prevented her from being close and connected to Joe and from being fully present and connected to me, both of which might be frightening or "stressful" to her. Jane said, "that might be". While not much of a reply, this was said in a heartfelt way that conveyed her honest acknowledgment as well as her genuinely engaging with what I said. Again, an important moment of analytic contact.

As we went along, I came to know more about Joe too. Joe was from a family in which he took care of everyone. Of course, I pointed out how he was now taking care of Jane. His father died when Joe was twenty. Joe's sister was in a car accident when she was a teen and was in a wheelchair, living with mother. Joe's brother was an alcoholic and came and went out of the family's life, creating misery and crisis. Joe was the person everyone counted on. When I asked about how this left him feeling, he said he was glad to help them out, but he resented them as well. He said, "They take advantage of me all the time." I asked, "And how about with Jane?" He said, "Yes, it can be that way too" and said he "even thought of leaving her sometimes, because it gets so bad". When Joe asked me in a helpless sort of way, "'So, what do I do, doc?", I interpreted that now he was making me be the helper and he could be the helpless one. I told him he probably wants a turn getting cared for, but this way might not leave him satisfied. He agreed and went on to say he wished Jane would pay more attention to him. So, here we worked with some of the pathological projective identi-fication Joe used to feel in control, yet also remained feeling controlled and victimized as a result.

Joe's resentment also came out later in a most interesting way. I had spoken with Jane about the idea of continuing to cut back on the drugs. She told me that she wanted to continue cutting back. Unknown to me, they agreed between themselves that it would be easier for Jane to cut back and eventually quit smoking pot if Joe would ration her pot each day. Suddenly, Joe was mercilessly making Jane wait till he got home from work to be able to get high. Then, he would arbitrarily decide it was time to cut back some more, so he would give her less. Once, when he didn't get home till the late evening, Jane got drunk. I interpreted how both of them were playing out this sadomasochistic game and seeking power and revenge over each other.

While certainly not a traditional psychoanalytic treatment in terms of one person on the analytic couch, this was very much a psychoanalytic process. As the treatment continued, I was engaged in a three-dimensional analytic exploration. One patient was Jane, one was Joe, and one was their marriage. Bit by bit, we discovered the deeper meanings of Jane's drug and alcohol addiction, the struggles Joe had with his family, and the difficulties they had in their relationship with each other. Of course, the transference was the central arena for all of this.

The main theme in each of these areas seemed very similar. Joe was anxious that without his help, his mother, sister, and brother would be unable to cope or maintain themselves. At the same time, he was resentful of this because he felt they controlled him and made him be their slave or servant with guilt. Finally, he was internally preoccupied with the idea that if he separated himself from them and found his own place in life, there would be an emotional attack from them, some kind of punishment, followed by some type of abandonment.[1] Joe said, "Sometimes, I feel like taking care of others is all I am good for. What would they need me for if I didn't run their errands? Would I still mean anything?"

So, Joe remained in this sadomasochistic relationship with his family to ward off these feelings and phantasies of loss, guilt, rejection, and abandonment. I interpreted that perhaps he felt an ongoing sense of loss with his family and his marriage. Joe said, "I never thought of it like that. I think I keep so busy doing stuff for everyone that I don't have to think about any of that stuff." I interpreted that he probably struggled with talking to me about himself because of those feelings and that it was easier to deflect it by talking about Jane's addiction. Joe replied, "Yes. I am so used to just obsessing about her that I never stop to think about how I am feeling, except that I am upset with her smoking."

With Jane, she felt controlled by her mother, who acted nice and was generous financially, but, attached many strings to the gifts. Jane felt she needed the money and the help because she thought she "couldn't make it without them". But, Jane also controlled her mother by presenting herself as a helpless child who needed all that extra attention, forcing mother to relate to her in that way. Jane was also worried that if she separated more from her mother, they "wouldn't have much to talk about". Without the sadomasochistic dependency that held them together, Jane feared she would lose her connection to mother. Again, this theme of loss and rejection was present and, as a result, Jane sought to control her object as a way of preventing her own internal collapse.

In the transference, there was a similar dynamic. Jane saw me, the analyst, as trying to control her, enforce limitations, and "make her grow up". She was also very polite and respectful to me in a way that turned out to be based in fear of my being unhappy with her if she didn't follow my ways. She told me she worried she wasn't "getting better quick enough". Of course, when Jane felt this phantasy of persecutory parenting, she grew both fearful and resentful. On one hand, she wanted to rebel and do as she pleased. Yet, she grew scared that if she did I would be angry and maybe even "fire her as a patient". So, the image of being held in a sadomasochistic relationship was comforting compared to the threat of being the recipient of anger and then asked to leave.

Both Jane and Joe acted out a combined sadomasochistic relationship with each other that seemed to be begging for my intervention. I interpreted that they both seemed to want me to intercede as a parent, to break them up from their ritualized wrestling match. I interpreted that maybe they weren't sure how to do that for themselves and certainly wanted to change, but this was hard as they both seemed to gain some sense of safety, strength, or power from it. This was the combined couple's transference. Over time, I interpreted that they tried to protect each other and gain some independence from their family troubles within their marriage, but they participated in the very elements of their troubles in doing so: addiction, sadomasochistic relating, mistrust, and the fear of loss. We worked on these issues over the coming sessions.

As the months passed, their relationship improved. Their communication was better and more open. They found ways to create boundaries with their families in ways that made contact more pleasant and less painful. Jane's pot smoking continued to decrease and she no longer drank. They started to do a few things together, going out and having fun. Jane's relationship with her friend and pot supplier remained a sticking point, but we continued to explore its deeper meanings in her life and how she might approach it differently.

In one recent session, they talked about their mutual struggle with family issues. Jane brought up some problems with her mother and Joe mentioned some issues he was having with his family. They seemed to be relating as a unit, helping each other with unique, but similar troubles. Also, Jane began exploring her chronic sense of emptiness and how she has spent most of her life thinking of others, doing for others, and being her mother's errand runner. She said, "I have no idea who I am. I am too busy thinking about others to know what I want." I interpreted that the drugs provided Jane with a chance to do nothing for anyone, a chance to be selfish. I also pointed out that maybe she felt guilty or anxious about not serving her objects because this attempted solution actually left her with nothing. I said, "Maybe you tell yourself, 'it's a dead-end, but at least it is my dead-end'." Jane laughed and said, "I see what you mean."

Jane continues to cut down her intake of pot and has recently taken on a new job with much more responsibility. As noted earlier, I think Joe's presence in the sessions helped to prevent Jane from an early transference flight into persecutory phantasies that might have ended the treatment. To continue being a successful case, there will need to be a gradual resolution of the sadomasochistic dependency they have with each other and on me. Part of the combined anger and sense of victimization from their respective families held their relationship together and allowed them a focus in the treatment to begin examining their internal worlds in the treatment setting. However, they will need to eventually dissolve this pathological link and find a new way to view the world.

Case material 8.2

Paul was in his thirties when he entered treatment for help in remaining drug free from an amphetamine addiction. During his twenties, he spent much of his time at the bars picking up women and getting drunk. He became an alcoholic, involved in numerous one-night stands. At age thirty, he was fired from his job for showing up drunk and found himself close to being homeless and broke. Six months in an intensive recovery program helped him start a new life. Paul stayed sober for another six months but felt "bored". He went out drinking one weekend and used speed. For the next seven years he remained alcohol free, but was a speed addict. This addiction resulted in a very large financial debt from charging everything to credit cards and led to an estrangement from his family, friends, and the support system he had built when in recovery. Also, Paul contracted hepatitis from his drug use and was looking at a life that might become shadowed by chronic illness.

When Paul began psychoanalytic treatment with me, several times a week on the couch, he had managed to put together sixty days without using drugs. Some of what I encountered while working with him could have been the result of the mental and psychical effects of stopping his addictive cycle. However, I believe what emerged in the short period I treated him was more a part of Paul's core personality and his internal, object-relational struggles.

Initially, he was both intent on "getting help to look at my deeper issues" and "making sure I stick with my recovery and don't find a way to rationalize any crazy behavior or getting high". On one hand, Paul seemed motivated and sincere. Yet, the way he spoke to me about "showing up to do the right thing" and the counter-transference feelings of "is he trying to put one over on me?", led me to say, "I think you may be here because you are scared of relapsing, but also out of some sense of obligation." In other words, my counter-transference alerted me to a possible problem establishing analytic contact with Paul. He replied, "You're right. I guess I should come clean. I try and impress everyone and make you think I really am into whatever we are doing. But, this is just something I think I need to do. It is certainly not what I would pick to be doing on my free time." I said, "It makes you angry or irritated to have to see me and to have to show your insides to me, as if you are being made to?" Paul replied, "Well, yes. But, I am not angry at you specifically. But, yes. I don't want to be here. I would rather be having a good time, mindlessly having fun and doing as I please. I know logically I had better do this, but I do feel obligated to change. If the drugs still worked for me, I would be doing that." So, this was the reluctant, conflicted nature of the transference from the beginning. Core elements of analytic contact, attachment, vulnerability, openness, willingness to change, and a sense of mutuality, were missing.

In getting to know Paul, I learned he was raised by a distant father who never had much time for Paul. His mother, on the other hand, was overly involved with Paul. According to Paul, she was a dramatic, self-absorbed woman who always had some crisis to share with him. He said he felt like her "dedicated crying rag, forced to listen to all her worries, complaints, and unmet needs."[2] Based on these bits of history as well as other information Paul shared with me, I interpreted, "You felt trapped by your dramatic and needy mother so you were happy to leave home and escape her when you were eighteen. But, it seems that with the drugs and drinking you became a bit like her, full of crisis and unsure of yourself. Sometimes with me you are dramatic and other times quiet and reluctant. Do you think you are showing me what she was like as well as what it was like to be with her?" Paul replied, "Oh God! I hate to hear that! I don't want to be like her but I know I have become a lot like her. And, I don't really know what to be other than that, except to be high. Or both!" I said, "So, this is a difficult challenge. You feel forced to be yourself with me, which is uncomfortable. It makes sense you are reluctant to share your thoughts and that you try and impress me instead of revealing the real you." Here, I was interpreting the projective identification process that made up the transference at that moment. In doing so, I attempted to bridge the rocky analytic contact we had.

This and other similar transference interpretations led Paul to elaborate on how he tried to impress others. During one session, I interpreted, "I notice you were trying to be very polite and nice to me as you came in from the waiting room. You ask how I am doing and seem very respectful. Is that part of how you try and impress me or make sure we get along?" Paul replied, "Oops! I think you busted me. Yes. I do that with you and everyone else. I try and sell myself." I said, "If I don't buy what you're selling, what are we left with?" Paul said, "That is the problem. I don't know. I never have." After some thought, he went on to say, "I don't think anyone is going to like me. I have spent my life feeling unloved and put down. As a young kid and as a teenager, they picked on me. I couldn't go to my parents about it and my mother was too caught up in her own problems to care. When I was drinking, I felt protected from all that. I didn't care what anyone thought. Then, I got sober and it all came back." I said, "You told me you felt bored." Paul said, "That too. I felt like a nobody. And I was bored with myself and with life. Then, when I found speed, it was like a miracle. I felt important. Instead of worrying about how I look and if people like me, I felt sexy and wonderful. I want that back." I interpreted that it was very difficult for Paul to be sober and drug free and to truly be himself as he would have to accept that he would never be the perfect, always likeable and sexy person he imagined himself to be on drugs. Instead, he had to accept that he was a man of many traits, some likeable, some in need of work, and some just the way they are. Paul said, "I know that is true but it is really, really hard to swallow." Paul resisted analytic contact because he had to face these hard-to-swallow aspects of himself and, because of projective identification dynamics, he felt forced to face them in a persecutory way.

There was a side to Paul that was far from the polite and nice image he tried to convince me of. It was a more manipulative, angry part of him that wanted things his way and demanded that his objects deliver. He would miss some of his sessions and not call to tell me what happened. So, I would call him and have to leave a message regarding the missed session and remind him that I would see him at the next meeting. My leaving a reminder was an acting out of my counter-transference feeling of uncertainty and mistrust. His actions left me with a sense of aloneness and confusion about our relationship. I was acting out the difficulties we were having maintaining analytic contact.

Paul's same lack of response and lack of follow through happened when he needed to call his insurance company to confirm his authorized coverage, but didn't. I began to question the stability of our connection. I said, "You know we need that authorization for us to continue meeting and I need it to be paid. When you seem to ignore it and not do it, it looks like you may not care about us or that you may feel we don't deserve this time." I also interpreted that it might be a way of relaying to me his own ongoing feeling of being ignored, devalued, and cast aside.

In other words, I assumed this way of treating me was the reflection of how he treated his internal objects and how he felt they were treating him, via projective identification. This pattern was confirmed when I would see Paul after a missed session and he wouldn't mention anything about his absence or about my phone call. When I drew his attention to it, he would dismiss it as his "being busy, absent minded, or overwhelmed". I interpreted that it could be that he was more comfortable having us be absent from his mind than to have to deal with the feelings of conflict he felt about our relationship and the issues we faced together. Paul replied, "I don't want to look at myself. I don't like myself. I don't want to have to do this. I get so frustrated. It doesn't seem fair that I can't go out drinking and womanizing. Why am I so far in debt that I will be broke for the next five years? And, you are right. I think I will just blow you off instead of calling. It is easier. I just want to have fun." I said, "It is hard to grow up and face yourself." Paul said, "I don't know who I am, I never have. I don't know what to say. Can you tell me what I should be looking at? What I should be talking about? What would you recommend I talk about to get over these feelings? I want to be done with it!"

In the counter-transference, I felt Paul was starting to move away from his feelings and put them into me by demanding a quick formula on how to feel good. I interpreted, "You want me to be like your drug, quick and gratifying. Maybe that is because you were starting to feel anxious about yourself and uncertain about who you are. Can you tell me more about those feelings?" Paul hesitated and then began to weep. He said, "I have always tried to hide from myself. All through my twenties, I tried to dress myself up in every way possible to feel good and look good. Whether I had to charge it or steal it, I had the best. My clothes were all designer label, my furniture was top of the line, my car wasn't so great because I didn't have the dough, but all in all I managed to put together a pretty nice-looking package."

I interpreted, "It sounds very fragile, like you barely passed the test each day. With me, it must be difficult, since you don't have the buffer of cars, clothes, drugs, alcohol, and so on. All you have to bring me is the real you. What is that like?" Paul replied, "The drugs gave me the guarantee. If the clothes or furniture didn't work, the drugs always did." I said, "So staying sober is really tough for you in general and maybe even harder when we meet to learn about you." Paul said, "I am just so upset with everything." He started to cry again. He said, "I know it sounds so cliched, but a lot of this goes right back to my mother. I did not have a chance to be myself, to find out who I was. I had to be there for her. I had to help her through all her little dramatic moments."

I had a sense of what this might have been like for Paul as he would come to some of his sessions and have emotional outbursts and fits that I would have to help him manage. He would come in and seem out of sorts and uptight. When I asked what was troubling him, he would unleash a torrent of resentments and frustrations, all based around an angry sense of entitlement. Paul shouted, "It just isn't fair! Why the hell do I have to do all this work? I am young. I should be able to be having sex, getting high, and enjoying life." I interpreted, "You feel restricted, unable to do as you please. I wonder if when you can't be like mom, doing as you please, you suddenly feel your wings have been clipped. You haven't discovered any place in the middle, yet." Here, I was referring to his use of pathological splitting and his inability to negotiate his phantasy of the narcissistic object or tolerate the lack of narcissistic entitlement within the analytic situation.

During one session, Paul cried and raged about feeling inadequate in front of a female co-worker. They had gone out to lunch on the weekend. Paul tried to approach her as a new friend instead of another sexual conquest. Without the sex, without his drugs, alcohol, or his identification with a narcissistic object (his mother), he felt lost, ashamed, and rejected. He wailed, "I can't believe it! I was so ashamed! I had to pick her up in my piece of shit, broken-down Audi and we went to lunch at this Italian place. It was OK, but I still can't get over that I don't have any money to spend. I am on a god-damned budget. I tried to dress nicely, but I feel completely out of shape and most of my clothes are out of date. I feel like a shitty loser!" I replied, "You focus on the clothes and the money, but I think you feel very ashamed of what is on the inside. You don't think I or your co-worker would ever like you if we see what is on the inside. Without the fancy car, money, clothes, or drugs, you feel exposed and inferior. You don't trust I would tolerate you without all the wrappings." Paul said, "Yes!" and was quiet for a long time. Then, he said, "This is so difficult!"

The next session, Paul appeared calm and even a bit happy. I interpreted, "You seem to have taken in some of what we talked about last time. You seem more calm." Paul said, "I feel better. I think I might make it. It is hard, but I think I could grow to accept myself." The rest of the session was more of this new tranquility. Paul shared his hopeful outlook and talked about a "new stability" that he envisioned.

My counter-transference during this session was much the same as it was throughout Paul's analytic treatment. I felt a peculiar experience of being held at a distance from Paul, unable to really connect with his presentation. I felt the thinness of our analytic contact. Paul seemed unable to trust either the negative or positive expressions he had. So, his thoughts about his "new stability" didn't feel completely grandiose or manic, but a bit in that direction. Yet, I did feel he also managed to balance himself somewhat as a result of our work in the previous session and take in some of what we worked on. The sessions in which he ranted and complained didn't feel particularly threatening or worrisome, but I didn't really experience his tears as completely poignant. Yet, I did believe he was frustrated, upset, and pained at those moments. When I did experience Paul as genuine and real, I thought he was a man who felt very inconvenienced and frustrated that his life had been put on hold. That seemed real. And, that is what he seemed to see it as, a life put on hold by external factors, not by his own emotional struggles and his own actions. In fact, I think to realize that and to own that meant something humiliating and very anxiety-producing for Paul.

Also, his relaying how he had grown up being his mother's "emotional crying rag" struck me as real and a piece of his past and present pain that was now embedded in his object relationships. When Paul shared his new positive feelings and hopes of the future, I didn't really trust it as a genuine change of attitude or outlook. It seemed to be a combination of some manic stance and a sudden reduction of anxiety from several successful interpretations in the prior sessions. The interpretations helped Paul for a period of time, but he was unable or unwilling to participate with me in further cultivating the interpretive direction so as to bring some more permanent clarity or balance to his internal world.

In many ways, Paul didn't want to change, because he felt doing so was not truly for him. He grew up feeling his life belonged to his mother and that what he did was to please her or to mange her chaotic moods. His years of drinking and drug addiction were a respite from this. His drug problems served as a way out from the ongoing lack of self-identity he felt and an escape from the servitude he felt toward his objects. At best, he could try to convince his objects that he was his own man, in fancy clothes, exotic tastes, sexual adventures, and wild ways. But, without all that, he felt a combination of emptiness, inferiority, and a lack of freedom. He felt forced to please mother and his emotional experience was constricted by that internal obligation.

After about six months of analytic treatment, Paul's insurance coverage ran out. Typically, I spend hours on the phone fighting with case managers who find the treatment "not medically necessary". They remind me that the coverage is only for short-term crisis intervention and then they terminate the patient. So, when this happened, I immediately saw the writing on the wall. Knowing how Paul was already in great financial debt, I felt the door closing on our difficult but worthwhile journey. There was a chance he could see me for a reduced fee, out-of-pocket, until the new calendar year started for his insurance coverage. At that time, he could possibly be granted another number of visits.

I presented Paul with this option, but I felt in the counter-transference less than optimistic about it. He told me he would think about it. The next session, he began talking about his job, his 12-step recovery meetings, his time at the gym, and how he was fixing up his apartment. I said, "You are talking a lot today about things that are going on outside of this room. But, you aren't mentioning our work together. You were going to think about what you want to do after today, since it is the last time the insurance covers you. Maybe, it is uncomfortable to think about us and how to keep us together, so it is easier if I bring it up?" In the counter-transference, I had felt ignored and felt I was waiting to see what he would do with us. It was as if he held our fate in his hands and didn't care much about it. This may have been his narcissistic identification with his mother and his projection of his ignored, excluded self into me. Also, he may have resented having to make the effort to bring it up since I think, in his persecutory phantasies, Paul felt that having to truly make the effort to be a participant in the treatment and devote his time, money, and vulnerability to it would be akin to giving to me. And, this would be experienced as more servitude to mother. Paul said, "I will let you know. I will call you." I said, "I have a sense that to continue coming to see me must feel like an obligation that you would resent. You felt indebted to mother and now to me. Does that make any sense?" Paul said, "Well, I have felt that from the first day here, but I have tried to not think about it too much. But, you are right. Now, I feel that way for sure. I will think it over though. I want some time to think it over. I will call you."

I can only speculate that Paul was unable to overcome those persecutory feelings. He never did call and when I called him, he said he wanted to "wait and see how things go". Again, I think Paul felt he would be having to give to me and please me by truly engaging in the treatment relationship. He wanted help but in his phantasies help meant obligation, painful dependency, and a lonely exposure to the critical way he was with himself that left him ashamed and depressed. In that sense, he had no choice but to not return to see me.

Both cases presented in this chapter involved patients who grew up in families where there was significant emotional and psychical abandonment. There was a loss of contact with a reliable, caring parent who could give rather than need to be given to. In both cases, the patients felt their primary objects were weak and needed help to the point of draining and hurting those around them. At the same time, both patients felt their objects could easily become attacking, controlling, and rejecting unless constantly catered to. The drugs provided an artificial break from feeling guilty for not serving the object, a break from the feelings of criticism, control, and punishment from the angry object, and a way to forge a symbiotic identification with the object.

When I say the drugs provided a break, I mean a false sense of safety, revenge, and comfort. The drugs were really part of a self-destructive projective identification dynamic that eventually brought on the very elements the patients were trying to avoid. The drugs also gave Jane the power to rebel and do nothing. Doing nothing was a victory against her demanding and disappointing objects, but also a desperate, shallow, and temporary respite in her internal obligation to the needs of others.

For Paul, he used drugs to pretend he had the admiration and love of others instead of facing the failure and loss of his mother's containment and love. Without the drugs, he couldn't deny these intense feelings. He wanted to act out and escape this painful state, even for a moment. Because Jane was still using drugs, lived with Joe, and was able to attend her analytic sessions with Joe, she had a much better secure base to operate from and a way to withstand the pain of her own sense of loss and persecution. Paul lacked these external factors and therefore faced a more precarious internal state, without a feeling of hope or any kind of emotional safety net. Yet, he was able to remain drug free for six months while in treatment. For both patients, drugs served to cover up the lack of self-integration, the guilt over not providing enough to their needy objects, and the rage at not being cared for and parented.

I think Jane's history and childhood experiences were not as devastating as Paul's. Therefore, she was ultimately more able to tolerate the anxiety and frustration that analytic treatment brings about in the healing process. She was more able to tolerate and utilize the dynamic of analytic contact. Paul was able to hang in there until an external situation came along that triggered his core feelings of resentment at having to serve others instead of being served and admired. For him, analytic contact was achieved in a brittle and brief way. So, while he achieved momentary insight and a period of stability, analytic contact also represented a persecutory deflation of his tender narcissism and that led to an eventual retreat back into his angry detachment.

Notes

1 Here, Joe demonstrated what Rosenfeld (1960) stated regarding patients who have only partially reached the depressive position. Joe felt a duty to help, rescue,

and heal the object and felt guilty about separating from the object to fulfill his own desires. But, in addition, he experienced a much more primitive, paranoid threat of loss, abandonment, and persecution from his objects if he chose to live his own life.

2 There were several other siblings, but for reasons of confidentiality, they will be omitted from the presentation.

Chapter 9

Psychic mutilation and the struggle for integration

Some borderline, narcissistic, and psychotic patients come into treatment acting out their anxieties of primitive loss, sadistic guilt, and persecution. These feelings and phantasies compromise the internal annihilation threat that Melanie Klein (1955) felt was at the core of human experience.

This intra-psychic panic state emerges from the simultaneous fears of losing that which is necessary for survival (the object) and of being destroyed by that object. Often, the dread of attack and persecution comes first, followed by a phantasy of being abandoned or shunned. This is the result of internalization of traumatic object relations as well as the projection of aggression and envy. Through projective identification, a hyper-vigilant state escalates internally until the self and the object are constantly embattled.

The life instincts and the death instincts normally exist in a state of balance. When the external and internal worlds create demands or threats to the ego, the life instinct can become more powerful and actively challenge the threat. Or, the death instinct can deny, erase, or neutralize the threat by shutting down the life instinct. By cutting off the link between the ego and the threat, the death instinct creates a defense, a magical sense of safety and omnipotence. Clinically, this may appear as masochism, martyrdom, and denial. Often, there is a seeming indifference to the cruelty of others because sadism exists as a part of splitting. Therefore, there is a denial of any important self-to-object link.

The fears that overwhelm the ego are sometimes external environmental trauma and sometimes the result of projections of strong feelings and phantasies. Invariably, it is both, each casting a shadow on the other. Through projective identification, there is an endless loop of fear, aggression, defense, and offense against internalized objects. Klein (1946) felt projective identification was the fundamental method the mind used to cope and communicate with itself and its objects.

The ego develops by constantly taking in and expelling its experiences of subjective and objective reality. In phantasy, the ego puts its feelings into the object, whether defensive, libidinal, or aggressive. The actual person (wife, boss, friend, analyst) can be influenced into this intra-psychic relationship via subtle interpersonal interactions.

In her clinical work, Klein (1959) discovered how the ego constantly takes in the object and external world by introjection. At the same time, the ego expresses its feelings, needs, and desires through projection. Shaped by its introjections, the ego creates new sets of projections which influence what is introjected. This projective identification cycle, the ego's developmental trajectory, produces personality and perception. In healthy development, projective identification forms a self-perpetuating loop of positive experiences of self and object. This builds strong psychic structure and a character based on hope, forgiveness, fulfillment, and trust.

In pathological situations, the same internal process generates endless despair, mistrust, emptiness, and persecution. The ideal object is experienced as shifting into a persecuting and abandoning object. The paranoid-schizoid ego feels at a loss as to why this takes place, which is another form of intra-psychic crisis and chaos. As the ego matures, it starts to feel a sense of responsibility, yet this is a primitive sense of ownership that can feel persecutory. This sadistic type of guilt involves phantasies of a vengeful, unforgiving object in an eye-for-an-eye world. These exaggerated superego demands can cause the death instinct to retaliate defensively, by extinguishing all striving for success, recognition, life, and relatedness.

Excessive reliance on projective identification, the pressures of superego guilt, and defensive strategies of the death instinct all leave the ego in a barren state of loss and annihilation. This is a loss of profound proportions. In the part-self, part-object paranoid-schizoid world, love becomes hatred, security turns into abandonment, and knowledge shifts to chaos and confusion. Through splitting and projective identification, the ego perceives an object that was a sleeping dragon, now awoken to become a rageful beast.

If life and intimacy bring on such dangers, it is best to be rid of life. The death instinct can serve a defensive function by neutralizing or destroying the life-affirming aspects of the ego. In the rational of the unconscious, if the object seems so easily enraged or hurt, it helps to extinguish any object tie or dependence on that object. If the object feels dangerous and loss seems imminent, it is best to erase any identification with or need for the object. Rigid control, manic defenses, and denial are all consequential symptoms of the death instinct being used, defensively, against the life instincts. Paradoxically, to prevent catastrophic loss, the ego creates an experience of isolation, fear, guilt, and loss. Chronic reliance on manic independence, projective identification, and the death instinct brings about self-abandonment and self-persecution.

For many borderline, narcissistic, and psychotic patients, acting out is an external manifestation of the internal workings of the death instinct and the superego. In turn, the death instinct and projective identification are used defensively to avoid an internal experience of loss and persecution. If the patient is able to stay in treatment, these layers and cycles emerge within the transference and can be worked through. The death instinct and projective identification can become the leading transference force that aims to dismantle or destroy analytic contact. The analyst must focus his or her interpretive skills in this area if the treatment is to survive.

THE CASE OF O: ACTING OUT AND THE FIRST PHASE OF TREATMENT

O came to see me when she was twenty-five years old. She had never been in treatment before. She felt so depressed and acted so absent-mindedly that her boss suggested she seek help. I was struck by the way she looked like a sweet, attractive, and polite young woman, but also presented herself as aggressive and provocative with her pierced nose and a tattoo of fire flames on her back and shoulders. O worked as a manager in a small company that hired her as a temp. She stayed on and was promoted several times, but also was on probation for her "bad attitude". This was her "day job" that paid the bills, but O really wanted to spend her time painting. She had almost graduated from a prestigious European art academy and wanted to pursue oil painting and watercolor as a career.

During her first session, O told me she felt suicidal, depressed, and hopeless. Her love of art came from her relationship with her mother, who was a well-known European artist. O had attended art school, but dropped out because it felt "too rigid and controlling". Presently, she wasn't able to paint because she couldn't execute the work to the level of perfection she wanted. "It must be just so! And, I can never get it perfect enough, so I feel it isn't worth it to try", she said.

During the last four years, O had been smoking hashish and drinking heavily every day. This led to countless, shameful experiences of being used by men. "I am an alcoholic and my life is out of control. I've screwed up my life before it ever got off the ground!", O said. I learned she had a history of cutting herself with a razor when she felt upset and burning herself with cigarettes. "When I was a teenager, I think I did it to get my father's attention. Later, I just did it to cope with feeling so empty and lost." O had tried suicide by overdosing on aspirin when she was thirteen.

Up until age twenty, O was anorexic and bulimic. Then, she became pregnant and had a baby girl, whom she gave up for adoption. I interpreted that her eating disorder stopped when she became pregnant because she felt filled with love and hope and wasn't alone anymore, but now felt empty and grief-stricken. I said I thought she now tried to stop that pain, anger, and fear with alcohol, drugs, and self-mutilation. O said, "For years, I haven't been able to sleep more than four or five hours a night. I am always exhausted. I try and not think of my baby." I said, "So hurting yourself is connected to missing your little girl." O cried and said, "I thought I was over that, but maybe not!"

In summarizing her plight, O said, "My drinking, my sleeping around, and the way I drag my lazy ass around leaves me feeling so ashamed and disgusted with myself! For as long as I remember, I have felt this hollow emptiness inside. I always feel lonely and like a huge failure. At the same time, I really want to finally deal with my problems and find a way to grow up. I feel so behind in life, I feel I had better figure out what the next step is and hurry up and take it before I get any more behind! I need you to help me set goals and figure out what the next step is!" O said all this in a way that left me feeling tense, pressured, sympathetic, and a bit overwhelmed. I believe she was using projective identification, interpersonally and intrapsychically, to put her sad, pushy, and rushed feelings into me. Given her turbulent history and chaotic background, part of me felt pulled to somehow rescue her and heal her. I also felt tension to do all that immediately. Noting these feelings and understanding them as her projections and my response to those projections, I made an interpretation. I said, "You are feeling anxious and out-of-control and want to get back in control. But now you are thinking the way to do that is to hurry up and get to it and figure it out fast, or else. If we don't perform well, then we will fail. You feel so anxious, it's a do-or-die kind of thing." O said she agreed and felt she probably does that with other relationships and with her painting. "If I feel there is a mistake in my painting, I work at it with such a vengeance that I often create more mistakes!" she said.

When she was late by ten minutes coming to one session, she started screaming at me to the point where I felt physically threatened. She claimed I was ripping her off financially, since she was being charged for the session and when she arrived my door was closed. She felt I was deliberately "messing with her mind" and trying to manipulate and control her for "kicks". She was clearly in the grips of a paranoid assault and felt so abandoned and attacked that she had to attack back. Eventually, she was able to explain to me that when she can't make sense out of something, she feels out of control and berserk. This insight only came when I slowly asked her to explain each part of her anger: "Tell me exactly how you felt when you got here", "Please tell me the details of everything that makes you feel so disrespected and abused", and so forth. After she explained her phantasies about my closed door, the fact that I always locked my office door, and how long it took for me to open the door, I responded to each one. Especially when the patient's paranoid phantasies disrupt the analytic contact so severely, it is vital to investigate and interpret each of the moment-to-moment disruptions in that contact.

Because she was so in the grips of this paranoid anxiety, I told her the reality of each situation before trying to explore her psychological experience of that reality. I told her I keep my office door closed for privacy from solicitors and from anyone that may be in the waiting room. It took me about one minute to get to the door. O started debating how long it took and said she was out there at least five or ten minutes. Rather than arguing with her, I told her I could see how angry she could be if she felt I was deliberately being so abusive, taking advantage of her, and "messing with her mind". I said I could only assure her that all the things she mentioned were done for a reason, but not the assaultive and manipulative reasons she felt. This calmed her down immediately. She explained to me that she was so angry because everything seemed out of control and didn't make sense. But, now that I had explained it all, it made sense. She associated to her childhood when she was beaten, yelled at, or locked in the closet and never understood why. She said this made her feel lost and panicked for days. Toward the end of the session, I told O she could, if ever late again, simply knock on my door and I would open it. She felt this was reasonable. So, analytic contact had been dangerously crippled for a moment, but with very careful interpretation and exploration, it was restored. Rather than it being a combative exchange between enemies, we were able to mutually explore why O had experienced me in the frightening manner she did.

In working with borderline patients like O, the analyst must pay close attention to his or her counter-transference feelings and phantasies. Occasionally, O managed to pull me toward participating in her phantasies of control, persecution, and guilt. Caper (1992) has described how the patient's projections may influence the analyst to believe he is omnipotent and capable of magically curing the patient. The patient's wish to be understood can be a part of a resistance to working through. In other words, the passive desire for care and cure is a fight against the active give-and-take of insight and gradual independent thought. Some patients would rather take from the analyst than give to themselves.

O acted out in the transference and in her day-to-day life. During the first six months of treatment, she continued to drink and be promiscuous. This resulted in her having an abortion, being fired from a job, and contracting Herpes virus. She felt surrounded by men whom she first felt were genuine friends, but later realized they were simply using her. O would often set out to practice her painting, only to end up calling up her drinking buddies for a late-night party. At first she felt excited to be the center of attention, but later felt "like a slut". But, most of the time she fancied herself as living a "free and modern" lifestyle, a part of the in-crowd.

Over time, we understood this as an internal rebellion against her mother and a way to escape her own persecutory superego. She felt pressured to paint perfectly so as to please her mother's actual lectures and advice to "get it together" and "build a career". At the same time, O criticized and nagged herself. The pursuit of perfection was always on her mind. In exploring this,

O described feeling not only pressured but alone and desperate. She said she felt a painful emptiness and a sad lack of direction. This inner void combined with the pressure to be an ideal painter until she felt so overwhelmed that she drank herself into a blackout.

As time went along, we understood O's acting out in more detailed intrapsychic terms. Through gradual exploration and free association to her feelings and behavior, she was able to see the symbolic meaning of her thoughts and affect. The drinking served her aggression, a way of exacting revenge on her objects. "I drink at my mother", O said. "When I feel pressured to figure out everything in therapy right away, I feel like, 'screw that!' and I get drunk." In addition, she canceled many of her sessions because of hangovers. Typically, O would stay out till three in the morning and sleep till late afternoon.

Also, we came to understand how O's oral desires and aggressive thirst for an ideal object led to her mentally destroying that object. At different times, she mentally attacked me, attacked us as a unit, and frequently attacked her mother.

O needed and wanted nourishment from her objects, but her intrapsychic attack on these objects left her abandoned and isolated. Through projective identification, she was spoiling the very thing she craved. This led to her feeling great despair as well as great rage. She split off and projected the rage into her objects and then felt persecuted all over again. Therefore, O perpetuated an internal cycle of abandonment, persecution, and the experience of annihilation.

O was able to gain insight into her destructive eating as being part of this internal object-related cycle. She told me, "I eat so much when I am lonely because then I can still feel a connection to the world. It is my way of controlling my connection to the world, a way of making sure I don't lose touch with what is important for me to survive. Actually, its more like I feel all the people I need or love are gone and the food brings them back. But, it is only temporary so I have to keep eating more and more to make them stay."

O's eating problem was the result of a breakdown in symbolic functioning and an excessive reliance on projective identification. In an effort to control her objects and prevent an overwhelming sense of loss, she was left with food as the literal source of her needs, rather than it being a symbol for her rejecting objects. The more we explored these phantasies and feelings and dealt with the transference aspects of them, the less she began to act out.

By the end of the second year of treatment, O no longer gorged on food and only became drunk on occasions, rather than daily. She also stopped mutilating herself and started to paint on a regular basis. She was able to support herself at a satisfying job. Also, O began to grieve for her baby.

PHASE TWO OF TREATMENT: THE SUPEREGO AND THE DEATH INSTINCT

At this point in the analysis, along with a great deal of counter-transference confusion, I had started to gather an understanding for who O was and the way her mind worked. She grappled with a shifting, twisting mixture of paranoid and depressive problems that left her feeling very guilty, but in a hopeless and persecutory way. This paranoid type of guilt was the internal experience of a hoped-for ideal object that was easily hurt or destroyed, and returned to hunt her down. She felt the degree of conflict or potential harm to her object was so great that understanding, forgiveness, or reparation was impossible. O's superego was hostile and unrelenting, operating with the paranoid-schizoid position.

For several years, O had volunteered at a guide-dog shelter. She had put in many hard and long hours doing physical labor and secretarial tasks. If she wasn't able to make it in to work due to sickness or prior commitments, she felt she was a "lazy loser" and raged against herself for "not following through with anything in life". My sense was that she had to destroy any pleasure she derived from her volunteer work, as it represented her expressing an identity separate from her objects. Then she rebeled by doing her own thing, in this case volunteering. O felt guilty in a persecutory way and had to deny and destroy her connection to her own identity. Also, she wanted to depend on her internal and external mother, but felt that meant she was sacrificing her own identity. Therefore, she felt in a continuous bind.

Volunteering with vulnerable puppies was part of her feeling neglected as a child. In other words, she identified with the helpless puppies who needed proper care and love. In devaluing and attacking her volunteer work, O also identified with an irresponsible, careless mother who didn't take proper care of the helpless, hungry puppy part of her. Of course, there is no way of knowing what really took place in O's childhood, so we were investigating O's current phantasies about her current and past objects.

O maintained the phantasy of an ideal object who betrayed her needy, hungry puppy feelings and then O raged against this useless mother object. I was struck by the intensity of O's self-criticism about her volunteer work and countless other aspects of her life. It wasn't so much a cycle of neurotic guilt as it was a demonic, relentless trashing of herself without any room for forgiveness. It was sadistic and created an intense level of persecutory accusation that generated more and more anxiety. I felt this was an expression of the death instinct, a clinical manifestation of one part of her mind attempting to silence or destroy another part.

O had a need to know the answer to things and felt very disconcerted if she couldn't figure everything out. I felt her become demanding of my knowledge and wanting answers right away. Through her projecting her superego demands, we both endured a sense of urgency or pressure. She didn't ever simply become curious and ask questions since this was admitting weakness or stupidity, so she was left to feel a victim to the unknown. She had the victory of admitting her defective mind, but at the price of losing a sense of self and meaning. O felt lost and frightened, and often very overwhelmed to the point of tears. I interpreted this as the loss of an idealized yet easily destroyed mother object.

She used projective identification to infect the transference with this lack of knowledge, so sometimes I felt stupid and behind in knowing what to do with O. Gradual self-analysis led me to interpret that she was defending against feeling all alone without any knowledge and consequently seeing me as a failure. She idealized me as a knowledgeable container-mother she could cling to, but then destroyed me and was left alone and scared.

O's desire for knowledge extended to her wanting to know how to paint perfectly and how to be the complete master of her life, immediately. When this ideal wasn't reached, as it never was, she reacted by devaluing herself and erasing the strengths she did have. I interpreted this as her wish for me to be an ideal mother who could be all-knowing and all-caring and when that didn't occur, she attacked me and tore me down. I interpreted that one part of her mind made unreasonable demands on another part and then proceeded to attack and reject that less than perfect part. So, in her phantasies and through projective identification, I was the failed container without knowledge. Sometimes, she felt we both were this disappointing emptiness and attacked us both. Here, her phantasies maintained a drain and a threat on analytic contact. When she was able to push us away from more successful analytic contact, it verified and justified her phantasies and need to see us as useless.

De Masi (Capozzi & De Masi 2001) outlined certain patients' destructive methods of dealing with mental pain. He discussed their psychic strategy of self-annihilation. I believe De Masi was describing a clinical manifestation of the death instinct, in a defensive posture. Rather than feel overwhelmed by trying to contain and tolerate its internal conflicts and the link to the bad aspects of the self and object, the mind chooses to pursue self-destruction and an attack on the personality and identity.

De Masi (Capozzi & De Masi 2001) explains how these types of resistance and attempts at intra-psychic mutilation require the analyst to pay great attention to containment and boundary clarification through ongoing interpretation. With patients like O, the analyst must continuously act as a filter through which the patient projects various split-off parts of the self and various internalized objects. De Masi states,

> Klein's introduction of the concept of splitting, alongside that of repression, gives rise to a modification of technique, which now concentrates on recovery of the split-off and projected parts of the personality. The analyst serves as the recipient of the projections and

split-off parts, so that in this type of technique the here and now is more important than reconstruction of the past. Through systematic analysis of the transference, classical Kleinian analysis sets out to help the patient to recover an image of the internal world in which libidinal aspects hold sway over their destructive counterparts. The libidinal aspects can emerge only when the split-off parts of the self which are unwanted owing to the unconscious destruction and envy they contain have been experienced and recovered and reparative processes have been initiated.

(p. 8)

O's more libidinal or even benign vision of the world, herself, and her objects was constantly darkened and mutilated by the more pathological aspects of the death instinct and her excessive reliance on splitting and projective identification. Thus, my task in guarding and stabilizing analytic contact had much to do with constantly interpreting this splitting and projection.

O was extremely demanding and unforgiving of herself. If she couldn't be perfect, she gave up in disgust. After two years of treatment, she was shocked that she hadn't straightened her life out yet. Gradually, she talked about her demanding mother and wondered if she had "copied" her mother's way of being in life. I commented on her pattern of pressing herself to be perfect, followed by periods of acting out.

After a drug and food relapse, I told her, "I think there is a reason you used all those drugs last night and wound up having unprotected sex. I think you are disappointed and furious with yourself for failing to meet your rigid expectations of how to be with me and what pace you should be at with your artwork." After we talked about this, I added, "Maybe your acting out is also a way to lash out at your mother: rebeling against her, against me, and against that demanding mother-part of yourself." O said, "Well, yes! I feel ganged up against from all those forces. I didn't see any way out!"

When the superego sets up such impossible expectations, the death instinct acts on the side of life by trying to destroy the demanding superego. Thus, an internal rebellion rages between parts of the personality. In these ways, the death instinct is sometimes an expression of the sadistic superego and other times a defensive experience of the ego.

The superego and the death instinct

Freud (1930, 1937) introduced the concept of the death instinct as the result of his clinical observation. He noted certain patients who seemed determined to maintain their illness and tried to continue their course of self-distruction. The idea of a death instinct was never fully embraced by the analytic community. In fact, some analytic "schools" have seen Freud's discovery as his misunderstanding of the patient's defensive masochism and other defensive compromises.

Without tracing the historical sequence of this concept, it is clear that the death instinct has been a vague and controversial issue. When used at all, it is often mixed together with references to the superego, to anger turned inwards, and to the analyst's blaming the patient for his own counter-transference problems.

Melanie Klein and her followers stand alone in taking Freud's discovery seriously. Klein felt the clinical evidence for the death instinct was over-whelming. Specifically, she believed envy was the direct manifestation of the death instinct and, as such, envy sought to spoil and devalue whatever seemed valuable or connected to life. Some analytic schools have debated whether the death instinct is simply another name for sadism or masochism. Klein felt the death instinct was a different phenomenon. While patients often express sadistic glee at squashing the object of their envy, the sadism is secondary to the goal of the death instinct rather than primary.

Many borderline, narcissistic, or psychotic patients face a dual struggle. Their internal world is torn apart by the forces of the death instinct and a pathological superego. Theoretically and technically, it is important to make a distinction between these phenomena. At times, this is difficult as the patient's paranoid-schizoid or depressive states of perception color and complicate each.

According to Freud and Melanie Klein, the life and death instincts are innate and constitutional, but are manifested as emotional id-based urges. Developmentally, these are transformed by the ego into intra-psychic, psychological phantasies that interface with reality.

Klein emphasized the psychological rather than biological nature of instincts and the resulting phantasies. These are internal dramas that involve dynamic relationships between the self and its unconscious objects. The superego functions as an independent agent of the ego, a collection of particular parental functions. It consists of the projection onto reality, the introjection of that distorted reality, and the intra-psychic reactions to that distortion. This is layered with the internalization of actual reality. Through the interplay of projection, introjection, external reality, and phantasy, the dynamics of the death instinct and the superego are constantly changing. All these internal situations are played out interpersonally via projective identification and thus lead to further mutation.

Normal development brings psychological integration and balance. As the result of ongoing internalization of good, forgiving, and supportive objects in balance with a normal level of competitive and envious aggression, the superego emerges as an understanding, confidence-building, contemplative agency. With ample containment from external objects, the superego becomes fortified with an internalized containing structure of its own. The superego then has a stop, wait-and-see, look-before-you-leap capacity. However, if the superego is a vicious, punitive force that fails as a guiding and flexible container, the death instinct may begin to function defensively.

During normal development, the death instinct and the superego operate in reciprocal balance, with the superego representing the life instincts. If the superego takes on pathological properties, with exaggerated use of guilt and self-threat, the death instinct will try to eliminate this ego threat.

The superego seeks knowledge, challenge, clarity, success, and autonomy. Curiosity, direction, and motivation come from the superego. When combating the sadistic, inflated, and pathological superego, the death instinct tries to eliminate thinking, dependency, differences, and need. Differences and awareness of separateness from the object are attacked. The superego demands unrealistic states of agreement and acceptance between self and object, so the death instinct tries to eliminate the connection and relationship altogether.

With patients operating mostly within the paranoid-schizoid position, this constant internal battle leaves the ego overwhelmed and in a state of collapse. Developmentally, many of these difficult patients are testing the waters of the depressive position, but experience their depressive phantasies through a paranoid lens. The paranoid-schizoid ego tries to not hurt its objects, but mostly out of self-preservation. Since the primitive ego is still struggling with strong levels of hostility, envy, and persecutory fears (based on excessive reliance on projective identification), the object seems easily enraged and prone to revenge. So, when these patients are overly nice in the transference, it is not so much out of love for the object, but fear of rejection and attack.

Within these primitive phantasies, reparation feels impossible. The hurt to the object feels permanent, the ego's own hostility feels too strong to contain, and the object seems too weak to survive any hurt. Precocious attempts at reparation lead to manic acting out. These patients project paranoid-schizoid anxiety into the object and then feel unable to rescue or heal that object. This creates new superego guilt and fear, along with unrealistic demands to make it all better. The death instinct has to war against this and destroy these demands. Often this creates a vicious cycle where the superego is demanding a perfect "ultra-life" and the death instinct must eliminate all signs of life to counterbalance this.

Klein (1927) felt the superego was formed by a combination of the parent's commands and prohibitions as well as the child's own sadistic phantasies. Repression, splitting, and projective identification freeze these internal conflicts into a repetitive cycle, not allowing for change or resolution. Because of the dynamic and mutative nature of unconscious phantasy, these cycles do shift in form but not in substance.

For O, the effects of both external and internal cruelty were significant. Her actual experience with her family had been harsh and brutal. She saw her father as having no capacity for leniency, understanding, or forgiveness. Her own sadism, both as a defensive reaction and constitutionally, was quite intense. She felt these hostile feelings were unacceptable, as it meant she was the same as her father. To prevent this, she systematically denied, projected, and destroyed those aspects of herself. These intense struggles prevented her from achieving normal psychic development from the paranoid-schizoid to the depressive position. In fact, many of her problems centered on the way she careened back-and-forth between these two internal worlds. Therefore, much of the analysis focused on the often shifting nature of her anxiety and pathological phantasy life.

To avoid feeling she was a carbon-copy of her bad father, O took a very passive position in her life. By projecting all of her active sexual and aggressive feelings into others, she felt less frightened of hurting me and others and more hopeful of being loved and cared for. Of course, this actually resulted in her being neglected or taken advantage of, so she felt persecuted and ignored. This created a great deal of envy, for she saw others as capable of openly and successfully sharing their feelings and desires.

This cycle of projective identification colored her transference phantasies. O was passive with me rather than direct. Over the years, we understood this as a way to reject or destroy any potential identification with her forceful phallic father, a way to feel dominated in a sexual way, and a way to manipulate me to rescue her and love her. So, when she felt overwhelmed and wanted to come more often, what she did was come in and tell me how wonderful her massage therapist was and how she was considering asking her physician for medications. When I said I thought she wanted to see me more and have me care for her extra during this hard time, but probably felt reluctant or vulnerable to say so directly, she yelled at me for rejecting her and not seeing how upset she was. We slowly talked about the mixture of control, love, domination, and loneliness she felt in our relationship. Gradually, she told me she felt ashamed to admit her "weakness", felt I should know how and when to care for her without her ever having to ask for it, and felt I might take advantage of her sexually if she appeared weak and helpless. Clearly, it made sense for her to fight against any movement toward analytic contact if it meant the actualization of these types of overwhelming phantasies.

I believe O was describing paranoid-schizoid phantasies of persecutory guilt and fear. It is only in later intra-psychic development that the ego is able to neutralize its own erratic hostile and libidinal forces, so that genuine remorse, guilt, and altruistic concern color the object relationship. To some patients, the experience of being "lost, solitary, and forsaken" is felt as a punishment for breaking the rules and making the parental authority figure angry. For more primitive patients like O, being "lost and forsaken" is equivalent to annihilation and promotes ego fragmentation.

As time went on, O told me about not only how furious she was at her controlling mother, but how fragile she felt her mother to be. O called her mother on a daily basis to "check on her". O felt her mother would collapse if she felt she wasn't in control of O and of others. Without this control, O said mother would "fall apart, lose her identity, become angry, and turn into my enemy". Many of their regular telephone talks involved O's mother telling O what a horrible marriage she had. Feeling in the middle, O felt obliged to agree and side with her mother against her father. If she didn't or if she disagreed with mother's complaints, O's mother would yell at her, call her ungrateful, and refuse to talk with her for weeks on end. In these and many other ways, O felt forced in the middle of her parents, with no way out.

My impression, over time, was that O turned most of her oral and anal phantasies, needs, and urges inwards on herself. In order to protect her mother, whom she saw as fragile and easy to anger, she put most of her needs and demands on herself. Any rage or frustration towards her mother was also turned inwards. So, looking to herself for nourishment, ideal acceptance, and knowledge was a way of protecting mother and protecting herself from mother's potential abandonment and attack. Again, this was a phantasy based both in internal and external reality.

Klein believed the infant's intense oral cravings and aggression evoke attacks from the object in phantasy, but also pose a mortal threat to that internal object. The ego mobilizes primitive defenses to protect both self and object. These include splitting, projective identification, and manic defenses, all mobilized within a projective/introjective framework. Therefore, control, invasion, submission, abandonment, and annihilation are the central transference themes with patients who still live within this primitive internal experience. Predatory and persecutory phantasies and the defenses against them dominate the psychic landscape.

Certainly these patients progress to higher levels of function, yet these patients often regress to phantasies of annihilating the object and being annihilated in return. This leads to an oral/anal emphasis on control along with strong urges to blame and punish someone, be it self or object. If forgiveness or understanding is unavailable, flight or fight phantasies dominate all relationships. This persecutory guilt leaves the ego in a constant state of vigilant anxiety. Somebody has got to be wrong and blame must be assigned.

While the paranoid-schizoid position is thought to gradually evolve into the depressive position, the psychoanalytic literature rather loosely defines the details of that transition as the consolidation of part-objects into a whole self/object matrix. The shift is seen as a move from persecutory anxieties to depressive oedipal guilt. This chapter focuses on patients, such as O, who make a much slower and disorganized transition, involving intense phantasies of permanent loss, sadistic retaliation, and attack from the object.

In the transference, O projected her phantasies of a demanding, rejecting, and abandoning mother. This pushed her to make manic attempts at reparation for what she called "her sins" against me. She missed many sessions in the beginning due to her drinking or from overeating. She would binge on food and sometimes stay in bed after vomiting. Gradually, we understood how she was treating me and our relationship in the context of her unconscious phantasies. She felt scared of my criticism and retaliation but also felt a certain amount of "I will show you!"

O projected her own demanding mother feelings onto me and then felt pressured to be the perfect patient. In the beginning phase of analysis, she told me, "I am sorry I am not better already. I will try harder. Please be patient." Later, she felt more anxious and offered to pay me more because of how difficult and slow she was. Exploring these ideas led to her phantasies of my being impatient, intolerant, and on the edge of fury. The same feelings came out around her drinking and eating. While I was happy she had started to reduce this destructive behavior, she felt I was probably at the end of my rope and ready to either "fire her" or yell at her and "give up on her".

Bicudo (1964) has discussed the concept of persecutory guilt, by which the ego projects its primitive experience of guilt into the object and thus feels hounded by guilt. Bicudo describes patients who have negotiated some of the obstacles of the paranoid-schizoid position, but have yet to fully achieve the depressive position and its whole object functions. They continue to use splitting and projective identification to cope with anxiety, but now mostly the anxiety of guilt. Rather than feeling guilty about the harm done to the object, the ego is overwhelmed by phantasies of an object that is forcing them to admit guilt and to give over any pleasure or achievement they possess. These patients have yet to develop a forgiving superego, capable of being repaired and healed by the ego. They struggle with a superego that demands allegiance, wants revenge, and will not take no for an answer.

I am expanding Bicudo's ideas with the concept of an ego that has one foot in the depressive position and one foot in the paranoid-schizoid position. Overall, these patients use paranoid-schizoid ego functioning to cope with primitive versions of depressive anxieties. Also, I believe these patients are continuously faced with the phantasy of an ideal object that is spoiled by the ego's needs and demands. The ideal object is spoiled and turns into an angry, destructive persecutor. Via projective identification, the ego faces terrifying loss as well as attack and punishment without any solution or rescue. Abandonment, domination, and persecution loom as constant threats. The ego constructs an ideal, all-loving, and perfect object, only to be disappointed and scared by its disappearance. Therefore, the analysis of these patients' hunger, aggression, and envy is critical to helping them build a new, durable, and forgiving object.

Usually, the depressive position is viewed as ego anxiety around losing or hurting one's internal object. Clinically, it may be wise to single out the more severe phantasies of critically or terminally injuring the object and then being hunted down by it as belonging more to the paranoid-schizoid position or as a primitive precursor to the depressive position proper. The depressive position proper is a whole-object and whole-self experience containing tensions of hurting an object that can and will tolerate the blows and bounce back. In paranoid-schizoid suffering, the part-object is vulnerable to being destroyed by the needs, aggression, or love of part-aspects of self. Other parts of the object are felt to attack and abandon the needy parts of the self and leave it to suffer forever.

Consciously, these phantasies come out in more separate lines of association. O told me about a boyfriend she wanted to leave because he always cheated on her and sometimes beat her. She presented such a list of abuse that I felt like saying, "You should leave this evil man at once! You are crazy to stay with him!" Of course, this is literally what all her friends and several attorneys had already told her. What was interesting was how she laid out all these atrocities and then acted uninterested. I interpreted her projection of helplessness, outrage, and frustration into me. Sadistically, she stood back and let me suffer with these feelings and acted like they were no big deal. She would say, "Oh, I will just wait and see if it gets better. At least he didn't put me in the hospital this time." I told O that she was doing this to me and wondered if this was similar to how she felt with her mother. O said, "Well, my mother always makes me suffer, and my father tells me to ignore it, that its probably a phase and she will get over it." I said, "That was probably confusing and upsetting to hear after you were beat or locked in the closet." O said, "Yes, but I keep trying to follow his suggestion and let things roll off my back." I said, "By now, your back is full of scars from all that rolling."

O went on to say that my comments about her making me suffer and her acting indifferent gave her an idea. She said, "I think of leaving my boyfriend all the time, but I don't because I would be so lonely. I get scared that I would be so lonely I would go crazy and kill myself." The more we explored these thoughts and feelings, it turned out that she felt so angry at times she thought of killing her boyfriend, but then pictured herself alone forever because no one would ever want to love her after that. "I would be branded as unlovable. That would be punishment for being so evil. I would be ignored and rejected in the worst way." Later, these same feelings and phantasies came out regarding her mother.

O acted out less and felt less anxious when I made interpretations about the moment-to-moment expressions of the death instinct and her punitive superego. In other words, I tried to point out how, in the transference and extra-transference, she would actively try to punish or pressure herself and demand impossible levels of perfection. She also had a part of her that tried to deny life, success, dependence, difference, and need. This part of O's mind kept a vigilant eye on any curious or needy feelings and tried to erase them. Denial, splitting, and projective identification were used along with manic posturing to make sure I didn't notice these feelings. When I commented on this process, O said "Those feelings are pitiful signs of weakness. Of course I want to get rid of them." This was a vicious cycle in which the more punitive her superego became, the more the death instinct battled against these exaggerated attempts at a perfect life. So, her internal world was a battleground between perfection and self-negation.

THE FINAL PHASE OF TREATMENT: PRIMITIVE EXPERIENCES OF LOSS

O exhibited intense mixtures of paranoia and guilt in the transference, but this shifted in the latter stages of treatment. Over years of analysis, our relationship changed in her mind from being mostly scary or dangerous (shaped by the death instinct and excessive projective identification) to a relationship colored by both depressive and persecutory concerns. Slowly, more whole-object depressive relating emerged, yet she functioned primarily within paranoid-schizoid functioning. Most of the early- and middle-stage treatment was taken up by more paranoid-schizoid experiences of guilt, and persecution. Now, she showed the more core phantasies of primitive loss. So, analytic contact was more a constant in the therapeutic relationship, but facing her feelings and phantasies of loss meant trusting someone who could abandon and hurt her. Therefore, O pushed against our analytic contact during this phase of treatment, but in a less destructive, paranoid manner. Her transference was more clearly one of loss, aloneness, and despair.

One example was her reflection on the incident early in treatment of coming to her session late and finding my door closed. Now, she told me she felt she had "totally lost me". She explained that I went from an ideal, ever-present person to a "disappointing human". The idea that I was human and capable of not providing her a perfect container with constant nourishment was very disturbing. "If you're not perfect, you won't be able to take perfect care of me", she said.

In this third and final phase of analysis, O was more able to identify and work through this core issue of loss, abandonment, and fear of annihilation. We were able to see how her own envy and outrageous superego standards led to the simultaneous creation and destruction of a beloved ideal self and object. What was left was a weak, undependable, and traitorous sense of self and object. This led to rage and revenge projected into the object, giving her a fear of persecution. This was a cycle of loss with a paranoid-schizoid experience, where both self and object were felt in pieces that easily shifted and changed.

O frequently projected these idealized yearnings into me and demanded more than I could produce. She would then be angry and disappointed and blame me for being incompetent. O thought I was failing to help her or understand her during these times, and sometimes thought I was deliberately manipulating or neglecting her. When she started to rail against me for being a bad analyst, I interpreted this as her attacking me before I could attack her. In other words, she was frightened that her hunger and her demands were hurting me so badly that I would retaliate by abandoning her and attacking her. So, she tried to beat me to the punch by attacking first. This particular projective identification dynamic of paranoid-schizoid loss was played out in countless interpersonal and intra-psychic ways over the years.

One example occurred in the sixth year of treatment. O needed surgery on her knee. This was elective surgery so she was able to plan for it well in advance. Three weeks prior to the surgery, I handed her the regular monthly bill. Normally, she would immediately write a check for the full amount. However, she had not given me a check last month and now this month she merely put the bill in her purse and went on to discuss her plans for the weekend. I felt awkward, dismissed, and manipulated. This sort of thing had happened before and led to protracted arguments and difficult moments in our relationship. Therefore, I felt like, "Oh-oh, here we go again." Reluctantly, I brought it up only to have O begin yelling at me. She told me how insensitive I was and how I was only proving that I cared more for her money than about the troubles she had. O went on to tell me I was incredibly callous to "demand money" when she was shortly going to surgery and feeling anxious about it. Analytic contact was hard to maintain as her phantasies and feelings took over as her experiential reality of the relationship. However, our hard work together over the years proved to have lasting effects, as she was able to gradually return from this dark place, allowing for analytic contact to resume.

Within a few days, I received a letter from O. She wrote,

> Given how you have shown me the importance of our relationship over the years, I am shocked at your total lack of compassion the other day. You used to tell me my fears of you only being after my money were unfounded, but now you reveal the real you! Now I see how much time, energy, and money I have wasted seeing you. I am sure you will deny any of my feelings and try to simply convince me that I am wrong and its all a part of my mental disorder. Its me, the fucked up patient, right? Seeing you being so insensitive to me makes me feel like less than a person, worse than before. I am tired of always exploring myself. I think you have helped me, but I need someone who can show more

compassion and humanness. I need more of an interpersonal relationship, someone to share my life with and someone who is willing to share their life with me. My last therapist did that and it felt good. Actually, I grew to hate it and thought he was sicker than I was, but I still need to feel like you will give to me. I feel at least as smart as you, but on a much higher plane. That feeling disturbs me a great deal. I feel you are very limited and below me and I need someone much smarter that I can aspire to.

The three weeks before her surgery were a turbulent time. Her letter helped us to explore how she saw me as an ideal mentor that failed her, leaving her lost and threatened. Her spite and envy were clearly spelled out in her letter too. Her shifting perception of me, including her acknowledgment that I have been helpful, showed her ability to access some depressive object relations, while still experiencing mostly paranoid-schizoid fears of betrayal and abandonment. We were able to discuss all this bit-by-bit over the three weeks.

O sent me another letter during this time. This one was even more indicative of the work we had accomplished in integrating the split off, conflicted aspects of herself. O wrote,

This relationship we have built over the years has been very intense. I often have strong feelings of love and hate for you. I wish I didn't have to feel anything for you, but I do. Sometimes I wonder if you have feelings for me too and what they might be. I wonder if seeing me helps you in any way to make your life better. At the same time, I don't want to know the answer to that because it would be too painful to find out you just see me as one more job to do, one more crazy patient, one more invoice. That makes me scared and angry and outraged, but mostly scared. It is hard to feel that degree of fear without turning it into anger. Love, O.

In this letter, it is easy to see O's advancement into depressive functioning. She is able to feel love and hate at the same time. She is able to withstand the pain of feeling for me without having to immediately get rid of it or destroy it. At the same time, O is still impaired by paranoid-schizoid anxieties. When she gets her hopes up that she might be helpful to me or that I may have feelings for her, that hope is thin and fragile. She "doesn't want to know" because she is frightened I may not love her or need her. Overall, O is clearly more attentive to her object, her analyst, and able to experience the phantasy of whole-object reciprocal relating.

As the time for surgery approached, she was able to explore other feelings and thoughts. I interpreted that her letters, her anger, and her disappointment towards me might all be part of her fears about the upcoming surgery.

I said she might be feeling extra vulnerable and trying to communicate that to me. O told me she pictured the surgery as a dangerous risk. She finally told me that she was worried when she was under the anesthesia the doctors would rape her. This was a fear she felt as a literal threat. O believed this was actually a possibility. I commented that it was interesting she didn't picture someone there to protect her or to intervene, such as myself, her boyfriend, her father, or any other person "on her side". O told me that she had never considered that. After some exploration, she told me she would not consider that possibility because it "was her mother's job" to be there and protect her. O explained how she felt her mother should be there to protect her and she is sure her mother is incapable and unwilling to do that. "She would never be able to get it together to do that in reality, so I surely can't imagine her doing that!" she said.

I interpreted that she was so angry at not having this ideal and supportive mother in her mind that she refused to have anyone else there either. Therefore, she created a lonely and scary place filled with anger. O said, "Of course! I would not want you, my father, or anyone there to help me! It would only make it more painfully obvious that my mother is always a complete failure at taking care of me. It is her job, not yours or anyone else's! If I can't have my mother to protect me, then no one will! I demand she be there. I will wait it out, even if I have to suffer in the meantime!" Obviously, these insights gave us much to discuss in the following weeks and months. We were able to see how O repeated her original childhood feelings of parental loss by preventing the internalization of other good objects, out of spite and rage.

The more we explored these feelings and phantasies, it became clear how O also refused to care for herself. She said, "I won't take care of myself, it's my mother's job!" This helped us understand many of the ways she neglected herself as well as how she put herself in harmful situations and waited for her ideal mother to rescue her.

Several months after the operation, O was doing quite well emotionally, but still suffered sudden setbacks. The proof of her progress was in how quickly she was able to regain her internal balance, her trust in her objects, and her faith in herself. One session, she came and seemed quiet and upset. I asked what was wrong. O told me she was troubled and sad that when I came out to the waiting room I seemed too "professional and cold". As we explored this, she was able to explain how she wanted me to greet her with excitement and warmth. She wanted me happy to see her and showing my love. "I guess I need you to show me that you love and accept me, or I feel brushed aside and alone", O told me. I commented on how this was a narrow, overly specific expectation and demand for me to be an ideal object who conformed to her needs. I said that her hunger, wish, and demand is so specific and strong that it destroys all the good that she does have with me, because it doesn't fit into this narrow ideal.

At this stage in O's treatment, she was more able to take care of herself emotionally, but still resented having to do so. Now, instead of this always being acted out in masochistic and sadistic ways that constrained her life, she kept it more contained. The conflict still influenced her life, but not as destructively. As we dealt with her feelings and thoughts about loss and the wish for an ideal mother, she gradually brought together the formally disjoined aspects of her ego. Depressive conflict and whole-object functioning were more evident. Although not finished with her analysis, O's ego was better integrated, she was consciously happier and hopeful, and mentally she functioned more in line with reality. She was no longer trying to unconsciously mutilate herself or her objects. The war was over and it was time to pick up the pieces. Now, loss and grief were the painful yet healing psychological themes. O managed to stay in analytic treatment long enough to benefit from internal, structural change.

Chapter 10

Fragmented attachments

THE DEVELOPMENTAL PERSPECTIVE

Melanie Klein conceptualized the paranoid-schizoid position as an intra-psychic experience that, under normal circumstances, evolves into the depressive position. These developmental shifts are viewed as a move from persecutory anxieties to depressive, oedipal guilt within a whole-self–whole-object matrix.

Klein thought the newborn infant made immediate use of introjective and projective mechanisms to relate to their maternal object. Phantasies of giving–receiving and attacking–defending foster early differentiation and, in turn, phantasies about what these interactions do to both parties. This moves the infant to the realization of a world of two or more agents impacting each other in various positive and negative ways. As the infant realizes he is dependent on the object, there is a fear of potentially damaging, destroying, or losing that much-needed object.

The infant's aggressive and libidinal urges can feel unpredictable and unmanageable, creating uncertainty about the consequences of relation-ships. Loss and destruction-of-the-object combine with loss and destruc-tion-of-the-self as two primal dangers. The ego fears being neglected and abandoned by the object or destroying the object and bringing on a retaliatory attack. The object's containing function (Bion 1967), when successful, provides the ego with trust and confidence in its object-related phantasies. The ego starts to understand that these urges and feelings are not only safe and non-destructive, but useful and valuable. With ongoing containment and processing, persecutory phantasies regarding annihilation and object destruction begin to coexist with phantasies of reparation, forgiveness, negotiation, difference, and tolerance. These experiences lead to increased creativity and symbolic ego functions.

In normal development, projection and introjection quickly weave a complex dyadic phantasy world where loving, aggressive, and needy urges are traded back-and-forth to build multiple and intricate self/object repre-sentations. This is defensive, adaptive, and creative. The infant hopefully acquires a majority of internal experiences where taking care of the object, protecting the object, and loving the object coincide with experiences of a loving, durable, tolerant, and forgiving object. These dilute and overshadow the more nightmarish phantasies within the paranoid-schizoid experiences. The mind moves into the depressive position and the infant starts to recognize his ability to influence and impact the object.

Phantasies of being able to feed, love, protect, and heal the object fertilize the emerging ego-ideal and superego structures. Equally present are phantasies of destructive powers. The child imagines himself erasing, destroying, or torturing the object in infinite and fantastic ways. These types of libidinal and aggressive phantasies comprise a fragile bridge between paranoid-schizoid and depressive anxieties. Unconsciously, the child is anxious about not being able to forecast, regulate, or control the positive and negative impact he has on the object.

Maturation of the ego and ongoing phantasy experiences of being able to "maintain" the object combine to help the ego feel more at ease and less on guard. Faith in the durability of the object increases and the anxiety over one's aggressive urges decreases. Continued familiarity with the survival of ego and object gradually builds trust in the internal environment. The infant comes to find out, through relationships with his objects, how durable he and the object are and how "full" or "empty" he and the object are of various libidinal or aggressive striving. The infant tries to "read" how safe or dangerous the self and object are.

The conception of self-agency and the ability to influence what is other than the self emerges. Libidinal urges and aggressive wishes begin to be something that can be directed outwards to the object rather than exclusively being experienced as emanating from the object. Phantasies are reshaped by introjection of what had been previously projected.

THE CLINICAL ISSUES

There is a group of patients, diagnostically borderline and/or psychotic, who have experienced trauma in early stages of life. The central theme of these tragedies is a deep sense of loss and persecution. These early experiences, both intra-psychic and interpersonal, are organized within the paranoid-schizoid position.

Once in treatment, the internal cycle of loss, fragmented attachments, primitive guilt, and persecution are repeated in the transference. These patients usually act out a great deal and are often struggling with multiple external stress: poverty, addiction, unemployment, divorce, and health problems. The combination of external chaos and unstable internal object relations often means a disturbed patient who enters treatment for a short time, involving the analyst in a lively, lurching, and taxing counter-transference experience. An abrupt, abortive termination often follows. Some patients do manage to stay in treatment and make significant progress. Nevertheless, the road to get there is quite bumpy. These borderline and psychotic cases challenge, if not make obsolete, any rigid theoretical ideas about idealistic states of analytic neutrality, working through, and termination. Melanie Klein's work, her followers' refinement of it, and the concept of analytic contact offer clinical hope for these difficult and often tragic cases. Analytic contact offers a degree of clinical flexibility that this group of difficult patients need to achieve gradual psychological transformation. Analytic contact honors the importance of transference and phantasy analysis over external criteria such as frequency and a one-size-fits-all view of what constitutes genuine psychoanalytic work.

I find that paranoid anxieties and desperate feelings regarding loss are often at the core of these brief and stormy encounters. By trying to explore these phantasies with the patient, some of these patients can stay in treatment and begin to profit from the experience. By adequately exploring loss and persecutory phantasies, analytic contact is built, maintained, and strengthened, turning volatile cases into hopeful treatments.

Case material

Mack was an intravenous drug user in his twenties. He was the youngest of nine children from a poor family. His father was an alcoholic and his mother was schizophrenic. She heard voices from the radio, telling her that her children were bad and to beat them. The voices told her that her husband was cheating on her so she would attack him as well. Eventually, he left the family and never returned. Over the years, two of Mack's brothers and a neighbor molested Mack. Mack started abusing drugs in high-school and became addicted to heroin. He led a scattered and lonely life, working odd jobs to get by. Two months before coming to see me, Mack had been diagnosed with terminal cancer. He became extremely anxious and delusional, leading to his second hospitalization. After his release, he fluctuated in-and-out of ideas about a vast conspiracy against him of strange devils, creatures, and the CIA. He also felt his friends and family were "just playing roles" and were really part of a conspiracy to kill him. In general, there were many people he wanted as friends and lovers, but they all seemed to turn against him or push him aside. He continued to abuse street drugs, sharing needles and engaging in other high-risk behaviors.

Mack could not find my office for his first appointment. It turned out that he had put all the phone numbers of his drug dealers into a pile and threw them away, vowing to not contact the "bad influence". He had "accidently" put the directions to my office in that pile. Later, I told him I thought he might be worried I could be a bad influence and he was not sure if he could think of me as a helper. Here, I made a comment based on my impression that he felt a good helper object could easily turn into a bad influencing or even deadly object.

This prompted him to elaborate over several sessions about his fears and doubts about the world. His friends, doctors, and girlfriend all seemed to be working hard to convince him of their care, while really planning to assassinate him. I interpreted that he felt all the people who tried to care for him, including me, were fragile and when he was afraid they turned into betrayers. This seemed to help ground him and he could tell me more about himself, while feeling less paranoid. Here, I thought Mack felt his needs and dependency were destructive and lethal. He projected this into his objects and felt surrounded by dangerous traitors.

Mack told me his lifelong phantasy of being a little goldfish swimming around, being pursued by a great big shark. This idea came up several times and Mack seemed to have a perverse, masochistic excitement about it. I interpreted that he wanted a caring, loving protector to pursue him, but his strong wishes to make someone care for him changed that person into a hunting shark. Here, I introduced the idea that his own feelings and phantasies were involved. He was not a passive victim. I also pointed out to Mack how he would passively float around in our relationship, waiting for me to swim in with suggestions on how to run his life. I said this was a way he changed me from a supportive helper to a controlling shark.

This prey/predatory theme colored the transference. Often, he would not show up for his session. Sometimes, this was because he was convinced I was out to kill him and he had to stay home for protection. Other times, he said he simply forgot. After a while, it became clear that if I did not call and remind him of the appointment or assure him I was not a CIA member, he just would not show up. He even suggested I call him a few hours before each session to remind him. Here, Mack became the greedy shark demanding I serve him. I suggested that he felt controlled and expected others to treat him poorly so he was trying to gain the upper hand. I explained that he seemed to act both passively with me but also had a way of wanting things to be his way. He responded by telling me how disappointed he was with his job and that he might quit. I said he was ready to leave his job and his analyst because they were not the way he wanted. Mack felt lost without things being as he wished and so he attacked them. He became the shark.

Also, I began interpreting that he wanted me to become a good helper shark and pursue him. However, he was so eager for my care that it scared him and he felt I was an aggressive enemy shark. Again, he seemed to become more integrated after these comments. What he most resisted in my interpretations was his desire to control me and make me into a servant shark. I think this was because it was too early for me to be interpreting his sadism and narcissistic desire for control. What I was interpreting were all examples of projective identification. Mack projected his needy goldfish self as well as his greedy, aggressive shark side onto me and then felt surrounded by them and needed to react against them. My interpretations of this projective identification process seemed to, on the whole, lessen Mack's anxiety and fragmentation.

Mack was suffering with financial crisis, emotional instability, and social isolation. Remarkably, he now decided to work full-time. He applied for a job that required long-term commitment and career development. This was in part a true sign of hope and motivation on his part, but also a way of denying his intense anxieties. Rather than face his despair and fear, he phantasized about ways to escape this life by mystical union with "the spirits" or by suicide, but feared what he would find in the afterlife.

Mack provoked me by not paying his bill and always having scheduling problems. I proposed he was replaying certain feelings of wanting to be pursued by a kind, supportive parent who would spoil him and take care of everything, but deep down he was scared he would find a crazy, mean, and demanding parent. I suggested that he suffered with those feelings himself and that they were getting acted out in our relationship. He was consumed with feelings of being abandoned and attacked. Mack seemed interested in these ideas and would then talk about his upbringing and how difficult his relationship with his mother had been. He brought in dreams about his parents. These were always gruesome nightmares.

During the five stormy months I met with Mack, two- and three-times-a-week, he struggled with how to relate to me. Again, fears of loss, rejection, and persecution colored the transference. He wanted to trust me but felt it would be a dangerous mistake. During one session, he said he wished there was a computer program that would tell me all about him so I would understand. I said he wanted me to know him and help him but he wanted to be in control and was fearful of getting too close. He did not want to have to share himself with me. Mack said that felt right and that whenever he started to get close with his former therapists, he quit. I said the computer program would be like a safe buffer or barrier between us, but it would also keep us apart. He said it would be an all-knowing, "totally comprehensive," and wonderful software program. I commented that he was describing an all-knowing, loving and understanding father for whom he longs. Mack said, "Of course! Father technology, Mother earth!"

Mack's ambivalence about getting near me came out in other ways. While he would not show up for sessions or always be late, he would also bring in stories he had written about himself and details about his life he had spent hours writing. He would give me twenty-page documents about himself, but he could not bring himself to spend time with me and let that knowledge be shared as we related. It was done in a rigid, protected way.

As the treatment went on, we struggled with Mack's frightening and aggressive feelings that were acted out in the transference and in other areas of his life. He continued to use drugs and put himself in risky situations. He paid me with bad checks and "forgot" to come to his sessions. Sometimes, he managed to get me to call and remind him to come to his sessions because I felt I wouldn't get paid otherwise. Here, my counter-transference was a feeling of persecution and worried strategy planning. Through projective identification, I was left with Mack's unwanted vulnerability. The fear and worry, along with desperate efforts to escape those feelings, were projected onto me and brought to life with interpersonal acting out. He had me involved in the internal bind he felt he was in.

A sign of progress was that he could gradually see me as not involved in most of the bizarre plots he felt surrounded by. I was not part of the CIA, FBI, or a disguised ghost from the next life. I do not believe this was the result of simply splitting me into an all-good object. I think Mack, through projective identification, had me be the safe repository, the lone outpost of what survived his psychotic attacks. He projected the wish for a safe place, a non-contaminated space where he could rest from the internal chaos and painful loss. I became the temporary peace of mind he searched for. Mack did not idealize me and he did not demonize me. He did not respect me and he treated me as if I had no value. But, I was not a part of the persecutory vision from which he fled. My ability to tolerate and interpret his ongoing feelings of intense loss, fear of annihilation, and psychotic paranoia was soothing and healing to him.

Over time, he disclosed the various overwhelming and quickly shifting delusions he felt. For a while, he felt he was part of a vast medical experiment in which unknown agents of the government were killing and studying him. Then, he felt he might be God or a special chosen agent to help lead humanity from crisis. Next, he was sure there was a "memory chip" planted in his brain. Overall, he felt the world was dying from pollution and that there literally was something bad and rotting inside him. While he could reflect on his more bizarre anxieties as "stress-induced", Mack was fairly convinced that psychotic states are really windows into how the world actually is. He felt everyone was being tricked into believing the world was as it looked, but psychosis provided a glimpse into the reality of "what was really going on". When I interpreted his ideas as related to his terminal cancer and the medical treatments he received, he agreed but thought that was only part of the truth. Mack believed he really saw the world as it was behind the "governmental trickery".

When I made transference comments, Mack often dismissed them with an air of surprise and contempt. It was as if any opinion other than his was laughable. When I made more genetic comments about the parallel of his current fears and anger to his childhood experiences with his parents, the reaction was striking. This was most potent when I brought up his mother. He would be reduced to tears and paralyzed with feelings of loss and confusion. He would sob, "Why did she not want me, why did she hate me so?"

Overall, Mack seemed to become less anxious and less psychotic when I made interpretations about his fears of loss and persecution, and how these feelings were always linked together. These interpretations led Mack to elaborate on his feelings about his family and his current hopelessness in daily living. He would start to talk about his deep fear and uncertainty about living life. He would talk a bit about his cancer treatment. But, this would be interrupted with manic denial and devaluation of those around him (myself and the various medical and legal professionals helping him).

Mack would try to distance himself from the painful memories of his abusive mother by telling me how physically ugly and repulsive she was. He told me how superior he was in light of her ugliness. This easily collapsed and he felt ashamed for me to see how "hideous" he looked. I interpreted that while he thought he looked hideous, he was actually feeling hideous. It was less scary to think of it as only "skin deep". Through projective identification with his internal mother, he formed a picture of an evil and ugly mother object that he now identified with. In other words, Mack projected his ugly feeling (rage, greed, dependency, and abandonment) into his memory of mother. This turned her into an ugly object. Mack could then feel manically superior. This excessive reliance on primitive defenses broke down, leaving Mack feeling ugly, bad, and inferior.

So, Mack spent many sessions telling me how ugly he felt. He thought I was trying my best to tolerate his "disgusting acne, his fat stomach, and his big ears". Mack saw these parts of himself as the literal outgrowth of evil inside him. He felt he had sinful evil "stuff" inside him that produced physical ugliness as a side-effect. He was worried that people would notice this evidence of badness and not like him. I interpreted the ugly-feelings–ugly-mother–ugly-self cycle to Mack. Also, I talked with him about his concerns that I would not accept him for whom he was and that I might hate him once I found out what was inside (the ugly feelings). This helped him talk more coherently about his fear of being unlovable. In other words, my interpretations of the projective identification process shifted it from a concrete phantasy to more a symbolic conflict.

Mack did reasonably well at his new job, but he hated everyone there because they seemed stupid and uninteresting. I commented that he felt they were not interested in him and he feared they saw evil in him. He agreed but said they were still stupid.

During one session, Mack said his head was clearer and not so full of what he called his "psychotic spaces". Mack noticed his dreams were easier to remember. He went on to tell me two dreams.

In the first dream, he was at an outdoor carnival. He was at a booth where there were small bowls of goldfish. He was looking at one and suddenly the goldfish started communicating with him telepathically. The fish pleaded for help. It told Mack that cruel scientists were conducting painful experiments on all the goldfish. The fish said he was being forced to swim in acidic water and that horrible, secret medical experiments were going on. As Mack was listening to this, the fish swam around and Mack realized the fish's face was his face. Mack saw the fish was himself.

When discussing this dream, Mack felt it was quite straightforward. He felt experimented on by the methadone clinic. During more persecutory moments, he felt much of the world, under the direction of the CIA and FBI, was conducting cruel experiments on him. In other words, the dream was not so much a symbolic expression of internal conflicts as a literal and very concrete mirror of Mack's phantasies. I mentioned that perhaps he was trying to tell me about the great pain he is in and is asking for help as the fish did. He immediately dismissed me and said, "I don't need any help. How can anyone help anyone? We are all going to die anyway." Here, Mack seemed to resist the acknowledgment of the fear, pain, and loss that made up his life. Narcissistic dismissal, denial, and persecutory phantasies helped him avoid the overwhelming anxiety, separation, and loss he felt every day.

He went on to tell me the second dream. In this dream, a group of scientists met Mack in a laboratory. After conducting blood-tests on him, they all sat around a table. They told him they had granted him a pardon and would take him to a wonderful place. They picked him up and flew to the North Pole to a secret palace. There were no other people there. It was a beautiful "utopia" and Mack was to live there forever in bliss.

Mack said he felt really good about the second dream and thought it meant he was being granted special things and finally could relax. When I had made the transference comment about the first dream, he dismissed me and denied any dependence or need. He kept the dream on a concrete level to keep me out. But now, when the second dream seemed to offer him forgiveness and rewards, he quickly felt a union with it as an ideal object, to the point of not distinguishing it as a dream, but more of a special cosmic "sign". I commented that while he still did not want my help, he felt so good about being pardoned. It was as if he had been accused of a great sin and now was forgiven. Here, I was thinking of his persecutory superego and how the dream might be a manic flight into feeling special and not needing anyone. Indeed, my counter-transference phantasy was of the comic book hero Superman going to live at Superman's secret home in the North Pole. In this arctic lair, he was independent and powerful, yet cold and alone.

Mack said that the idea of being pardoned made him think of all the sacrifice he makes in his life and how he gave up on ever being loved. Instead, he thought if he let others dominate him he would be loved for that. "I gave up on anyone ever loving me for me, but I thought if I did what anyone wanted, that payoff felt close enough to love. I guess I settled for that. I wanted love, but all I found was pain. The dope is my lover. It takes care of me."

I thought to myself that his caring lover has also destroyed him, much as he has internalized his mother in a destructive manner. So, I said it sounded like he was describing what happened between him and his mother. In response, Mack recalled a particularly gruesome time with his mother when he was ten. She had gotten drunk and was yelling about aliens invading her mind and started to beat on him. He ran away but she caught him and pulled a clump of hair out of his head. When he went to school the next day, he had a black eye and a clump of hair missing. The teacher called the child protective authority and they questioned him. Mack said he was so scared of his mother and so embarrassed at school. He cried.

At this point, the session was over. It was one in which Mack had been especially open and revealing to me. He showed me a great deal about his fears and his terrible childhood memories. All this was done in a fairly trusting manner and I think this sharing reduced his immediate anxiety quite a bit. Mack was much less psychotic during this hour. We had achieved analytic contact and that contact brought a degree of insight, integration, and relief. However, Mack reacted to this vulnerability.

As he went to the door to leave, he stopped and began to ask me a series of demeaning questions. Mack started to devalue me. He wondered if my license were current. Even if it were, it was not nearly as good as other licenses. He wanted to know if I were familiar with several different schools of body therapy and hypnosis and he wondered why I hadn't used these obviously superior techniques on him yet. He told me he was thinking of going to a local guru who could talk with dead spirits and did a special "laying on of hands". Mack said these approaches seemed best suited to his condition. I felt defaced and taken by surprise even though he had done this many times before. I had to think on my feet, literally, as we stood at the door. I said I thought he was feeling anxious and divided. On one hand it felt good to have shared so many painful feelings with me and he wanted to stay with me now, for protection. He did this by his keeping us in the room past our ending time. Mack listened to all this quite interested. Then, I said that while being dependent on me and showing me his feelings felt good, now he was worried I might turn on him like his mother did. So, he was trying to push me aside as not very important or valuable to protect himself. If I were not as good as the guru and not well licensed or knowledgeable, then I probably couldn't hurt him. I told him he was worried if he was in good hands or not and whether he could trust me or not. Mack looked at me and said, "well, I have to check out these things!" I told him I would see him next time and opened the door. Analytic contact was restored, if only for a brief time.

Here, Mack was showing his reliance on paranoid-schizoid defenses. He used splitting to divide the object into good or bad, important or worthless.

He used manic devaluation to avoid the change of his idealized good object into a bad, attacking object. Finally, he used projective identification to first put painful, hurt little boy feelings into me for safekeeping and then projected angry betrayed feelings into me. He then felt faced with me as a worthless, dangerous object that he needed to protect himself from. My interpretations of this seemed to calm him down and offer some reassurance and insight.

During another session, several weeks later, Mack brought some photographs for me to see. They were of him and some friends at a punk music festival. He told me about some of the people and how he wanted them to like him and see him as special. However, they all seemed aloof and distant. He said he felt hurt by them and wished they were not all so "stuck-up". I was struck by how, in most of the pictures, Mack seemed to be deliberately and desperately posing in a way that said, "Look at me, I am special and fantastic!" I said he was showing me how much he wished to trust me and feel close. However, it was difficult to reveal how isolated and powerless he could feel. I also said he must hope that I see the specialness inside him and that these photos showed me how special he wants to be and how sad he feels.

Mack immediately responded by telling me I should consider using more up-to-date techniques than "this psychoanalytic crap". He went on to say that I treated him with a weak and useless type of therapy and I should consider some of the alternative therapies he knows about. My countertransference was a feeling of irritation at his brisk dismissal and devaluation. I felt like retaliating, but mostly I felt sorry for him. I said, "You took a step and showed me some parts of yourself that are vulnerable. You showed me how fragile and lonely you can feel and how much you long for someone to love you and praise you. I think you frightened yourself and now you're jumping back and putting up your shield by putting me down and calling me a weak analyst. You want to be with me and feel safe but it's hard to do. You think I will reject you or put you down, so you put me down first."

At first, Mack said my comments were wrong and that "this transference crap is not what I need. We should talk about everyone else, not me!" He went on to tell me how he sees the world as filled with losers and that there are only a few "elite" people in the world. He is one of them. "I am a powerful, handsome, smart man and I want to be loved by someone as smart as me. But, all I see are losers and assholes." I told Mack he felt his power was fragile and that he had to work hard to maintain it. I said he was afraid of losing the ideal image of himself, much as he fears losing the ideal relationship he wants with his mother and being attacked instead. Mack said he had come from a "family of ultimate idiots" and he could never trust his mother's love. He went on to tell me about his vision of what life should be like. "I want to live forever, be perfect in every way, and be surrounded by wonderful, smart people. I want to never be sick and to always be happy. I want the sun to shine every day of the year. If I can't have that, I would rather kill myself. It isn't worth the trouble to be around all this mediocrity."

I told Mack he is looking for an ideal bond with me, his mother, and his friends. He is afraid to want this because he thinks they will reject him, betray him, and hurt him. To avoid this, he tries to think of himself as ideal. That way, if people don't turn out to be loving, it's their fault and he is still superior and strong. Yet this leaves him alone and different, which feels like another form of isolation and persecution. I also said that he was having to frantically maintain this ideal self but he is always feeling it nearing collapse from his own doubts and self-loathing. I said he probably longed to not have to be so vigilant and instead wishes he could just relax and feel safe. While I did not directly mention his feelings about the cancer, my comments were meant to address that painful lack of perfection as well.

At that moment, Mack fell asleep. He slept the rest of the session in a contented and relaxed way. I was struck by how he left the session without having to depreciate me or question the treatment. He seemed more calm and fortified.

About three weeks later, Mack called and left a message. He said he had been fired from his job "by the managers and partners in trickery". He said he could not afford to continue treatment and felt fine without it. He never returned my calls.

I felt disappointed but not surprised. I think he probably fled from the painful loss and insecurity we had been working on. Patients like Mack are driven by such extreme paranoid phantasies that they often flee treatment almost immediately. If they stay, they present difficult and stormy transferences, are overwhelmed with anxiety and conflict, and often end the treatment abruptly. Analytic contact was tenuous in general and tedious to maintain at any given moment.

Some of these difficult patients successfully terminate after symptom resolution and a better understanding of themselves. However, this is less frequent and usually after a very rocky and erratic treatment process.

Given how many cases end like this one with Mack, it is important for the analyst to not become pessimistic. Optimism can be maintained by realizing that we see very troubled people who have a hard time interfacing with life. We may be just one more threatening or frustrating relationship that ends before it solidifies. However, we may be able to offer a great deal of help in this chaotic process. The analyst should be cautiously optimistic with each case he sees, always striving for as much analytic contact as possible for as long as is sustainable. This cautious faith can help both parties during difficult treatment periods and fortify the analyst after premature and abrupt terminations.

Reflections

Mack was a tragic and troubled patient who was only able to make contact with me for a limited time, in a limited way. During the first two or three months, he used acting out as a primary defense. The external forms of acting out were numerous. Mack failed to show up or was late to his sessions. He neglected to pay me. He continued to abuse narcotics and was involved in high-risk sexual behaviors. In our analytic relationship, he would refuse to talk with me or he would belittle the idea that we could learn from talking. These ways of acting out were manifestations of his internal core conflicts. Mack wanted to establish contact with me, but dreaded it, scorned it, and saw it as brittle and threatening. This was his paranoid-schizoid phantasy about all objects and his reaction to that phantasy. It was acted out emotionally and interpersonally.

As the more major acting out subsided, Mack took another stance. His associations and his transference manner showed a defensive use of the death instinct. It served to ward off or destroy the life-affirming aspects of our relationship and his need for me or others. The additional hardship in this case was Mack's terminal illness. Physically he was dying and mentally he tried to kill off the life connection between himself and his objects. Like all things, this was not absolute. Part of Mack wanted the opportunity for closeness, trust, and understanding. However, he was so in the grips of persecutory visions of abandonment and manipulation that he tried to destroy or neutralize those risky opportunities for warmth and help. To this end, Mack had the phantasy of a computer program to safely manage our relationship, taking the life and the threatening closeness out of it. His 20-page reports killed off any spontaneity or real relating to me, but kept him safely in control and still in proximity. His ideas about government plots depersonalized us and his emphasis on how ugly he and his mother were served to cancel out any experience of yearning, admiration, separation, or loss. In fact, this ugliness strategy also gave Mack a sense of control. Instead of the love he wished for suddenly turning ugly and attacking, he was the one making it that way, giving him mastery rather than becoming a victim to it.

Mack's drug addiction was also a demonstration of the death instinct, in both a primary and defensive manner. It was a way that Mack was literally killing himself. Also, it was a way to kill the life-affirming wish to be with a good maternal object. Thus, the death instinct acts as a shield against the terrible risk of being vulnerable and dependent, only then to be attacked and abandoned. Finally, I think the narcotic high he sought symbolized a union with a cruel, tormenting object that could also have momentary soothing qualities. He kept coming back to that union in the sad hope of isolating those soothing, maternal qualities, but ultimately became addicted to the overall painful betrayal of that object/drug. So, Mack demonstrated the essence of the conflict between the life instinct and the defensive nature of the death instinct. He searched for scraps of a good maternal object that provided life, but also destroyed those efforts out of self-survival.

All through the analytic treatment, Mack displayed his struggle with feelings of loss and fear of annihilation. However, these issues were more prominent toward the end of our time together. In a relatively short period of time, five months, Mack showed the ability to internalize some of my interpretations. He introjected parts of our relationship and this led to a degree of integration and stabilization. With this new vulnerability, he was more able to share himself with me. So, he let me into his inner world a bit and when he realized it wasn't so dangerous, he showed me more. He also started to have more access to his dream life and made more reality-based associations in our discussion. What began to emerge over time was a man suffering with great sadness, loss, and dread. Mack's dreams illustrated the stark loneliness and sense of despair he lived with. Mack shared more of himself through stories, photos, and spontaneous expression.

But, the essence of these more interactive, relational moments was loss, pain, and fear. His story of being beaten by his mother seemed to sum up the ongoing terror and sorrow Mack felt as he made his way through each day. I think part of the reason he stopped coming to his sessions was that this new exploration and working through of loss and persecution was so overwhelming that he needed to retreat. He did this by regressing to acting out, the death instinct, and the consequent psychotic phantasies. I believe he didn't trust me enough to talk about this anxiety and look to me for some reassurance or pacing. He felt he needed to deal with it himself so he fled.

Rather than seeing this as a treatment failure, I think it was a positive move for Mack to enter into a relationship with me and maintain it for a period of time. Despite the overwhelming odds, we were able to build a degree of analytic contact that offered a temporary psychological shelter and a brief opportunity to learn about himself. During our meetings, part of him tried to keep a safe, status quo, via acting out and the dynamics of the death instinct. However, he was able to partially face the core dilemmas in his life and momentarily work on some of his extreme feelings of impending loss, attack, and suffering.

Part IV

Clinical reality, psychoanalysis, and the utility of analytic contact

Chapter 11

Loss

For some patients, their internal world is focused around a search for an idealized object to be with. When this hoped-for state of union fails, and by definition it always does, their idealized objects crumple like fallen angels. The ideal object either becomes a quite ordinary human without any special sparkle or the fallen object rises up as Satan's right hand. In other words, the infantile ego's natural attempts at union with an idealized object can collapse into disappointment, loss, and persecution. This psychological and clinical phenomenon is quite disruptive and destructive to the pursuit of analytic contact. Splitting and projective identification play a prominent role in the psychic life of such patients and for analytic contact to be operable, these two defenses need to be consistently interpreted and worked with.

Splitting is an important ego function in the paranoid-schizoid position. It is necessary for normal ego development. Splitting keeps the bad away from the good long enough for the early ego to feed on the goodness, identify with it, and create a firm psychic structure. A whole sense of self and object emerges. If the ego is overly tilted in the direction of oral aggression and desires for immediate gratification, if there are not enough mitigating good objects to offset early primitive anxieties, or if the infant's external environment is lacking in certain critical ways, there will be a deconstruction or foreclosure of early ego phantasies of a union with the ideal object.

A feeling of betrayal and envy of what could have been, and righteousness about what should now be, combine with despair and loss to leave the ego ready to fight with and fight off any available object.

The ego is then pushed in several possible pathological directions. Some patients will exhibit psychotic fears of being attacked and tortured by what used to be a good object but now is a relentless persecutor. Danger is the patient's constant preoccupation and safety is their chief concern. The experience of an attacking and intruding breast is paramount in their psychic memory.

Other paranoid-schizoid patients are ruled by borderline anxieties that fluctuate between the loss of the ideal object and more paranoid fears of being judged, used, or attacked by that object. Their principal concerns are dualistic. They fear the loss of what is needed and the return of something ominous. This results from projective identification mechanisms in which the ego pushes angry parts and loving parts of the infantile superego into the object and then feels filled with persecutory objects and empty of positive feelings or a sense of hope. Therefore, the transference is like a see-saw that shifts the relationship between a fragile trust that is easily crushed and lost and an angry, confrontational type of contact. Loss of the object and loss of ego integrity are constant threats. Thus, analytic contact is precarious at best and constantly being tested.

Finally, some paranoid-schizoid patients will exhibit more narcissistic ways of organizing their inner life. These patients are marked by the memory of loss and shaped by their defenses against it. They feel denied access to the breast and feel deprived of a union with the idealized mother. In narcissistic spite and protest, they now refuse to let the object in. Retaliation and revenge color the transference. The patient stubbornly refuses to let the analyst into their mind. This stubborn "keep out" policy hides a terrible sadness. They are overwhelmed by the loss of the ideal object and union with it. If they allow themselves to partake in a relationship, the gratification reminds them of what they lost. Therefore, it feels better to go without. These patients subsequently make use of narcissistic, masochistic, and altruistic defenses to hide these painful feelings. Indeed, the ego can project its experience of deprivation into its objects and empathically and skillfully fix or heal the object. This dynamic brings some patients into the field of psychology and they defensively and creatively shift from patient to analyst, handing off their pain to their patients for them to now skillfully cure.

Usually, denial of the loss and devaluation of all past and present objects is used to bolster the patient's sense of self. Omnipotent self-idealization and other manic defenses characterize the transference. Relationships are intolerable unless controlled in these ways.

Separation and individuation is difficult in the paranoid-schizoid position and whole objects are not yet fully available to the ego. Indeed, for these psychotic, borderline, and narcissistic patients, separation or difference between self and object is threatening.

Psychotic patients can feel that anything which is not "self" is a tormentor at best. Annihilation is felt whenever separation looms. Hostility, judgment, and cruelty are the essence of this "non-self" object. Therefore, the ego uses massive projective identification to meld self and object together for safety. This usually backfires and the ego feels filled with poisons it cannot escape from. As analysis progresses and the psychotic patient enters the depressive position, guilt is often the most difficult treatment issue. These patients have such sadistic superegos that they feel they have done terrible things to their objects. Their sense of liability and shame can be so unrelenting that they retreat back into psychosis, as a temporary shelter.

The borderline experiences separation or individuation as a fundamental abandonment and a vindictive attack. Clinging and needy behavior is common, as well as righteous counterattacks. Again, the sense of betrayal and rejection is felt when separation seems to turn the good object into the bad object. Therefore, the transference is often an acting out of both parasitic and rejecting behaviors along with intense projective identification mechanisms. As the borderline integrates and shifts toward the depressive position, he will encounter the sorrows of loss and experience mourning. This pain will be defended against with acting out, splitting, and more projective identification. Development, in this sense, is thwarted. The anguish of the depressive position will sometimes trigger a negative therapeutic reaction.

The narcissistic patient feels humiliated and impotent in the face of differentiation or separation. His anxieties are not so much about being attacked but more about the knowledge that he is unable to have what he so much pines for. These patients experience loss of the idealized self once they lose the phantasy of fusion with an idealized object. When narcissistic patients improve during treatment, they will often resort to omnipotent manic defenses to prevent depressive anxieties. As they reach the depressive position and realize their impact upon their objects, they will deny this by grandiose posturing and manic devaluation. They will deny the value of the object and their need for it, thereby trying to ignore the injury they have inflicted.

If loss is so massively entrenched in the internal landscape and good objects shift into bad, persecutory ones at any moment, all intra-psychic efforts are focused on the avoidance of this suffering. The ego resorts to destructive splitting, excessive and ultimately self-defeating projective identification processes, denial of internal and external reality, and a vengeful erasing of basic self-observing, cognitive functions. The death instinct is used to disassemble and cripple any part of the mind that can acknowledge and investigate these painful experiences of loss. Insight becomes intolerable and the analyst's interpretations are felt to be deadly attacks. Analytic contact is the enemy. Acting out or fleeing altogether are common reactions. Patients will become paranoid and furious when insights are offered or transference comments are made concerning loss or separation. So, while analytic contact is the very thing that will gradually calm and heal this frightening inner state, it is also experienced as the creator of loss and separation. Therefore, the analyst must constantly combine his or her efforts to establish analytic contact with interpretations regarding the patient's paranoid experience of that contact.

Again, paranoid-schizoid loss entails both the loss of good part-objects followed by their simultaneous rebirth as deadly enemies. Klein discussed this point in 1935 when she wrote,

> the absence of the mother arouses in the child anxiety lest it should be
> handed over to bad objects, external and internalized, either because of

her death or because of her return in the guise of a "bad" mother. Both cases mean to the child the loss of the loved mother, and I would particularly draw attention to the fact that dread of the loss of the "good", internalized object becomes a source of anxiety lest the real mother should die. On the other hand, every experience which suggests the loss of the real loved object stimulates the dread of losing the internalized one too.

(pp. 266–7)

Internal phantasies of not being able to gain entrance to the mother's body lead to an identification with a closed off and unavailable idealized object. Therefore, in the transference, these patients will show a resentful reluctance or refusal to let any positive objects in, whether it be interpretations or other parts of the analyst.

Early experiences of losing the desired union with the mother's body can lead to a disappointment or failure in envy.

In other words, envy is part of normal developmental forces that build intimacy and other important mother–infant bonding. With unsuccessful envious efforts at union and control of the breast, deprivation, annihilation anxiety, and bitterness set in. Desperate, rigidly repetitive efforts at "one last try" combine with hopelessness. In the transference, the patient will make intense overtures to know, join, and control the analyst. These efforts fluctuate with despair and feelings of "what's the use". These patients may stop treatment while demanding extra sessions at the same time. It is a terrible bind they feel. To let the good object in is to remind themselves of the original loss. Therefore, they turn the tables and the ego becomes the gatekeeper, denying the analyst entrance.

These patients have such strong aggressive oral desires, envy, and rage at not having complete access to the idealized object that they seek to destroy or devalue that object. Through projective identification mechanisms, this results in their experiencing the object as both rejecting and persecutory. The object, now full of the ego's rage and loneliness, appears to betray and attack the helpless ego. Loss and persecution dominate the internal world.

Treatment is of course very difficult with such patients and many stop prematurely. Analytic contact is tenuous and unstable. Even when such a patient engages analytic therapy for years, they may suddenly and without notice quit. These are individuals who suffer in most aspects of living and are never really happy or contented for long. They crave, demand, and pine for the special object of their desire to provide, give, and feed them. Change is traumatic as it signifies an aborted union with the object. When the analyst provides good food in the form of an interpretation, it is often soured by the ego's projections of rejection and rage. In turn, the patient then feels controlled, attacked, or judged by the interpretation and proceeds to deny, erase, or devalue the analyst's offering.

Case material 11.1

S was caught in a chronic bind that left her hopeless and frustrated. She wanted to be successful in her career and feel powerful in her field. Miss S often felt superior and contemptuous over her co-workers, seeing them as pathetic and not in tune with what she felt to be "common knowledge". However, each time she had an opportunity to move from a more secretarial position and temp worker to a more prestigious job, she declined the offer. She cited her need to avoid becoming "part of the system". She felt others were controlled by the "corporate structure" and were left without any freedom or creativity.

In the transference, S avoided any feelings of dependence and would ward off my interpretations. Again, she did not want to be controlled and felt it was best to be independent. This left her in a bind with me just as she was in a bind at work. While she could feel free and in charge of her own destiny, she was lonely and unable to use my knowledge. If she took in my interpretations, they were intellectualized as a way of diffusing the dangerous emotions she felt or they were converted into her own property. If she already knew it, then my saying it was meaningless. A significant part of analytic contact involves the mutual interaction around interpretations, the analyst's understanding of the patient, the expression of that understanding, the patient's reaction to that expression, the mutual exploration of that reaction and association regarding the interpretation, and so on. S managed to bring that progressive, exploratory aspect of analytic contact to a halt with her need for intellectual ownership and neutralization of my contributions.

Growing up, S felt her mother was extremely controlling and used her children to make up for her own emotional void. At the same time, S felt she had to protect her mother and bolster her fragile self-esteem. Therefore, she felt her mother was sometimes controlling and manipulative and other times was weak and needy and therefore needed to be rescued. Unconsciously, S felt she was denied union with a healthy, strong, and independent mother and instead was engulfed by her mother's faults. The close, trusting, interdependent relationship that she craved with her mother was denied and belittled, as it seemed to be far too risky. These threats to S's autonomy were recreated in the transference over and over. She would use humor to put me down if I brought the subject of our relationship up. Again, analytic contact is the process of investigating intra-psychic and interpersonal relationships. S avoided and dismantled my attempts to facilitate this important aspect of analytic contact, the investigation of the transference. Therefore, the treatment was stuck in these different ways.

In S's phantasy, our making progress meant I was becoming the controlling mother who had total say over the relationship. For us to not make progress meant she was once again being kept out and away from the union she so much desired. The way these two dilemmas combined in the transference was that she could keep me as a neutral object that fed her as she pleased, under her omnipotent control. She said, "I pay you to make me feel good, that is your job. I have no connection to you other than as a commodity." As soon as she needed me or phantasized us as being intimate, together, or important, it triggered feelings of loss. Hoping for a successful, happy union with me where we both would be benefited was too much for her to ask. This wish unleashed her oral desires. Being so intense, they are projected into the object. This leads to the phantasy of not only losing the good object but of being controlled and attacked by a hungry, aggressive bad object.

S would date men who were well beneath her in most ways. This gave her a feeling of control and superiority. Like in the transference, she felt safe and powerful. However, she would eventually become depressed when she realized that while in charge, she would never be able to receive much from these men. To avoid this painful predicament, she would have affairs. This temporarily restored her sense of confidence until the cycle repeated. Her hoped-for wonderful union with a perfect object turned into a disappointing and ugly mismatch. She lost her hopes and found herself pinned by her own need to dominate.

Some patients, like M, are always on the verge of being overwhelmed with feelings of being denied access to the mother and subsequently controlled or attacked. Their oral phantasies and desires are so strong, as the result of projective identification and subsequent defenses against the hungry object, that each step in the analytic relationship is questioned, challenged, or fought. These are individuals who expect loss and defeat and react accordingly. They assume they will be banished and forgotten. It is very difficult for them to trust. Trust seems to rust, corrode, and turn into something evil. Indeed, many of these patients are overcome by these frightening feelings so quickly that they may not make it past the initial consultation. All these treacherous feelings and phantasies make the intimate attachment and patient learning of analytic contact formidable.

The idea of committing to a particular time each week or the idea of having to pay money to receive help is experienced by these patients as submission. They feel they are at risk for being manipulated or humiliated. Betrayal, humiliation, and persecution loom in every aspect of their relationships. Patients who are more paranoid or psychotic will experience the analytic commitment as a loss of self-regulation and an attack on the foundation of the self. One patient was incredibly passive and compliant.

Gradually, it came out that she felt she had better conceal all of her needs and wishes for understanding and help from me. She believed I would become enraged and torture her, like all the "other devils" in her life, if I caught wind of her wanting something from me.

Borderline patients can feel the fee and time constraints of treatment are a betrayal of basic trust. Their thinly held hope for an ideal object is broken and dangerous aspects of the object emerge. Narcissistic patients see the frame of treatment as denying them their natural birthright. Therefore, to ask them to give, via free association, fees, and time commitment, feels terribly humbling and demeaning.

The loss of the idealized object and its return as a vicious or callous bad object is particular to the paranoid-schizoid position. This is when oral desires and oral aggression are at their height. The ego projects grandiose wishes and strong love feelings onto the object. Equally strong aggressive feelings and intense desires to own and join with the breast and the mother's body predominate. Splitting keeps these two domains apart until the ego can slowly integrate them. The idealized object is huge and powerful, yet hollow. Because of splitting, it is not a mixture of all the infant's feelings. It is lopsided and fragile in its omnipotence. Therefore, it is easy prey to the ego's aggressive yearnings and oral attacks.

Segal (1974) writes:

> paranoid anxiety is due to the projection of the death instinct into an object or objects which are then experienced as persecutors. The anxiety is lest these persecutors should annihilate the ego and the ideal object. It originates in the paranoid-schizoid position.
>
> (p. 125)

She continues, "Depressive anxiety is the anxiety lest one's own aggression should annihilate or has annihilated one's good object" (p. 125). In these two quotes, she makes an important distinction. In the paranoid-schizoid position, the object is idealized and therefore subject to envious attacks by the hungry ego. In addition, the ego and the object are in parts and somewhat undifferentiated. Separate, whole object relationships are not yet achieved. Therefore, the attacks upon the idealized object endanger the integrity of the ego. Annihilation of self and loss of the ideal object are parallel threats. The mutual exploration and relational honesty that is part of analytic contact can often be experienced as part of these threats.

In the depressive position, the ego's destructiveness is a threat to the good object. Depressive anxieties concern injury inflicted on the object and restitution to be offered. Since a good object is more stable and resilient than an idealized object, the overall threat to the ego and the object is experienced as different and not as catastrophic. Hope remains. In paranoid-schizoid functioning, hope is replaced by omnipotent magic, which can easily fail.

During the natural development of the ego, both loving and hateful feelings are exchanged over and over with the object through projective identification. This is the process of early structural integration and ego consolidation. A balance of good and bad is gradually obtained and ego stability emerges. Segal (1974), following Klein's ideas, outlined the process by which the child in the oral sadistic phase attacks the breast by projecting hate, envy, and desire. The infantile ego then introjects a breast which is both destructive and destroyed. This is a pivotal point in psychic development. With the internalization of plentiful good objects and gradual ego integration, these phantasies of a destroyed, lost breast and the phantasies of a revengeful, destructive breast are neutralized. However, certain factors may prevent this balance and lead to lifelong struggles with loss and persecution. This can be the result of either overly active oral urges and destructive amounts of ego hunger for union with an ideal object or it can be various degrees of external trauma. Often it is a combination of both. Segal (1974) writes:

> If early envy is very intense, it interferes with the normal operation of schizoid mechanisms. The process of splitting into an ideal and a persecutory object, so important in the paranoid-schizoid position, cannot be maintained, since it is the ideal object which gives rise to envy and is attacked and spoiled. This leads to confusion between the good and the bad interfering with splitting. As splitting cannot be maintained and an ideal object cannot be preserved, introjection of an ideal object and identification with it is severely interfered with. And with it the development of the ego must necessarily suffer. Strong feelings of envy lead to despair. An ideal object cannot be found, therefore there is no hope or help from anywhere. The destroyed objects are the source of endless persecution and later guilt.
>
> (p. 41)

Here she is outlining how internal desires, aggressive in nature, can corrupt the important developmental process of splitting. The ideal object is attacked and destroyed, leaving only a bad object to identify with. Segal makes a critical point when she explains how these destroyed idealized objects are the source of endless persecution. Certainly later on in the depressive position, this brings on feelings of guilt and remorse. However, in the paranoid-schizoid position, the loss of the idealized breast is followed by the entrance of relentless angry and unpredictable objects. The ego experiences this as two separate events, the loss of one object and the attack from another. In reality, this is the transformation of the ideal object into a bad object through the breakdown of splitting. Destructive processes of projective identification aimed at the ideal object eventually break it down and undo the important mental divisions created by splitting.

Segal (1974) has shown how if hostile and anxious impulses are too strong, projective identification switches from a healthy developmental process to a destructive and vicious cycle. Under great feelings of persecution and anxiety, the ego tries to erase or obliterate the hated object and the aspects of the ego which relate to that object. In addition, feelings of envy make the ideal object seem unreachable and tortuously distant. This is intolerable and triggers more attacks from the ego, through projective identification. All these internal difficulties put enormous strain on the natural splitting of the ideal and the bad. As the oral aggression and destructive projective identification peak, the differences between ideal and bad are eroded. The ego experiences quick and frightening losses of ideal and sudden emergence of bad.

Loss of the ideal object as well as the experience of the ideal object turning into multiple attacking objects makes the ego crave, miss, and envy the ideal object even more. In fact, the feelings of loss and subsequent persecution create a sense of entitlement and outrage in some patients. Others merely give up and are overwhelmed with fear and grief. This sense of entitlement will cause some individuals to demand the presence of an ideal object that is under their control. Klein (1946) spoke of this,

> the phantasy of forceful entry into the object by parts of the self in order to possess or control the object creates problems with normal introjection, which the patient may find difficult to distinguish from forceful entry from the outside, in retribution for his own violent projections.
>
> (p. 11)

This becomes a technical difficulty when such patients experience interpretations as the analyst trying to force his way into their mind. At the very least the patient becomes upset and feels judged. More often, they become highly defensive and paranoid. For analytic contact to survive, the analyst must be consistent in interpreting this sense of invasion and intrusion.

Case material 11.2

Rose was a patient who shifted unpredictably between the depressive position and the paranoid-schizoid position. In much of her life, she functioned quite well, but was relating to life through obsessive-compulsive defenses and manic grandstanding. While these coping styles certainly involved oedipal issues of competition, control, and power, she also struggled with paranoid-schizoid feelings of grandiosity, loss, and persecution. This involved the wish to be joined to an all-knowing, all-powerful ideal object who would take perfect care of her. When she started to want everything her way, immediately, she felt overcome by envy and greed. Her ideal couldn't possibly live up to her demands and expectations. Therefore, her ideal object was destroyed by her oral aggression and she was left to identify with a weakened, deflated object lacking in knowledge or power. This filled her with great anxiety and she used manic defenses to regain control. The following are case notes from a session that illustrate the quest for the ideal object, the downfall of that object, and the effects such phantasies and transference have on analytic contact.

Pt: I want to bring up a new topic. I have been thinking for a few weeks now of going back on medication. I think I will go back on an anti-anxiety agent. I felt way better on it years ago when I went through my divorce. After I felt better, I decided I didn't need it any more and stopped using it. What do you think? [I am struck by how she has kept her thinking to herself for weeks. She has kept her anxiety, her thinking about it, and the possible solution all to herself. I am also struck by how controlling and provocative she is, telling me what she has decided to do.]

A: I think you've already made up your mind. [She has eliminated the relational tension analytic contact contains.]

Pt: No. But, I would like to try something, maybe experiment. Perhaps an anti-depressant, or a combination of agents. That would be interesting. I know how long it takes to work in the bloodstream, so it would take some time to fully get the effects. [She tells me the pros and cons of different brands of medication and what dosage she would put herself on. This is all done in a quite provocative way.]

A: I think you are setting us up to debate. [I attempt to rekindle the analytic contact with a comment about how she is relating to me and how she might be using the relationship.]

Pt: Well, I don't know. I really do want your opinion. If I really wanted to take medications I would. It would be easy. I don't see the problem.

A: You are inviting me to put you in your place. You are presenting yourself as a pharmacist and that you know better than I do. One of us has to be above the other, rather than equals.

Pt: No, not at all. [She goes back and forth about it.]

A: You're asking for my opinion but you have already decided what you're going to prescribe yourself.

Pt: I feel strange, fuzzy. It's all kind of confusing.

A: I think you're feeling overwhelmed and anxious and not sure how to deal with it.

Pt: I have felt that way for three years now. Therapy helps, but only so much. What if I do have a mild chemical imbalance? What if I do have some type of biological problem?

A: But, you are not sure. [I am emphasizing her lack of knowledge and lack of control over her objects. I think this is her current anxiety, felt and experienced as a loss of the ideal object and loss of identification with the ideal, leading to a feeling of instability and inferiority. Therefore, she uses manic defenses to compensate.]

Pt: No. I am not so sure. All I have to go by is my prior experience. After my divorce, I felt so bad and medication helped me. After my sister died, I could hardly go on and I started taking it again. Again, it helped. I sure wouldn't want it to be public knowledge that I was on medication, but if it would help it would be worth it. [Here, she is alluding to phantasies of being exposed or exhibiting herself. However, I felt the leading anxiety was her lack of knowledge/power, her sense of loss, and her needing me.]

A: So, maybe needing my opinion, my ideas, might be uncomfortable. If you are feeling uneasy about needing me, maybe you're deciding you already know everything and don't need me.

Pt: I guess what I meant is that I don't think I need something as strong as what I used to take, but I think I need something. I figure Prozac wouldn't be quite right, but maybe a newer mood stabilizer.

A: Again, you are diagnosing yourself.

Pt: Why not? Anyway. Last time I went to a psychiatrist I simply told them what I saw as the problem and what I felt would be best to take and they wrote me a prescription.

A: You ignored my comment.

Pt: It doesn't feel comfortable.

A: You seem to want to have total knowledge of everything.

Pt: It's control, total and absolute control! That is where I go when I feel anxious and stressed. It's coming out at work lately and with my friends too. They still drive me nuts. They do stuff that seems so stupid. I can't believe they are so dumb. So, yes! I feel like a control freak and a nagging bitch. But, some of it is totally justified.

A: Right now there are a lot of things in your life you have no say over, no control. Whether you get the new position at work or not, if you are going on the trip out of town, and how you are getting along with your mother. These are all things you feel you're not in command of. Right now you are trying to control our relationship, maybe as a way to not feel so lost.

Pt: I am letting go of these things and it makes me feel crazy, horrible. But, I am trying to let go. It makes me feel very nervous, my life in general.

A: It's difficult to realize you're scared and don't have power over me or anyone else.

Pt: Yes. That is true. I think it's more about these ugly weird feelings that are finally coming out. The fear is there, but there is some real hatred too. That is very frightening.

A: Tell me more.

Pt: I only see it in bits and pieces, but I feel really furious about how I have only lived half a life. I feel ripped off and used. I hate how my father treated me when I was growing up, how he used to beat me and molest me. I always try and control those feelings. I worry that if they come out I will be dragged off to hell. I feel really bad that I have such hatred, but it is there. I want to sort it all out and understand it. It's just so damn hard.

A: So, you wanting medication and trying to overpower me about it is a way to hide from all the hatred and pain. It's really a struggle for you to not know everything and not control everybody in your life. It makes you very anxious to be in the middle of all these unsettled and unknown things.

Pt: I want to be able to not know, I want to be OK with not controlling everything. But, I feel so lost and worried when I am not.

A: Based on how hard you try and control us, it looks like you feel your world could easily fall apart and bad things could happen to us.

Pt: I feel confused and frustrated. I came in and told you about medications in a cold, scientific, and controlling way so it got ignored. What if it is important? What if I really need them? Different therapists have different ideas about medications. I don't want it ignored and swept under the rug.

A: If I thought medication would be helpful, I would not ignore that need. But, when you relate to me in a controlling way, you end up seeing me as weak and needing to be reminded of how to take care of you. You have to remind me of how important it is to assess you, diagnose you, and treat you. So by controlling me you don't see me as very competent or able to take care of you. I hear you saying that you don't want me to ignore you and sweep you under the rug.

Pt: Yes. I end up feeling worried that I am on my own and have to take care of everything, which I am sick of.

So, while the first part of this session was rather rocky and analytic contact was difficult to maintain, my persistence in making transference interpretations and inviting my patient to explore the deeper, more frightening aspects of her mind led us both back to a useful climate of analytic contact in which progress and change were again possible.

Case material 11.3

Jay was a psychotic man in his twenties who wanted to find out why he could never have a meaningful relationship with a woman. Immediately, he tried to control me and organize my thoughts. Jay did this by bringing in several binders full of poetry he had written so that I could have "an opportunity to understand him better". He also told me what topic we should cover the next session, reminded me what time it was during the session, and brought in the results of recent consultations he had had with various other therapists and internists. At home, he tried to control his anxiety by studying astrology charts and searching the internet for information about learning disabilities. He is convinced he has an organic learning problem that may have something to do with the nature of his "cosmic constellations".

Jay recalls a scary upbringing with two very hostile and abusive parents. He felt they would attack him for any reason and were usually unpredictable in mood and deed. They locked him in his room for hours on end and "plotted" with each other on how to discipline him. Jay felt he could do nothing right in their eyes. His two sisters are institutionalized and he has cut off contact with his parents.

In the transference, it quickly unfolded that while he wanted my help he had to be in charge. If I presented some idea or interpretation to him, he felt attacked and pounced on without warning. This led to paranoid views about my technique and frequent threats to quit altogether. Jay instructed me on how to carefully spell out anything I was doing or about to say so he had plenty of warning. He told me that without warning and prior knowledge, everything was "a storm". So, the brittle analytic contact that was present was constricted by his attempts to control me and my way of working.

My sense was that he was continuously on the verge of losing the symbolic functioning of an idealized internal mother. Similar to what Bion (1959) has discussed about the need for and the potential loss of the maternal container, the infant needs the experience of a symbolizing function within the receptive idealized object. If the result of projective identification feels like an angry boomerang where raw frightening material is taken by the object and vomited back up without some type of modification or digestion, the ego is threatened with a return of its own split-off venom. Therefore, it is crucial to normal development that the ego trust in the idealized object to serve as a symbolizer with which the ego can gradually identify.

Jay, organizing his experience within a paranoid, psychotic framework, was lacking a symbolic ego function. When I offered him an interpretation, it was distorted and poisoned by his projections and left without any symbolic value. This meant our relationship took on a very concrete, limited, and dangerous character. If everything was not clear and taken at face value, it became "a storm". So, it was a constant struggle to maintain analytic contact without our relationship simply becoming a storm in which we both sought refuge from each other.

An example of this came up regarding the word "hour". I usually call the analytic appointment a "session". I have learned from patients like Jay the need to be clear about such things. Jay came in to one session with a glazed look in his eyes and began telling me off. He said he had been up all night pacing, furious with me and the mental health system. The idea was that many therapists called the session "the therapy hour" when it is actually only 45 minutes long. This felt like an outrage, a lie, and a deliberate act of arrogance by therapists. Jay had lost touch with the internal, symbolizing ideal object that he longed for. In the transference, I was the hoped-for symbolizing ideal object that would show him how to shape his concrete terror into something more manageable. However, that aspect of me quickly vanished under his aggressive, oral projections and out of the destruction emerged a critical, untrustworthy object. I was now part of the bad system that used him instead of protecting him.

This was a difficult treatment as Jay was sure of what he felt and knew it to be real. There was no as-if quality to it. Analytic contact was overwhelmed by his paranoid vision of us. My fall from grace, from being the idealized object that would save him, was fast and ugly. We spent many hours going over the minute details of various events where he felt I had turned on him and betrayed a fundamental trust. He told me how I should be and how he wished I was. Much of the analysis concerned the moments when he felt I suddenly shifted from what he hoped for to something quite menacing and disappointing. This was the most important work in that it was not only the heart of the transference but also was the core of what stabilized the analytic contact with Jay. Interpretation was helpful in two specific ways. First it served as an ongoing detoxifier of projective phantasies and secondly it represented a potential new object for Jay's ego to introject. Analytic contact is, in parallel, the ongoing psychoanalytic exploration of the patient's archaic object relations and the conflicts surrounding them along with the investigation of the patient's current reactions to a change or shift in those objects, through the medium of the psychoanalytic relationship, the transference.

Chapter 12

Looking at films for perspectives on structural change

This chapter examines two movies, *Secretary*[1] and *Mostly Martha*.[2] Drawing a parallel between the two plots by examing psychic loss, this chapter focuses on the two lead women's struggles with troubled father–daughter relations. On one hand, the case can be made for a simplistic profile of a healthy working-through process in *Mostly Martha* versus a pathological solution in *Secretary*. However, the author shows how normal mourning and aspects of paranoid-schizoid pathology can overlap, providing certain internal bargains that work adequately and serve to maintain a functioning ego. The corresponding psychoanalytic concepts of acting out, sadomasochism, and working through are reviewed.

This cinematic comparison and psychoanalytic perspective of the films' deeper message is useful in understanding the place of analytic contact in the healing process. Part of establishing analytic contact is viewing the exploration of transference, defense, phantasy, and conflict as essential to treatment, regardless of frequency, diagnosis, or use of couch. In addition, the clinical concept of analytic contact includes the important need of the analyst's acceptance in our stance with patients. There can be an optimal degree of analytic contact, but that is always changing, always fluid, because of the patient's involvement or lack thereof. Each patient's level of ego functioning during the course of treatment as well as at termination will never be fully integrated, perfect, or finished. We must accept this in order to provide our best assistance to each person. However, we do our best to be psychoanalysts, interpreting the patient's feelings and phantasies about their experience of analytic contact and their methods of retreat from it. The clinical encounter that takes place within the realm of analytic contact provides each patient the best opportunity for psychological healing, integration, and a sense of personal balance in the world. How the patient interacts and reacts to the experience of analytic contact is something we can try to navigate through interpretation. Ultimately, the patient's transference will determine the course of treatment and its outcome. Much like the two movies this chapter explores, the interface between a psychoanalyst practicing their craft to the best of their ability and the patient's phantasies, defenses, and transference state produces a compromise in which some new ground is established and some old ground remains.

ACTING OUT

Freud (1914) believed the patient, in the grip of unconscious wishes and phantasies, brought their conflicted internal state to life by some sort of immediate action, usually external. In the psychoanalytic setting, this acting out of psychological conflict was fortified by the patient's denial of its existence. Often aggressive in nature, acting out is directed at others or at the self. Freud thought this action was best understood as related to the transference and often served as a method to deny the transference.

Contemporary Kleinians have widened and deepened Freud's ideas concerning acting out. The term is now also known as acting-in, in reference to the transference aspect of it rather than the general acting out the patient may do outside of the treatment setting. In addition, Kleinians note how this acting out that takes place outside of sessions is often still a transference communication. Joseph (1975, 1978, 1985, 1989), Riesenberg-Malcolm (1986), Segal (1982), and other Kleinians have explored the manner in which the transference always involves an element of acting out, usually by the patient but sometimes by the analyst as well. They have outlined the importance of noticing and analyzing the moment-to-moment unfolding of various forms of object relations in the analytic relationship that constitute what could be termed acting out. Complex forms of projective identification and other psychological mechanisms are understood as not simply a method of instinctual discharge or a reaction to repressed memories, but complex methods of defense, reparation, aggression, connection, play, resistance, and retreat. Both the life and death instincts come into clinical view when acting out is sufficiently analyzed.

SADOMASOCHISM

Sadomasochism is a psychoanalytic concept that tries to explain the interplay between sadism and masochism and how they are interrelated. The individual engages in self-punishment as well as domination of the object in phantasy. This is also usually part of a person's interpersonal life, in which people play out the domination and the submission, often exchanging roles in some manner.

Freud wrote about these matters in 1920 as well as in other essays. The sadist gains pleasure from hurting the object as well as masochistic pleasure from identifying with the victim. The sadist may feel the need to be punished for those deeds and the masochist may inflict guilt upon his tormentors. Pleasure and pain mix as the erotic and aggressive phantasies are combined.

Rothstein (1991) states that sadomasochism is best understood as a series of pathological compromise formations. Therefore, they would lend themselves to standard analysis and working through. Rothstein also reminds the reader that, in some cases, the mind is able to form effective compromise formations which produce adaptation and growth. In other words, all compromise formations are not pathological. Grossman (1991) states there are three ways to account for the phenomenon of sadomasochism. Pain and the painful affects and phantasies that come with it complicate the normal resolution of psychic conflict. Subsequent ego and superego distortion creates cycles of repetitious aggressive behavior toward the self and others. Next, Grossman states that pain and painful affects are part of an aggressive drive which has its origins in bodily sensations, much as the pleasure or sexual drive does. Finally, he notes that a history of trauma brings about impairment in the ability to use phantasy to further development. Instead, repetitive behaviors and sadomasochistic mental imagery take over as a way to undo or master the trauma. This effort at mastery can sometimes be effective and sometimes destructive, leading to a fixation of pathology.

Melanie Klein drew attention to the sadistic qualities of the infantile superego, particularly evident in the more severe pathologies. Kleinians postulate superego sadism to be a way to turn aggression onto the self rather than onto its original target, the mother and the mother's body.

WORKING THROUGH

Freud (1914) thought the patient would need time and help to work through the resistive nature of id impulses. The process of psychoanalytic work was thought to go contrary to the repetitive, unconscious forces that create pathology. Therefore, change was slow and often halting. Working through was Freud's answer to the question of why treatment took so long.

To achieve a genuine working through, interpretations must be consistent and insights need to be revisited many times from different vantage points. The nature of the patient's resistance must be examined and confronted in its numerous forms. Eventually, the patient comes to acknowledge, accept, and transform certain previously repressed or disavowed areas of his character.

Fenichel (1939) saw working through as a process in which the analyst dealt with the patient's defenses by showing, through interpretation, that it is the patient who is responsible for his actions, thoughts, and feelings rather than something outside of him. In addition, the patient must be shown how he evades that knowledge of personal intent and tries to project it out externally. Finally, the historical origins of that evasive pattern are gradually examined and integrated. Just like Freud, Fenichel noted the importance of repetition in these matters, as the working-through process needed numerous demonstrations in the analytic setting before the ego would internalize the new outlook.

Greenson (1965) thought that the concept working through served as an umbrella term for whatever it took to overcome the patient's unconscious resistance. He pointed out that any success in this area was only possible if an effective working alliance had been established between patient and analyst. Dewald (1976) explored the need for the analyst to be tolerant. It was this new, welcoming object relationship that made change possible, but only if experienced over and over again. Dewald stated it was the repetition of this new, more favorable relationship that undid the patient's resistant defenses. Valenstein (1983) thought that insight alone was not enough to produce psychological change. He saw working through as consisting of the patient's translating their insights into action, over and over until it became a familiar part of their personality. He thought this insight into action formula was especially important for those patients suffering from a more grave diagnosis. Brenner (1987) thought that the concept of working through was unnecessary. He saw the slow, often halting nature of analysis to simply be the way analysis is. Brenner advocates the simple, repetitive use of interpretive work that provides insight, which in turn leads to lasting therapeutic change. He took working through to be the general term that embraces the analysis of all psychic conflicts and thus was not special enough to be singled out as a special procedure. Brenner thinks patients come to treatment with pathological compromise formations that need to be analyzed. Resistance to that procedure occurs within the transference, which in turn needs to be analyzed.

Melanie Klein (1961) elaborated on the clinical specifics of working through and how new insight can occur one day, but be denied or attacked the next. She pointed to the necessity of continuously interpreting the transference as the critical method to shed light from multiple angles on the patient's unconscious issues. This gradually brings about awareness, acceptance, and integration. It is thought that this repetition of transference interpretation will bring about lasting change, rather than temporary shifts in behavior. O'Shaughnessy (1983) discussed how the patient communicates with the analyst via words, but much more by less developed ways such as projective identification. As the patient feels understood by the analyst's interpretations, especially transference-based interpretations, he may become more aware of these subtle and manipulative methods of communicating. With time and assisted by the analyst's patient interpretive efforts, the patient is able to shift from these more primitive ways of communicating to relaying his own insights about himself to the analyst in words. This new use of words to relay insight about oneself is both indicative of growth and promotive of growth. O'Shaughnessy states that interpretations put the patient into a position to be able to change. They offer the potential for change. The patient then must make an active transformation by combining self insight and words to convey to the analyst their thoughts and feelings. In a sense, I see this as the patient's returning the analyst's interpretation to the analyst after internalizing it and personalizing it. By then returning it in this modified form, the patient is now sharing in the interpretive process of the analytic relationship. This is necessary for enduring character transformation.

INTERNAL BARGAINS, WORKING WITH INTERNAL BARGAINS, AND THE CREATION OF PSYCHOLOGICAL BALANCE

I will present two film reviews that explore loss, sadomasochism, and the use of creative or restorative acting out. Acting out can be used to create a reasonable adaptation to internal conflict. Rothstein (1991) noted the healthy nature of some compromise formations. I choose to see this in terms of internal bargains (Waska 1999) that come out of pathological relationships between the ego and its objects. The ego establishes the best possible stance to its objects, based on the particular phantasies that surround it at the given time.

The term working through connotes moving past something by either bypassing it or by passing directly through it. The term also conveys the process of undoing the old as a journey is made into the new. These ideas are all valid, but don't necessarily serve all the clinical circumstances that are found in day-to-day psychoanalytic practice. In many cases, there is no dramatic transformation from old to new, but more of a modification in the patient's internal object-relational bargains. Intra-psychic phantasy states become less pathological and the ego becomes less reliant on primitive modes of relating. However, the link to the object often retains its original cast. Therefore, the patient may still act out, but in far more subtle ways that are less destructive and often more creative and adaptive.

This idea of acting out as progressive is explored in Grossman's 1991 paper on "Sadomasochism and Psychological Growth". He states that playful fantasies of domination and submission, when acted out, help reassure the patient that the object can survive the full expression of the subject's sexual desires. Also, the subject's harsh superego and guilt regarding sexual wishes can be avoided by submitting to the domination and then secretly identifying with the aggressor in the pleasure of being able to express desire.

Hasui (Hasui & Kitamuca 2004) points to the constructive use of aggression during the process of mourning and how therapists often consider it a hindrance rather than part of psychological healing. This is similar to Grossman's (1993) idea of mastery through sadomasochistic acting out.

I think acting out is actually an unavoidable aspect of working through, as well as a necessary and important component of progress. Betty Joseph and her followers (Hargreaves & Varchevker 2004) speak to this when describing the almost ubiquitous presence of acting out in the transference relationship and how acting out is often the needed clue for the analyst to provide the right interpretation. Certainly, some types of acting out can be very pathological and destructive, leading to analytic standoffs, dead ends, and the replay of painful, pointless cycles. But, as I will explore in two films, sadomasochism is one of many methods in which the ego constructs object-relational bargains in which acting out both repeats certain dysfunctional postures but also is a method of solving, adapting, or mastering loss.

Secretary

In the movie *Secretary*, the main character, Lee, has an unavailable, alcoholic father. Lee feels sorry for him and loves him as a pathetic disappointment. Various scenes of father coming home drunk, of father calling Lee from a phone booth after being kicked out by his wife, and father on his death bed all convey the hopeless, sad object he was for her.

Lee's mother treats her drunken husband as an infantile failure, yelling at him and belittling him. In a projective identification process, the wife also treats her daughter, Lee, in this infantile way. Lee, in identification with her father, is dependent and weak, needing her mother to give her rides and take care of her. This slowly changes throughout the movie.

Lee's conflictual feeling about her father is acted out in a sadomasochistic fashion. She develops a ritualistic perversion of cutting, burning, and hurting herself. She even has a special kit of tools for the process. This outwardly destructive behavior seems to serve as a vehicle for Lee's feelings of self-blame, rebellion, hostility, revenge, and the sexualized organizing of fragmented object relations. There may be a crude striving toward separation, independence, and mastery involved in her self-harm. Yet, its function in the beginning of the film seems to be mostly defensive. Without this destructive focus, a painful abandonment and rage is all that is left of the father–daughter bond.

Lee finds a job as a secretary to a domineering, sadistic lawyer. Mr Grey, the lawyer, produces a replacement for her self-destructive behavior. Her external acting out shifts from cutting and burning to being a slave/secretary, but her internal struggles continue. Now, Mr Grey punishes her in a sexualized manner instead of her doing it to herself. Through a mutual projective identification process, the lawyer embodies Lee's conflicts: the longed for, caring and attentive father, the continuing withholding of love and approval she longs for, the split off aggression and desire for power that Lee carries on behalf of father, the forceful punishing mother, and Lee's own search for personal truth. She finds her lost father as well as all her internal struggles within this new relationship.

Mr Grey, the lawyer, serves as Lee's surrogate father-analyst, but one who uses suggestion and transference manipulation to create a cure. After witnessing her cutting behavior, he tells her, "You will never do that again! Promise me that!" In complying with this suggestion and urging, she finds a cure to her masochistic symptom by putting herself in a subservient role to him. In other words, internalized sadomasochism is replaced by externalized sadomasochism. The actual inner conflict is not addressed. However, over time Lee begins to change the way she relates to herself and her objects.

Toward the end of *Secretary*, Lee seems to want something more than a mere replica of her family history. She wants love. In trying to convince Mr Grey of her intention and wanting to prove her love, she confines herself to his office chair for days, urinating on herself and going without food. Masochism is the vehicle for her attempt to shift her father–daughter relationship with the lawyer to a more healthy bond of love. She also has to try and cure her father-lawyer of his own pathology and create a happy, normal family with him. The movie ends with both characters seeming to be happier, healthier, and not as confined to rigid methods of intra-psychic solution. However, when we see Lee putting a dead bug in the bed so as to invite a sadomasochistic sexual union later that day, we know some things get better and other things remain the same.

Mostly Martha

In the film, *Mostly Martha*, we meet an isolated woman named Martha. She is a chef who maintains a masochistic life of cooking for others, many of whom are not appreciative and others who outright insult her talent. She often is overwhelmed with anxiety and takes refuge in the walk-in freezer of the restaurant's kitchen. We learn she was taught to cook by her father, but the absence of any other reference to her father being a part of her life as well as Martha's lack of boyfriend or husband, makes the viewer wonder about the loss of an important father–daughter bond. Trying to understand Martha's personality and her internal experience through this absent father–lost-daughter lens shows the film to be a complex, dynamic story about inner life and psychological conflict.

When Martha's sister is killed and Martha has to care for her sister's young daughter, Martha is unsure how to cope. After being away from work for a while, she returns to find that an Italian man has been hired as an assistant chef in the kitchen. Martha takes this as a humiliation and a narcissistic blow. The antagonistic relationship she quickly develops with this man may be a transference replica of her internal relationship to her father.

Martha's new surrogate daughter is depressed and angry about the loss of her mother. For a period of time, Martha finds this agitating and difficult to deal with. However, I think that when Martha was able to identify with this little girl's suffering about her mother as Martha's own suffering about her own father, a transformation began. Martha started to mother this child and be understanding. In other words, the little girl served as a projective identification vehicle for Martha. Once Martha allowed this internal grieving to open up, she also was able to let the Italian chef into her life. He served to be a father replacement of sorts. At the same time, by the end of the movie Martha and the Italian chef gave the little girl the second chance at a loving family that I believe Martha had been hoping and searching for as well.

In Martha's psychotherapy, several interesting events occur. Martha dominates her analyst by reciting endless recipes and always talking about food. It is done in a complex way that makes her delivery boring, irritating, alienating, and sexy all at the same time. Her analyst seems to end up feeling useless, pressured, powerless, and bound by perverse rituals of cooking. In other words, through projective identification, he begins to experience what Martha struggles with. He is also unable to establish a true connection with her, which I think is Martha's underlying problem *vis-à-vis* her father.

In Martha's psychotherapy treatment, there is a sadomasochistic match, much like the characters in *Secretary*. At first, Martha acts like a servant and cooks meals for her analyst. Then, he feels forced to eat her meal and begs her to "at least eat with me".

At the end of the movie, the projective identification process in Martha's therapy has run full cycle. The viewer sees Martha's analyst desperately trying to fulfill the recipe requirements for a dish Martha suggested he cook. He is longing for her approval. He realizes he has failed and appears to become despondent. In panic, he gets up and exits, presumably into the figurative walk-in freezer to hide.

Here, one can speculate that perhaps Martha was recreating within her analyst, via projective identification, the experience of being taught how to cook by her own father. In this teaching, there was a caring, a sexual tension, a pressure to please, and a feeling of failure to win approval. The vehicle of cooking served to bond her with her father-analyst in a sado-masochistic way that left her in a state of loss and constant emptiness. Her reliving this throughout her adult life by unhappily cooking and refusing to allow men to get close to her kept this internal struggle intact. Her experience with her sister's child and her new Italian husband seemed to allow her to work through much of that. Yet, in her psychotherapy, she seemed to still be a part of this inner struggle. Rather than working out these feelings, she expelled them into her analyst. She acted them out in such a way that the analyst became a part of the masochistic cycle. We are left with the impression that Martha's father–daughter turmoil has been deposited in the analyst and Martha will abandon him and enter her new life as wife and mother. This may be similar to what happened to Martha as a child with her father. So, in the end Martha achieves a marked shift in her life, but may still carry the leftovers of her past.

These two films show a use of acting out that serves to create a level of growth, progress, or undoing within the context of pathological object relations. The characters demonstrate the fluctuation and coexistence of pathological internal systems of relating and growth-orientated object-relational bargains that aim at change and mastery. Examining the two movies together provides another way of understanding how complete analytic contact is never fully reached. However, a degree of optimal analytic contact is possible if the analyst consistently interprets the patient's retreat from that contact, including the acting out that distorts and destroys it. By monitoring and struggling with the transference–counter-transference matrix that unfolds around the establishment of analytic contact, a degree of successful contact can be made that in turn produces a level of integration and change that is helpful and healing.

Martha and Lee are similar characters, struggling with similar problems and locating solutions that are satisfactory, yet partial. These two women's love for their father is caught in a web of loss, anger, and despair. Through projective identification and the adaptive use of sadomasochistic acting out, both characters manage to work through much of their traumatic inner world and find a way to heal. This healing utilizes a mix of new capacities as well as old yearnings for revenge, acknowledgment, and approval. We see two people find their way out of loss and into love, still colored by the past but perhaps in a more creative way that allows less restriction of thought and feeling. In this sense, these two movies provide a masterful rendering of what happens so often in our offices and every day in life. Clinically, this is the way analytic contact unfolds with most of our patients, in a less than optimal, often chaotic, and confusing movement forward. Some of the old remains, but hopefully enough analytic contact has been found, tolerated, and sustained to gradually shift or integrate some fundamental aspects of the patient's mind.

Notes

1 Director Steven Shainberg; producers A. Fiereery and A. Hobby; starring James Spader and Maggie Gyllenhaal; country of origin, USA; distributor, Lionsgate Films, 2003; running time 111 minutes.

2 Director, Sandra Nettelbeck; producer C. Friedel; starring Martina Bedeck, Maxime Foerste, Sergio Castellitto, and August Zirner; country of origin, Germany; distributor, Paramount Entertainment, 2002; running time 106 minutes.

Chapter 13

Psychoanalysis or psychotherapy? Shifting the debate to a clinical focus

Merton Gill has left his mark on psychoanalysis in multiple ways. Rather than provide a review of his many years of theoretical contribution to the field, which can be found in both his own many writings and various summaries by others, I want to focus on his 1994 view of what constitutes true psychoanalytic work. In this phase of his life, he strongly adhered to the idea that psychoanalysis is a procedure that involves the analysis of transference and does not need to rely on what he called the extrinsic factors of couch and frequency. This stance was the culmination of views he held from 1979 onwards.

In reading over Gill's numerous papers and books, it is striking to note that he never includes any of his own case material.[1] While Gill does use the clinical material of other analysts and supervisees to further his theoretical perspectives, he does not allow us into the realm of his own analytic work. So, I believe we are left with a brilliant theoretical view of what psycho-analysis should be in the clinical setting, without the clinical setting. It is just not the same to use other people's case work to make your theoretical point. Something is lost in the process when one's case material isn't there to carry the theoretical message. In this sense, Gill's work, in particular his 1994 work, goes untested. I wish to provide the missing piece to his brilliant puzzle by looking at my own Kleinian-influenced psychoanalytic practice.

Tuckett (2005) notes that the three lines of great impact Melanie Klein and the Kleinian tradition have had on psychoanalysis involve the concept of psychic reality and conflict, the idea that the patient's past and their core conflicts can be best understood and resolved through analysis of the present relationship to the analyst, and the importance of always linking theory to clinical evidence. Tuckett states that psychic reality consists of a constant effort to manage unbearable affect that occurs over the conflicts between love and hate. I wish to follow Tuckett's recommendation regard-ing linking theory to clinical evidence and Klein's focus on the patient's current relationship to the analyst by using my Kleinian clinical stance and Gill's formulations to show the importance of what I will term analytic contact.

What helps to bring clinical life to Gill's theoretical stance includes the Kleinian technique of the total transference (Joseph 1985). Joseph has expanded on Melanie Klein's believe that everything a patient brings to the session should be considered as part of a transference communication. Prior to Klein's stance, transference was seen as limited to direct verbal references from the patient concerning feelings toward the analyst.

Analytic contact is essentially the sum of what Gill saw as essential in psychoanalysis. It is the establishment of object-relational contact with the patient through exploration of the transference, phantasies, and defenses. It is the investigation of the patient's unique personal experience of psychic reality. Regardless of setting, frequency, or use of couch, the analyst strives to create a mutual curiosity about and discovery of the patient's object-relational world, which naturally includes the connection between patient and analyst. During this ongoing attempt to find, understand, and analyze the transference, the analyst is also looking at how the patient avoids this type of contact.

Finally, Gill used the term analytic process to describe his view of what the psychoanalyst's therapeutic goal should be. I am using the term analytic contact instead of analytic process because it better describes the close intimate bond and psychological touching of minds that must be a part of the transference–counter-transference relationship. The term analytic contact embodies the emotional and psychic contact of two parties, struggling together. I use the word struggling because for many if not all patients, every moment of analytic contact is a moment of dread and despair, as he or she struggles with change and a new way of being with his or her objects. Therefore, successful analytic work always involves the patient's moment-to-moment retreat, attack, hiding, and attempt to shift the treatment into something less than analytic, something less painful. Thus, the analyst must include in his interpretations an understanding of this retreat and attack, while attempting to steer the treatment back to something more analytic, something that contains more patient–patient and patient–analyst contact. The support that we give our patients is a subtle and sometimes not so subtle belief that we will help them survive this painful contact. We are implicitly promising to stay with them until they get to the other side of this frightening process of change. Therefore, I believe analytic contact is a term that better reflects the flesh-and-blood clinical reality of psycho-analytic work.

So, in this perspective, what defines a treatment as psychoanalytic is whether or not the analyst is attempting to create analytic contact, making interpretive efforts to maintain it, and exploring how the patient is either working towards this contact or against this contact. In other words, what are both parties doing about the transference? What are they doing or not doing to understand the various aspects of the immediate relationship in the room? Are matters other than the immediate relationship being used to further a mutual understanding of psychic reality, transference, and phantasy or are these others matters being used to defend against, cover up, or attack the potential for analytic contact? These are the clinical questions that help classify a treatment as analytic or not, instead of theoretical matters of frequency, diagnosis, couch, or other external features.

Gill's (1979, 1994) ideas about the importance of analytic process over the less important extrinsic factors of frequency and couch have been verified through Ablon's (2005a) reseach in which he showed that an analytic process (what I am terming analytic contact) can be established without sole reliance on frequency or use of couch. In addition, Ablon (2005b) has noted from his extensive research into what actually takes place in psychoanalytic treatment that "psychoanalytic treatment is not applied to patients. Rather, our patients are coauthors of the treatment process. For this reason, thankfully, there can never be one proper analytic process; rather, there are change processes unique to each dyad" (p. 593). This is again an example of clinical research that backs up Gill's theoretical constructs about the mutual construction of the therapeutic process and what I believe is the constant cycle of projective and introjective indentification that goes on in analytic treatments, which brings about either pathological enactments or opportunities for working through. Another way of saying this is that interpretation of the transference, phantasies, conflicts, and defenses such as projective identification can foster analytic contact and reduce those forces that seek to attack and eliminate analytic contact.

Case material 13.1

Analytic contact is not a phenomenon restricted to an individual one-to-one treatment setting. It is something the analyst can strive for in any clinical setting.

Bob and Frances came to see me after they had been together for five years. She was ready to get married and have children. He was obsessively undecided on those matters as well as most things in his life. After meeting once with the two of them, I suggested, as I often do, that we alternate between meeting individually and as a couple so we could begin to understand how each person functioned as well as how they related together. The second visit was with Frances. She started off telling me of her relationship to Bob and her frustration over his lack of commitment. The more she talked, I had the sense from her story, as well as from my counter-transference feeling, that she kept much of her feelings to herself. She seemed to provide me with a little clue about her emotional state out there and then not follow up on it.

The first way this came into the transference was when she was telling me about their living arrangement. For the last year, Bob had not worked because he was not sure about what direction to take with his career. Since he had no income, Frances invited him to stay with her. After living together for six months, Bob took a job that paid a decent salary. After five months of his not offering to contribute financially to the rent or utilities, Frances became angry and insulting, after which Bob began paying her a small sum. But, a month later, he announced he was moving out into his "own place". The message of Frances's story was clear. She felt they had been living together for a year and that made her happy. But, when she realized Bob never saw it that way and only viewed living with her as a temporary, free hotel until he could get his own place, Frances was angry and hurt.

The way Frances told me the story seemed to dilute and muffle her angry, hurt feelings. I said this to her. She replied, "I was very upset. I thought we were going ahead with our relationship, getting more committed and close and then he just leaves!" She started to cry and said, "But, he did pay me some money at the end, so it was OK. It was helpful to have some help with the utilities and a few other small things." I said, "You are relating to me in a particular way right now. I asked you about your deeper feelings, feelings that are important to you. You told me how upset you are and then you suddenly switched to how he gave you money and how that made everything alright. You are having a hard time relating your true self to me without going off in other directions." She replied, "So, I should ask him for more money and then I will feel better?" I said, "No. I am showing you how you are relating to me. Perhaps it's the same way you relate to Bob. You showed your inner self to me and then you retreated and brought up something that isn't about your feelings. Maybe you aren't sure how I will be if you continue to just be yourself and share your feelings with me." Frances said, "I don't ever feel like I am worthwhile enough to have an opinion. I usually keep quiet about things." She went on to talk about how she "retreats" from expressing her needs and ideas with others. I commented that the more she kept her feelings and needs to herself, she might feel in control and safe, but she was never letting me or her boyfriend in on who she is and what she needs, so the odds of getting us to care for her like she wishes are slim. Frances nodded and cried. She said it was hard to express herself and she was angry with herself for having feelings and needs.

I said she was angry with herself for having feelings and needs with me and after she expressed them a bit with me, she was now attacking herself. I asked her if the way she was relating to me and her boyfriend was a pattern she had ever noticed before. Frances said she thought it came from her childhood and the way she was raised and "the things that happened to me". I asked her what she meant. She says that she has always felt there was something that happened to her as a child, "something sexual". She said, "I tried to get at it in therapy before, but I could never identify the person or when it happened or exactly what took place. I just have this feeling that has always been there of someone coming down on me, holding me down, and I feel like I am suffocating." Frances started to cry. Then, she suddenly started to tell me about her theories about Bob's childhood and how his early experiences have made him not want to make commitments. She went on to discuss this for a while, saying she felt sorry for him and how much his past influenced his adult life. Then, she switched to telling me about her theories about her mother's childhood and how her mother might have been abused and how that might explain her mother's distant and angry ways. I said, "You started to share something very important and personal with me, but then you felt over-whelmed and upset and switched to telling me about other people and hiding yourself in the background. That way of relating to me is protective, but I think you are all alone now with your pain and focusing on other people's pain instead of getting help with yours. That is the same thing you did a minute ago about your boyfriend moving out on you. So, it looks like it's very uncomfortable to stay focused on yourself and be present with me, sharing your hurt and your needs."

Frances replied, crying, "I do that a lot. I zig-zag all over the place. I have always done that. I don't know what to do instead." I replied, "We can work on that together. You brought up the molest memory right after saying you are angry with yourself for having needs. Could it be that you blame yourself for that too?" She replied, "I don't know if that is exactly true, but I do feel I am somehow to blame for most things and wrong to be myself. And, I feel there is no one there for me when I have that memory." She began to sob.

This case is an example of my using interpretation to address the trans-ference. Specifically, I was addressing the transference retreat from analytic contact. Frances was able to make an initial move toward me to establish meaningful contact and begin to explore something about herself with me. Then, she bolted from that expressive contact into a not-me topic that disconnected us and distanced herself from the anxiety she was feeling. So, I interpreted that disconnection. In doing so, I brought back the potential for restoration of analytic contact. Indeed, Fances was able to continue to explore her feelings and thoughts and tell me that she has noticed these patterns throughout her life and has noticed how helpless they make her feel.

Instead of simply interpreting her defense of intellectualization, dis-placement, and so forth, I chose to interpret the total transference (Joseph

1985) in which those defenses were part of how she was using me, relating to me, and experiencing our connection. I was interpreting her engagement or disengagement in the analytic process. In other words, I was interpreting her retreat from analytic contact.

Case material 13.2

Jake was a twelve-year-old boy brought to treatment by his parents. They were concerned about his lying to them and his gradually worsening grades. I met with the family first and then with Jake by himself. After that, I alternated between meeting with the family and meeting with Jake as it seemed to provide both the opportunity to deal with the family dynamics at play as well as Jake's personal psychology. This arrangement was once a week. Relatively soon, I was struck by how the "lying" problem was essentially Jake not being honest about what he wanted or didn't want. His parents seemed loving and well-meaning, but also determined to have Jake make As in all his classes and have him participate in numerous extra-curricular activities. "Making sure his mind is stimulated and his potential is reached", was their motto. After about two months of meeting with Jake and his family, I made interpretations based on those ideas. I told them that I saw them as loving parents who seemed to want a bit too much out of their son. I said that they had a remarkably well-behaved young man who did need to do his homework without procrastinating so much, but they seemed to ignore how good they had it. I was providing a confrontation and interpretation of the dynamic or conflict I observed.

With Jake, I told him, in front of his parents, that he seemed a bit too well-behaved. It was a mystery why he was so compliant on most matters and seemed to not have much problem with his parents' rather rigid requests and guidelines. An example of this was that his parents didn't allow him to go out to the movies with his friends, unless they went with him and deemed the movie as appropriate to his age level. They weren't religious or politically conservative, but their actions with Jake made them seem like a religious, conservative stereotype of some sort. I questioned Jake's lack of protest about the movie restrictions.

In my counter-transference, I noticed myself wanting to suggest rebellious behavior to Jake, for him to stretch the envelope and do his own thing. I felt like conspiring with Jake to do naughty things behind his parents' back or to outright demand freedom from them. In thinking about my feelings, I came to the conclusion that there was a projective identification process occurring in which I was being given Jake's desire for more freedom and his hidden wishes for a bigger self-identity. I interpreted that he wanted me to understand how he was trying to please his parents and make them happy, but in the process he had to deny who he was and what he wanted. He had to lie about what he really thought and felt. I said that he wanted me to be his messenger, to tell Mom and Dad that he was a good boy, but also to tell them he had a life that didn't always mesh with their wishes. The following week, Jake's parents reported that his lying had altogether ceased and they were much happier. This improvement has held up over time. They still wanted to see me because they felt Jake was "not living up to his potential".

During a recent session, eight months into the treatment, I met with Jake by himself. He began by telling me he had gone to a cousin's home for the weekend with his family. They went there to celebrate the baptism of the cousin's new baby. Jake said, "We went to this church and I didn't know what I was supposed to do. We had to sing and I wasn't sure what book to sing from so I didn't. I tried to do the proper thing but I didn't know how. It was the first time I had been to a church service and it was all new to me. Do you go to church?" I asked, "Why do you want to know?" Jake said, "I just wondered. Anyway, it was a whole new experience. I had to learn how to kneel down at a certain time and we all got bread and wine to share. I didn't really drink wine, but the bread had some on it. I was unsure of how to be because no one told me what to expect." Then, he went on to tell me about other aspects of the weekend and how he was glad it was a celebration because his parents let him have a candy bar. Normally, they don't approve of sweets but allow it on special occasions.

We went on to talk about other things for a while, and then I said, "You know, you never really told me how you felt about going to the church. You sound like a good boy, doing what good boys do, but I think that is possibly a way you are lying to me about who you are." After a pause, Jake said, "I don't want to hurt your feelings. But, I couldn't stand it. It was incredibly boring. But, I don't want to say something to offend you. What if you go to church a lot? But, if I have to be honest, I would have rather been stung by a thousand bees! What a waste. I was bored stiff." I interpreted that he had to lead a secret life and hid himself from me in order to save me from what he thought was his hurtful, nasty self. Jake added, "I feel that way toward my parents too. I even do that with some of my friends. They want to hang out at the mall sometimes and I don't feel like it. But, I don't want to hurt their feelings so I say I can't because I have so much homework, which is ironic since I never do my homework and would rather be at the mall than sitting at home doing homework!"

So, here is a once-a-week treatment in which there is a combination of individual therapy and family therapy. It would be easy to assume there is not much psychoanalytic work that will take place. However, as a psychoanalyst, I did my best to establish analytic contact with this family. I used the principles of the psychoanalytic method including the exploration and interpretation of transference, defenses, conflict, wishes, fears, and repetition of object-relational patterns. While each session was not punctuated by numerous examples of these principles, I kept my analytic eye open and strove to maintain an analytic focus. In the examples above, I located and interpreted the projective identification process that helped explain why Jake was lying to his family all the time. This was a moment of analytic contact which in turn led to symptom improvement, insight, and I believe the beginning of some structural change. And, I interpreted Jake's transference in which I was a fragile object that he needed to protect by lying about his true feelings regarding the church. This was a moment of analytic contact that also paved the way to structural and behavioral change.

This case material shows that even in a setting in which one would not immediately assume psychoanalysis was being practiced, an important analytic contact was made in which deeper, unconscious, object-relational conflicts were addressed through careful focus and analysis of the transference. The way the family related to itself and to the analyst was the center focus and out of that came answers to the emotional difficulties they came to treatment for. Psychoanalytic contact was established, if only here and there, and the psychoanalytic method proved helpful to this family.

Case material 13.3

Louis was a thirty-year-old black man who drove a taxi for a living. He came to see me because his girlfriend had left him and told him the only hope for their relationship was if he dealt with his "anger issues". Initially, Louis seemed defended and shortsighted in terms of his goals. He told me, "All I want to do is get her back. You got to help me, Doc." We began meeting once a week, due to scheduling constraints, money problems, and his reluctance to attend more frequently. The first few times we met, I saw him as somewhat simplistic in his thinking and possibly lacking in psychological mindedness. So, in the counter-transference, I quickly felt a combination of frustration and lack of enthusiasm. I reflected on this and wondered if, through the transference, I was getting a view of what others saw and felt when with him. I asked him, "Louis, you don't seem to want to look at what makes you angry, what is behind it all. Instead, it seems you want a quick fix, for me to make it all better. Is this part of your troubles with your girlfriend? Does she want you to participate in the relationship more?" He said, "Well, that is kind of what she says. She is always wanting me to talk and explain myself. She says I won't take ownership of myself and what I do. Then I get angry and we argue." I said, "So, I am on to something, but it probably makes you angry to hear me say it." He said, "I don't like to be told I am doing wrong." I replied, "When you use the word wrong, it shows me that you took what I said personally, like I was putting you down. How does that work? Tell me about feeling that way." He said, "Everyone tells me that. My girlfriend and my friends always tell me I take things too personal and get too angry. I don't know what the fuck they are talking about!" I said, "You are getting worked up right now I think. So, it looks like you are feeling blamed for something and don't want to have to look at yourself and feel wrong. Is that accurate?" Louis said, "Yeah. You have something there. I just don't like to have to talk about this stuff. I feel like I am being singled out and then I react." Here, he was reflecting on himself and noticing a pattern in his thoughts and feelings. My interpretations and transference comments led to a moment of analytic contact.

In the next session, Louis told me he wanted to admit to his problems with anger and wanted to find a way to get over it because everyone is telling him about it. He went on to talk about how he realizes that he gets "very defensive" and doesn't want to "take accountability" and that he has "always been like that, even as a kid". I asked him what he meant about always being that way. He explained that "Since I was a kid, I always felt like I would be losing if I admit to something. So, if I don't admit to it, then I win." I said, "So, you see things as a competition where you are either right or wrong and you try to never be wrong, even if it means you are angry and defensive." He agreed and added, "I feel like I am being accused of something, so I don't like to take that on." I added, "You take things personal, then you don't want to admit to being bad or wrong." He agreed and then said, "So I want you to tell me what is wrong with me and how to fix it." He said this in a way that made me feel like he had handed me a foul-smelling package and he sat back and waited to see what I would do with it. So, I interpreted that he was wanting me to take over and be like a parent to him so he could be a kid with no accountability and in doing so he was dumping his unwanted problems on me and not wanting to take the blame for them. Also, he was painting a target on himself and saying, "tell me what is wrong with me". I said, "So, you are doing exactly what we have been talking about with me, right now, in the room." Louis laughed and said, "I see what you mean. Yeah. OK." Then, he associated to being that way all his life and said, "I don't remember a time in my life when I was not trying to escape the blame. I have always seen everything as a contest and I don't want to lose!"

So, what initially started out looking like a case where there would be little self-reflection and not much psychoanalytic process possible turned into a situation where analytic contact was possible. We were examining the transference, exploring his defensive method of relating to me and his objects, and he was making links to the past. Over the next few months, this process created a gradual psychological shift or change in which his symptoms began to ease as well.

Case material 13.4

S was a forty-year-old woman who came to treatment after separating from her boyfriend of several years. He had cheated on her for the third time and she'd finally "had enough". Over the course of several months, we dealt with her grief, anger, and doubt about the breakup, the rocky relationship, and her "tendency to get involved with men who disappoint her". She met a man at work and became involved and this led to a fulfilling relationship. There were a few rocky patches and we explored how she once again was convinced she would be disappointed, but things worked out and she felt very happy with him.

In the treatment, S often came in and told me of some recent incident with her mother that left her furious and upset. So, our focus was often on S's ongoing tension with her mother and the frequent arguments they got into. These fights were usually over discussions that mother seemed to quickly take over and make her own. "The spotlight always ends up being on her!", S told me. S saw her mother as very self-absorbed and not able to think about S in a way that felt soothing or comforting. However, over the course of S's two-year treatment, this feeling lessened and she reported seeing her mother as more able to focus on S and "we got along better and she was more of a mother and less of a self-centered friend". I don't think that mother changed as much as S did. In other words, I think S suffered from a phantasy of a depriving mother who cared more about her own well-being than her child's.

S's analytic treatment was paid for primarily through her health coverage from work. We used the couch and met twice a week. Throughout the treatment, S questioned, complained, and criticized the work we did. She called me an "old school Freudian" who wasn't "hip with all the new ways of helping people". She consistently told me she didn't see the point of coming to me and never saw any change or progress. However, over the course of our work together, she also reported that many of her friends saw her as "way less volatile and not as uptight as usual". As mentioned, her fights with mother were greatly reduced. S also spoke more about her anger and sadness about her father, who had left the family when she was six.

The more we explored S's internal life and her past, the more a picture of a lonely, angry little girl emerged. When she was growing up, mother was a waiter in a nightclub and was prone to leaving S and her older sister at home without a babysitter. This was a memory that brought S to tears many a time. S "felt utterly alone and scared", "but tried to pretend otherwise because it was too overwhelming". When S's mother did provide a babysitter, S remembered "strange men, drunken old women, and teenagers who didn't give a fuck". This intense sense of abandonment was something that seemed to extend from when father left the family to when S was a teenager. At that point, she began hanging out with a rough crowd and often didn't come home at night. There was also some question as to whether S had been molested by one or two of the babysitters, but she couldn't recall much and efforts to engage her about it went nowhere.

The central theme of the majority of S's treatment was as follows. She would come in to the session, lie down, and begin talking about random matters at work or what she did with her boyfriend over the weekend. Then, in short order, she would bring up something related to her hurt feelings about her mother or about her childhood. I would ask her to tell me more about her feelings and thoughts on the matter. Then, she would quickly end up sobbing bitterly about the "lonely, unfair situation" her mother put her in growing up or the "disappointing, shitty relationship" she had with her mother as an adult. I would ask questions and explore these sensitive and painful memories and views with S. But, at some point, she seemed to become overwhelmed with emotion and turned her anger and upset onto me. She would say, "Here we go again! All we ever do in this useless therapy is talk about how shitty my childhood was and then nothing happens. I just am left feeling crappy and nothing comes out of it. I don't learn anything and nothing changes. There is no point in this therapy. I only end up upset. You never give me any direction or tell me what to do. What is the use of rehashing all the crap that happened back then?"

I took several approaches with this. First, I told her she was probably very upset and wanting to get rid of the pain by blaming me. In other words, I interpreted her projective identification stance of attributing me with the pain and anguish. As a result, I said she was now seeing me just like she saw her mother: disappointing, painful, and useless. S responded to this by telling me how I was indeed just like her mother, not helping her and "steering things to your direction and ignoring me". Sometimes, she would settle back into her painful memories and begin exploring them for a while, but to make a link from those lonely experiences to today seemed impossible or simply something she didn't want to do. So, I stayed in her moment-to-moment psychic experience with her. I would interpret the way S put me in the role of her disappointing and hurtful mother and then she would feel helpless, angry, and without help. Sometimes, S would agree with my interpretation and make a few associations to how she does that with her boyfriend on occasion. But, most of the time, she simply took her projective identification experience, this angry, sadomasochistic transference, as reality.

This is very much representative of Gill's (1979) description of patients who will not let go of the transference. They see it as reality. Because S stayed in treatment for as long as she did, I had the impression that she achieved both a comforting, healing closeness from this type of mother–daughter relationship with me, as well as a perverse, sadomasochistic relationship. In this dual stance, she was held close by my attention and interest in her pain and suffering, but also felt controlled and persecuted by having to be the one who suffers. She saw me as making this happen by bringing up her past over and over again, when in fact she would spontaneously shift into childhood memories and deep experiences of family pain that she then stayed in and felt trapped in.

Even though S felt I was a bad analyst providing useless therapy and causing her constant pain, our work made certain important inroads. As mentioned before, S's relationship with her boyfriend was smooth and without much turmoil. Her friends told her she seemed "way more mellow" and "not prone to mood swings anymore". S, in a manner similar to the transference, told me she couldn't understand what they were referring to. Also, she managed to acquire a major promotion at work and felt proud and excited at her new position. Finally, she reported that her mother and she were starting to visit each other on a regular basis and they often got along fine and S felt happy and fulfilled afterwards.

So, S demonstrated important external changes that signified new internal states. However, when her health coverage changed and she would have to pay for treatment out of pocket, she elected to stop. She said she "was done" and "didn't see the point of it" and "was tired of me dragging her back to a bunch of painful memories". In terms of looking at this treatment and assessing it to be analytic or not, the concept of analytic contact is again helpful. The transference was explored and interpreted, even though it was not successfully resolved. The patient's phantasy state and ongoing pattern of internal conflict were investigated and her defenses were confronted and worked with. However, the analyst did most of the work in these areas because S hung onto the transference as reality. S did not want to let go of the transference or even acknowledge it; it just was. This was an unconscious effort to avoid the analytic contact in which we mutually would explore the painful relationship S had with her objects. This would mean not having the sense of total masochistic control over them that she did in the persecutory state she was in. Change would mean loss, lack of control, and acceptance of deep, chronically held grievances.

So, this was a case in which analytic contact was not just resisted but also converted, perverted, and distorted into a replica and reenactment of past trauma. This was a clinical example of what Feldman (2000) has described as a manifestation of the death instinct in which the ego attacks its own sense of reality and judgment, using their now distorted perception as a vehicle for phantasy gratification. Analytic contact was taken over in the service of acting out. As the analyst, I was unable to intervene successfully to resurrect the process from a pathological one-to-one with potential space for exploration. The analytic contact we did establish along the way was hijacked.

Case material 13.5

Todd was thirty-three when he began seeing me for help. He had been feeling depressed for years but suddenly had taken a turn for the worse when his girlfriend found out he was secretly checking her phone bill and then she broke up with him. He had been worried she was seeing other men and had become so insecure that he "just had to find out the truth". It turned out that while they had been casually dating for almost a year, she had never wanted the type of close commitment Todd longed for.

Todd had a history of "wanting to be loved by someone". Over the course of his five-year analysis, at twice-a-week frequency on the couch, I consistently interpreted this need and demand to have someone provide love and parenting for him. Specifically, I focused on how Todd wanted me to be that lover, that unconditional parent, and that magical rescuer for him. But, I was still only "someone" who provided that service. His desperate wish was also a narcissistic desire for someone, anyone, to serve that function for him.

This desire for my love and attention was a wish to be idealized. This was paired with a sense of fragility. It was easy for him to think I didn't love him and was uninterested. In the second session of the week, during the fifth year of analysis, Todd came in and said he felt like he didn't want to come in today. I asked why. He reflected for a bit and said, "I think it has to do with what we talked about last time."

This was a positive sign in that he linked both sessions together, he linked his feelings to the material we had discussed, and he kept the connection between us intact in his mind, even if tenuous. These were signs that he was gradually emerging into the depressive position (Klein 1935) and was seeing himself and his objects in a more integrated manner. However, this was easily corrupted by his manic and reparative wishes that often were tainted by paranoid-schizoid (Klein 1946) phantasies. What I mean is that he relied on manic ways of relating and phantasizing to see himself as always right and never wrong. This was in part to avoid the object's judgment, attack, and abandonment. So, he pictured himself as superior to avoid the loss of approval, love, and connection.

This brings us back to what Todd shared with me. He said, "Last time we met, I was going on and on about how I am furious with people who don't recycle properly, people who don't use their turn signals, and people who don't vote. Then, I told you I thought all those people who lost their homes in the terrible hillside fire last month were stupid for having built their homes in the middle of so much dry grass and they ought to have to pay the fire department for all their work. When you said I was quick to make certain assumptions about them and quick to find them at fault, I felt you were being mean to me. But, later I thought about it a great deal and realized I was being very judgmental and mean. I saw a follow-up news report on the fire and they interviewed some of the families and you are right. They didn't all purposely live in a dangerous area! It was the coming together of a lot of circumstances: the wind, the heat, the lack of rain this year, and someone throwing a cigarette out of their car. But now, I think you have seen the reality of who I am. I am a bad person! If you think that way about me, you won't want to be with me and I look just like anyone else." "Not special in my eyes", I replied. "Yes. That feels lonely", Todd said.

During Todd's analysis, we dealt with his desire to be viewed as perfect so he would be noticed, praised, and loved. There were times he felt I was telling him it was OK to "be deviant and break the rules", which in his eyes meant being an outcast who would not be loved. So, when he was talking about how "dirty" he felt after going out dancing and occasionally picking up a woman and sleeping with her, I would say, "You really are taking yourself to task for that, by the way you are talking. You must worry I disapprove. It is like you are confessing to me your most recent sin." Todd took this as my giving him absolution for his sin. He said, "You make it sound like no big deal. It is like you are condoning that kind of behavior. It kind of scares me. It is like you are telling me that is OK." Based on my understanding of the transference, I said, "It scares you to think its OK to not be a perfect little boy because then Mom and I might not love you."

Here, I was using my knowledge of how he interacted, in phantasy, with his mother, both in the past and currently. This was based on what he told me about his childhood and my knowledge of how he related to me in the transference. Part of this transference was a false image he wanted me to buy into, of a well-behaved little boy who followed the rules and did things right.

This, in his phantasy, would convince me of how good and lovable he was and then I would praise him and be present for him. When I interpreted this, Todd told me, "I have myself convinced that I am perfect and good, but I know what you mean. If I don't do that, I do feel you would be uninterested in me and even want to leave me."

Establishing analytic contact with Todd was, in one respect, an easy matter because of his dependency and his urge to possess and be possessed by his object. He wanted to talk about his feelings toward me and the various meanings of our relationship. This satisfied him on a deep level. He saw it as having me be a nurturing parent as well as a way to be controlling and acquiring. So, while he was more than willing to explore the transference, it was often done in a way that took the transference as fact. Again, Gill's (1979) work on the patient's reluctance to give up the transference is helpful. This is a clinical example in which analytic contact is corrupted into a vehicle for the domination of phantasies and object domination. For Todd, this meant an ongoing way of him acting out a dire feeling of "I need you and I will not loosen my grip on how I see us because then I might have nothing." The difficult aspect of Todd's treatment was to help him question the nature of his transference while working with his fears of my abandonment and his loss of power and perfection. Part of this was his fear of letting go of his idealized mother and to work on how this idealization protected her from his anger and him from her disappointing normality.

While only attending twice a week on the couch, Todd established and maintained a strong analytic contact throughout his treatment. It was the nature of our specific psychoanalytic work together and his particular set of unconscious object-relational phantasies and defenses that allowed this to occur. Kirsner (2001) notes that there is no universal distinction between psychoanalysis "proper" and psychoanalytic therapy. He goes on to propose a less theoretical, more clinical distinction in which "psychoanalytic therapy takes place when the psychoanalytic method is used, when the psychoanalytic stance is adopted" (p. 120).

I would add that the psychoanalytic method, when applied, creates the potential for analytic contact to occur. Then, it is the task of the analyst to explore why and how both parties are fostering or eradicating that analytic contact.

Note

1 It would be interesting to know why, but that is not the focus of my chapter and probably involves personal matters that are best held private.

Summary

Analysts struggle with a great variety of patients in day-to-day private practice. Some of these patients are trapped in internal conflicts over grievances, complaints, and entitlements with their objects and this pattern emerges within the transference (Weintrobe 2004). Others present more depressive concerns and bring the internal confusion, despair, and rage of oedipal struggles into the transference. Successful working through and the co-creation of meaning with the analyst is a sign of current, present-day oedipal resolution of infantile oedipal conflict. This progress can and often does trigger phantasy attacks on the analyst, the analytic couple, and the analytic work (Rusbridger 2004). Therefore, some patients begin their treatment appearing to be higher functioning, but then begin a more primitive and obsessive standoff against growth, change, or attachment within the analytic situation. Indeed, many patients, if not all, display a marked reliance on projective identification at one time or another in their treatment (Waska 2004). This internal method of relating to the object is usually part of a constellation of complex defenses, phantasies, and unconscious bargains with the object that make for complicated and difficult treatments that can stall out, break down, or come to *impasse* unless understood and gradually interpreted (Waska 2005). These different patients often use projective identification as a primary vehicle to avoid their deeper anxieties and unacceptable feelings and thoughts. The gradual and consistent interpretation of the transference is vital, but only fully curative if the vehicle of projective identification is interpreted as well. The analyst serves as translator of this projective stance. How that translating function is used by the patient is critical to the better understanding of deeper phantasies and the analysis of the transference. The relationship between analytic contact and the patient's method of relating to that translating function must be constantly examined for the treatment to be a viable psychoanalytic vehicle for change.

Bion (1962) has explored the concept of alpha-function in which the mother or analyst serves as a modifier, transformer, and container of unorganized, overwhelming, and confusing mental states. These states are, through the alpha-function, transformed into integrated, endurable moments of experience and knowledge. Chaos is turned into knowing. Patients look to the analyst for this and gradually internalize this function as their own. However, some patients see this as unwanted, undesirable, and even dangerous. These patients will use various defenses, including the turning of meaning and symbolism into concrete and ego distant non-meaning, as a way to fight off the alpha-function of psychoanalytic work (Sandler 1997). Again, the patient's reaction to the establishment of symbolism within the transference and in their phantasy world must be part of the treatment investigation, as this reaction so often determines whether analytic contact can be obtained and sustained.

This book has highlighted patients who avoid the analytic contact that psychoanalysis works to establish. Instead, these patients try to enlist the analyst to be the one who does the emotional work of analysis, including the alpha-function, the containment of undesirable affect, the voicing of uncomfortable thoughts and feelings, and the work of point man for all object-related conflicts. The analyst is pushed to be the messenger, the announcer, and the one who faces unwanted psychic reality. Through projective identification, the patient tries to enlist the analyst to be the parent who takes care of the child in every way, without asking for anything in return. Tuckett (1983, 1997), Sandler (1976), and others have noted how that while projective identification is an intra-psychic phenomenon, it is often brought into the external world through various provocative, actualizing, interpersonal dynamics which enlist the analyst to act out the intra-psychic phantasies. The analyst is asked to believe the patient is helpless, unable to voice his own concerns, and in need of a supportive parent figure to step in and take over. This type of projective, interpersonal pull on the analyst can lead to various types of non-helpful supportive actions that promote this pseudo-dependent object relationship.

At times, the analyst will no doubt be drawn into this way of relating to the patient, finding himself or herself voicing the concerns, fears, and aggressions that the patient has him hold. Once the analyst realizes how much love and hate he is holding, enduring, and speaking on behalf of the patient, he can hopefully realize the projective identification dynamic taking place and begin to interpret it rather than play it out. Otherwise, analytic contact will fade and the acting out of archaic object relations will take precedent.

We are the temporary parent for some patients and the translator of unconscious phantasy, but all in the service of helping the patient take a balanced hold of what they either see as too dangerous to touch or that they cling to so hard that they crush in the process. If we notice ourselves clinging to the patient's material too tightly or trying to discharge it too quickly, it is a clue that we are being enlisted to do the dirty work the patient is reluctant to take on themselves.

Psychoanalytic treatment, conducted from a Kleinian framework, links the patient's current psychological experience to early infantile and childhood interactions with the internal and external world (Steiner 2004). As a result of greed, envy, frustration, and desire, the immature ego feels hatred toward the object, resulting in phantasies of an injured or dying object. As a result of identification, to ward off loss and guilt, the entire world seems to collapse and annihilation seems imminent. At that point, the history of contact with good objects is crucial to bring balance to this internal catastrophe. With ample good object experiences, the ego is able to approach and transition to the depressive position. There, mitigating factors such as guilt, integration of love and hate, reparation, restoration and forgiveness, compassion, and acceptance make it possible to make it through those overwhelming anxieties. There is a happy ending to the story. The self and the object are whole, good, and able to tolerate the inconsistencies, disappointments, and flaws that life, self, and others bring.

However, if there has been a lack of good object experience, or if the good object has been tainted with abusive and painful experiences, the ego may not be able to tolerate the natural pain, despair, fear, and rage of living. This causes a breakdown of the internal world in which the very qualities that were potentially growth-enhancing become disabling. Guilt feels very persecutory, reparation seems impossible, hate overcomes love, and compassion seems like a lie. Mutuality or dependence is deadly. The regressive qualities of the paranoid-schizoid position take over, making it feel worse, more ominous. So, the ego tries to block off both methods of relating and simply hides out or sets up a last-ditch standoff against the good object. This often creates a breakdown of analytic contact.

All the patients presented in this book created analytic standoffs in which they felt threatened by the presence of the good object and rebeled against the emergence of goodness and autonomy in themselves. These types of patients often demand magical cures from the analyst as a way to avoid the real, painful work in which they would need to grieve the loss of their ideal vision of perfect objects taking total care of a perfect self. They need to accept the mix of good and bad within themselves and within relationships. Control, rigidity, and unidimensional relating are common, often turning into sadomasochistic power struggles with the analyst if internal change begins to occur. Analytic contact represents a threat to their inner status quo.

The desire for genuine love, of self and with another, is held hostage by the quest for idealized versions of parental figures that were unavailable in the past. For these patients, psychoanalytic contact and working through represent the aborted hope of admiration, rescue, and soothing by a perfect object. In these cases, the patients see a good object or a good self as a poor second choice and therefore fight off the analytic process and contact with the analyst.

A genuine working through and acceptance of mutual dependence combined with independent growth and creativity is essential, yet slow and difficult to obtain. In a successful treatment, states of fluctuating union and separation are gradually integrated to allow for tolerable levels of loss and guilt that do not inhibit growth, striving, and self-expression.

The complicated cases illustrated in this book are typical of the difficult patients analysts see in private practice. They don't have one glaring behavioral symptom to focus on. However, they all have this central psychological theme of avoiding the good object at all costs. Often, the analyst can feel excluded, misrepresented, or ignored in favor of a very distorted transference image. As Brenner (1970) suggests, treatment should proceed as it does with any other case of transference analysis. Yet, I think that focusing on interpretations that address the tangled mixture of paranoid-schizoid features and immature depressive functioning can offer the analyst some degree of direction. Noting and interpreting the defensive, anti-growth use of the death instinct to fight off the life-affirming good object is essential. Also, exploring the way the patient has felt forced to prematurely take care and protect his objects while still under the burden of strong oral wishes and aggressive urges most be exported.

Bringing the patient's transference fight against the good object into the very center of the analytic exploration and working-through process is critical in turning the corner in these difficult cases. The components of analytic contact, intimate mutuality, sharing of deeply held feelings and thoughts, and the examination of the immediate relationship, are often equated with the good object and therefore attacked and shunned.

In many of the cases presented, the patients illustrated a specific mix of phantasies, defenses, and object-related dynamics that made up a psychic shelter or retreat. This retreat unfolds in the transference setting as a fight against the good object of the analyst and the analyst's interpretations. Therefore, the analyst becomes restricted to being seen, heard, and internalized as a force to be avoided, blocked, or defended against. As Steiner (1993) states, these patients seem to simultaneously suffer the anxieties of both paranoid and depressive positions without any respite. There is no clearing, no hiding, no retreat for them. The best they can do is to refuse entrance to goodness, growth, or love while under the sway of their phantasies about the treacherous nature of the good object. Specifically, they see the death instinct as the best method of coping with the constant phantasies of primitive guilt, catastrophic loss, and persecution. This reliance on the death instinct and the intensity of these specific phantasies create a very particular and hard-to-reach psychic shelter in which the ego hides itself in a last-ditch standoff.

Following the Kleinian method, the author uses interpretation as a tool to modify or reduce the patient's anxieties and as a way to explore the unconscious phantasies at play. Frequently, projective identification serves as a vehicle for the patient's phantasies and transference (Waska 2004). This dynamic inevitably draws both patient and analyst into some degree of acting out which in turn must be interpreted. This continuous back-and-forth process provides the foundation for joint learning and the discovery of new knowledge about the patient's mind and personality. This creative aspect of treatment is part of the working through (Hinshelwood 2004) and serves to protect and nurture the ongoing analytic contact.

Once the analyst decides to make an interpretive intervention, it is crucial to observe the consequences. What happens after an interpretation will guide the analyst in understanding the patient's current object relations, the nature of current phantasy states, and how and why projective identification might be the central mode of defense at that moment. All these factors constitute the better understanding of the transference, if not actually comprise the very elements of transference analysis.

Many of the more difficult cases presented in this book represent individuals who have not achieved a full engagement within the depressive position (Klein 1935). These paranoid-schizoid patients are not able to access a secure relationship to an internal object which would alleviate the need for splitting and pathological projections. Frustration tolerance is difficult and separation from the idealized object or the object of the ego's sadistic control is felt to be overwhelming. Togetherness is both hoped and longed for, but also experienced as traumatic and persecutory. Linking thoughts and feelings is threatening, so mutual exploration and reflection with the analyst is seen as dangerous. Therefore, interpretations can be experienced as an assault or as a lack of understanding (Bell 1992). Here, a very core element of analytic contact, interpretations, is viewed by the patient as dangerous and to be avoided. Fortunately, analytic contact is a clinical concept that entails a psychoanalytic approach which is flexible, capable of tolerating and solving many otherwise difficult or impossible moments.

Some of the other patients presented in this book represent more neurotic, depressive cases that involved a fear of damaging one's object, guilt, and a need to serve and please at the cost of independence and autonomy. While these individuals displayed a better degree of frustration tolerance and inner integration, projective identification was still a factor in their attempts to deny certain anxieties by projecting unacceptable or unresolved feelings into their external relationships.

In psychoanalysis, the aim is to uncover the deeper meaning behind seemingly ordinary comments. By doing so, we quickly encountered the underlying transference and in many cases this projective identification process that fuels the transference phantasies.

The analyst needs to always be aware of his or her possible collusion, with both paranoid and depressive patients, in the avoidance of transference and projective identification dynamics. For all patients, the careful and systematic analysis of the transference is essential for the modification of their internal world. Change and growth are in direct ratio to the ongoing interpretation of the projective identification cycles in the relationship and the overall transference climate.

The main elements the psychoanalytic literature has identified as common in addictions were certainly present in the cases I presented in which drugs were an issue. Difficulty in affect tolerance, object substitution, narcissistic rage, and compromise solutions around issues of powerlessness were all elements in the analytic work. However, there was also another factor that shaped the internal lives of these individuals. As Rosenfeld (1960) noted, there is a depressive aspect of the ego that is combined and often overshadowed by paranoid dynamics. Specifically, I think the ego is operating within phantasies of an object that is injured, weak, and needing care as well as disappointing, intimidating, withholding, and aggressive. Actual historical experiences with parents who were prone to fluctuating moods, needy and demanding ways, as well as volatile and controlling manners combine with the ego's strong infantile cycles of projective identification and splitting. Forced to face and deal with objects that must be cared for and forgiven, manic defenses and pathological identification are also used to cope. These internal and external experiences mix to create a rigid method of dealing with objects that is highlighted by approach–retreat cycles, passive–aggressive standoffs, retaliation strategies, and a desire to control others through a pattern of strict anti-growth and anti-change ways of relating.

This approach–avoid transference translates into an intra-psychic stance in which the patient longs for a soothing, quick-fix-drug type of love from the analyst and retreats from the more genuine yet vulnerable aspects of analytic contact that constitute the mutual exploration and relational honesty making up psychoanalytic treatment.

A wish to heal the self and stop the addiction is initially helpful in bringing the patient into treatment, but this often switches to paranoid feelings of being forced to "be better" which can be traced to resentful feelings about having to heal and serve the object.

Many addicts, as well as other difficult patients who are not troubled with drug problems, exhibit the particular mix of paranoid and depressive dynamics found in cases presented. Steiner (1993) has explored patients who find a respite or psychic retreat between the two psychological states. I am noting the cases in which the patients have not been able to successfully integrate the paranoid position and were compelled to negotiate the depressive position prematurely. They end up faced with the more pathological aspects of both positions and attempt to emotionally escape by avoiding, disconnecting, and refusing contact with the object in a desperate attempt to free themselves from the burden of their own conflicts and the pressures of an unpredictable, unsafe object. Drugs provide one temporary method of hiding from the object and preventing attachment or growth, both of which are seen as threatening. Therefore, addiction can be understood as a specific form of psychic retreat. Drug addiction and the psychic retreat it engenders make progress in psychoanalysis difficult. However, the clinical stance of analytic contact enables the analyst and the patient to have a fair go at it and often find a foothold in which to reach the underlying issues and slowly change.

The psychoanalytic method, as defined by analytic contact, is well suited to many individuals seeking help with problems that at first glance appear external and behaviorally maladaptive (Sulzberger-Wittenberg 1970). With exploration, deeper psychological issues are revealed that fuel the destructive behavior. Patient, consistent interpretation of the internal phantasies, feelings, and defenses that produce these addictions and interpersonal drama provides relief from paranoid and depressive anxieties. This leads to a better understanding of the addiction and a start to eliminating it.

With this analytic understanding and the support of ongoing transference interpretation, growth and change become possible. The addictions create great difficulties for both patient and analyst and demand a level of perseverance that patient and analyst cannot always bear. However, if the psychoanalytic method is utilized, the basis for the destructive, addictive cycle is better understood. Then, the direction of what is needed is more clear and the chances of change become more within reach. While these difficult cases are not always salvageable, the psychoanalytic method, as practiced within the realm of analytic contact, provides the patient hope, support, and a strong opportunity for a shift in the addictive process. This is a shift not only in the external symptoms but the underlying psychological base of the problem. The analyst must realize these are complex cases that often fail or only show partial resolution. This should not be cause for counter-transference despair, but merely a confirmation that we often work in the trenches with the most trying of human suffering and don't always see transformation or a complete turnaround in our day-to-day private practice experiences. But, we can offer a hand to these patients during a most painful period of their life.

While self-injury and substance abuse are difficult symptoms for both analyst and patient to cope with, and relapses are frequent, the emphasis does not have to be on managing crisis. The initial ego support and therapeutic boundary setting in these difficult cases must be matched by psychoanalytic exploration. In working with these patients, I find that through mutual projective identification processes, the analyst and the patient are frequently resurrecting certain aspects of the patient's archaic phantasy life as defined by various self and object representations. Therefore, the continuous analysis of the transference and the counter-transference is certainly essential. However, the additional willingness on the part of the analyst and the patient to explore the frequent and mutual interpersonal–intra-psychic acting out is paramount. This is a cornerstone of the clinical approach of analytic contact.

The book's case material has shown the various ways patient's transference and phantasy processes are constantly in motion and how these phantasies are constantly shaped by reality factors. Mental functions, including phantasy, are woven into and around all internal and external factors; this allows the analyst many chances to gather information as to the exact nature of the patient's psychic structure and the accompanying phantasy elements. The analyst is then in a position to make usable interpretations and begin to unravel the phantasy material in the context of the clinical transference and the projective identification processes that are ubiquitous to the analytic relationship.

Through the clinical material, Kleinian technique is shown as helpful in a variety of analytic situations, within the flexibility of analytic contact. Projective identification is often the leading mental mechanism patients employ within the transference setting. Therefore, the interpretation of projective identification is essential and figures prominently in any discussion of technique. Melanie Klein offered fairly specific theoretical concepts on how the mind functions and how anxieties shape internal dynamics. Her method of treatment and her theory of mental processes provide the clinician with a clear map of how to proceed. This set of guidelines is flexible enough to be applied in a way that takes into account the complexity and uniqueness of each patient–analyst pair. In this sense, the elasticity of analytic contact is compatible with the comprehensive approach of contemporary Kleinian technique.

Patients in the depressive position relate to whole objects that have a certain lasting quality to them. The ego's aggression is balanced and the object can tolerate it and bounce back. The stabilized ego projects its own remorse and guilt into the object and finds a forgiving and trusting object in return. Love and trust are projected and introjected. Disputes occur and relationships have pain, but things can be counted on and wounds heal.

In the paranoid-schizoid position, internal experiences are more frightening and fragmented. Splitting protects the fragile nature of the early ego and its part objects. Good is separated from bad until the ego is stable enough to withstand its own ambivalence and stormy relations to itself and other objects. Oral aggression, envy, and the intense desires to unite with and own the mother's body place stress on the splitting process. These instinctual forces can drive the ego to use excessive and destructive forms of projective identification. This type of projective identification, aimed at achieving union with the idealized object, can break down the process of splitting and lead to destruction of the ideal object. The ego is left with the bad aspects of the object and self-fragmentation. The internal experience is one of loss. The ego loses the ideal object, which is replaced by a bad, persecutory object. Within the paranoid-schizoid position, this leads to ego de-stabilization and feelings of annihilation. Therefore, this experience of loss in the paranoid-schizoid position is quite different than the type of partial loss and restoration encountered in the depressive position.

Paranoid-schizoid loss is complete and leaves no hope. The threat is to the ego, not to the object. Not only is restitution unavailable, but the loss is automatically followed by the arrival of an angry or rejecting persecutory object. A two-fold sequence of loss and attack bring the ego to a state of fragmentation and implosion.

In analytic treatment, patients experiencing these states of loss and persecution can develop near-intractable transference conflicts. The work is slow and the patient often has difficulty staying in treatment. Hope is absent and the analyst is felt to be a constant threat. Analytic contact is difficult to maintain in these settings, but crucial to consistently reach for. In the successful cases, this involves a slow process of exploring these frightening phantasies, via examination of projective identification and splitting within the transference. Acting out is frequent.

Interpretation is helpful in two specific ways. First it serves as an ongoing detoxifier of projective materials and secondly it represents a potential new object for the patient's ego to introject. This of course entails a working through of the particular ways that the new object will be experienced as lost and then returning as bad. This is the essence of the working-through process and is a lengthy task. Once in the depressive position, mourning may present a significant threat, enough that regression to paranoid-schizoid defenses is evoked.

The case material in this book shows the three overlapping phases of treatment that occur with some borderline, narcissistic, or psychotic patients. These patients are dealing with paranoid-schizoid experiences of the self and the object. In this part-self, part-object world, many shifting, opposing, and contrary states of feeling and thought occur.

Acting out is the first phase of analytic treatment. This is an externalization of persecutory anxiety, primitive guilt, and phantasies of annihilation. Projective identification, splitting, and denial are common and tend to make for difficult transference and counter-transference problems.

During the middle phase of treatment, pathological superego states and manifestations of the death instinct color the analysis. The death instinct reacts defensively to the sadistic superego. Technically, the destructive internal conflicts created by these two elements must be clarified and interpreted in the transference. Flexible analytic management and containment is a crucial supplement to ongoing interpretation. If these chaotic patients are able to stay in treatment for a period of time, the acting out and the superego/death instinct phase gradually give way to phantasies of loss. This is still a paranoid-schizoid perspective of loss, making it a persecutory experience. While depressive anxieties do enter the picture, these still involve pathological and destructive states of guilt and all-or-nothing threats of abandonment and attack.

Many patients have the occasional feeling of being influenced by outside forces. Indeed, it is a reality of life that we are all influenced in some degree by the good fortunes of life as well as the slings and arrows of misfortune. Some patients are driven by strong phantasies of influence and view themselves as virtually controlled and manipulated by most of life. Many psychotic patients struggle with primitive phantasies of persecutory guilt, loss, and annihilation. These phantasies are difficult for both patient and analyst to bear, but hopefully are explored within the transference and reshaped into something more tolerable, fulfilling, and creative.

Susan Isaacs (1948) viewed phantasy as the bridge between the instinctual and the psyche. Additionally, phantasy involves complex relations between self and object linked by affect and thought. Libidinal and aggressive conflicts are played out within this intra-psychic arena. Projective identification is the most basic method of discourse for this intra-psychic exchange. For some patients, the need to evacuate the unmanageable aspects of self and/or object leads to a concretization of conflict in the external environment. At its extreme, this results in the lack of symbolic function.

During treatment with these types of patients, the analyst is frequently called on to struggle with, detoxify, and translate the patient's projections into something less anxiety-producing or disorganizing. This is often the most difficult aspect of the treatment, as patients do not want to take the projected parts of self or object back. They feel threatened by re-internalizing them. Analytic contact involves consistent interpretations regarding this refusal of new knowledge and self-reflection. These patient's fight off the ownership of these unwanted aspects of their personality. Therefore, they often react to these interpretations with acting out and other defensive maneuvers.

With many psychotic patients, their core anxiety centers around issues of primitive guilt. This is a paranoid-schizoid experience of persecutory guilt, where the object retaliates with revenge. The ego's oral aggression attacks the idealized object and converts it into a dangerous betrayer. Due to the nature of idealization, the object is fragile to begin with and easily toppled by the ego's demands. Without a supportive and containing good object, the ego feels fragmented and anticipates annihilation. In order to be effective, psychoanalytic treatment must address these fears of persecutory loss and primitive guilt in order to slowly contain and modify the patient's psychotic phantasies. Regardless of frequency, use of couch, type of termination, or severity of diagnosis, analytic contact is focused on the clinical exploration of these phantasies and the ways they emerge within the transference.

Many hard-to-reach patients struggle with strong phantasies of persecution, loss, and primitive guilt. As illustrated with abundant case material, borderline, narcissistic, and psychotic patients exhibit three overlapping phases of internal and externalized part-object relations. Acting out is the focus of their early transference dynamics. If gradually contained, this phase shifts to a battle between certain ego–object relations and the dynamics of a defensive death instinct. Once worked through, these patients show more core issues of loss and fear of annihilation. Analytic contact is about the specific focus on and understanding of these deep phantasies, regardless of external factors that may or may not assist in the healing process.

In conclusion, the ageless debate about what defines genuine psychoanalysis need not impede the clinical space. Utilizing interpretation and analytic exploration, analytic contact can be cultivated and sustained. The analyst must examine and work with all transference or countertransference attempts to corrupt or pervert analytic contact. A better way of defining the differences in treatment modalities (psychoanalytic versus therapy versus counseling) might be to ask whether analytic contact has been established and maintained or whether it is avoided, lost, or stolen by the patient's or analyst's intra-psychic and interpersonal stance.

Tuckett (2005) states that psychic reality is a constant effort to manage unbearable affect that occurs over the conflicts between love and hate. In this book, I have highlighted the way in which that management of unbearable affect can come in the form of attacks on analytic contact which reduce the treatment to something less than analytic. And, the analyst's job therefore becomes the interpretation of the patient's efforts to either foster or disengage from analytic contact. Again, I use the word contact to emphasize the critical component of inter-psychic contact between the patient and their objects and the interpersonal exploration of that contact. I believe this is the optimal clinical definition of what constitutes psychoanalytic work, rather than frequency or use of couch, and also informs us how to understand cases that either don't get off the ground and flounder or turn into a more supportive counseling situation. Feldman (2000) touches on this when he describes patients who seek to distort or erase their capacity for reflection and perception, sometimes to bring themselves to a state of inertia and other times to restructure their experience in a new and perverse way. I think this clinical manifestation of the death instinct is also an example of how the patient can determine what sort of treatment is taking place. If the transference is such that unconscious efforts are made to strip the analytic relationship of any meaningful contact, the deeper, more informative process of psychoanalysis can be rendered impossible. This is where the analyst has to be constantly vigilant, interpreting the patient's fears, aggression, and overall avoidance of the very things that constitute analytic healing.

There have been many inquiries and debates in the field of psychoanalysis as to the relevant importance of setting, frequency, diagnosis, use of couch, and length of analysis in determining if a healing, intra-psychic psychoanalytic experience has taken place between patient and analyst. Merton Gill, particularly in his writings from 1979 onwards, has taken a theoretical stance that pushes past these stagnant debates and the professional infighting to make a bold statement about what should be considered analytic about psychoanalysis.

Caper (1997) states, "Analysis of the transference in the analytic relationship allows patients to experience their role in the formation of their experience of the world, 'live' and as it happens. This promotes the integration of the patient's personality" (p. 18). He goes on to discuss how the resolution of transference is the resolution of confusion between internal and external reality. In describing his approach to the analysis of the transference, Caper states that successful analysis of phantasy and transference places patients in contact with their role in forming their experience of the world and their shaping of their relationships with their objects.

Caper's view of transference and its working through is helpful when considering analytic contact. Caper mentions nothing about frequency, diagnosis, use of couch, and so on. He is simply addressing the psychological goals and analytic process that take place within the relationship between patient and analyst. I think this is the core of what makes a procedure psychoanalytic. Analytic contact is the embodiment of these concepts and clinical tasks. The analyst assists the patient in understanding the differences between external and internal, points out the conflicts the patient has in making that realization, and shows how those conflicts are lived out in the therapeutic relationship. This is analytic contact. Frequency and use of couch may sometimes help facilitate it, but are only adjunct factors to what is truly a relational journey.

A growing number of analysts (Sechaud 2000) believe there is no useful theoretical difference between psychoanalysis and psychoanalytic psychotherapy when the same treatment process can be identified in both modalities. Suman and Brgnone (2001) noted that what is crucial in these debates is that the setting, whatever one wishes to call it, is one that promotes, allows, and maintains the analytic process. I would add that the nature of the transference must be examined as a factor in what promotes, allows, and maintains analytic contact. The setting must include the transference and counter-transference as aspects of what may help or hinder the growth of analytic contact. This thought is echoed in Carere's (1999) paper on the differences between uncovering and remaking treatments. He distinguishes them as attempts to either maintain neutrality and allow an analytic process to unfold or a directive stance aimed at changing the patient in some form determined by the analyst. I would argue that uncovering treatments are those in which analytic contact is promoted by the application of the standard analytic method of interpretation and transference exploration while remaking is often the result of pathological or perverse analytic contact that has been unnoticed and uninterpreted, leading to acting out by the analyst, under the disguise or justification of remaking the patient.

Aisenstein (2001) came to the conclusion that comparing or contrasting psychoanalysis with psychoanalytic psychotherapy is useless because "they are mere variations on a single method, based on the same theoretical environment and with the same aims" (p. 31). Here, I would add that if the aim in a procedure is to create, cultivate, and encourage analytic contact, the procedure is psychoanalytic and the treatment deserves to be called psychoanalysis.

References

Ablon, J. (2005a) On Psychoanalytic Process, *American Journal of Psychoanalysis*, 53: 2, 541–68

Ablon, J. (2005b) Reply to Blatt and Fonagy, *American Journal of Psychoanalysis*, 53: 2, 591–5

Aisenstein, M. (2001) Psychoanalytic Psychotherapy Does Not Exist, in *Psychoanalysis and Psychotherapy: The Controversies and the Future*. London: Karnac, pp. 19–31

Bader, M. (1993) Adaptive Sadomasochism and Psychological Growth, *Psychoanalytic Dialogues*, 3: 279–300

Bell, D. (1992) Hysteria: A Contemporary Kleinian Perspective, *British Journal of Psychotherapy*, 9: 2, 169–80

Bell, D. (2001) Projective Identification, in *Kleinian Theory: A Contemporary Perspective*, ed. Catalina Bronstein. London: Whurr Publications, pp. 125–47

Bicudo, V. (1964) Persecutory Guilt and Ego Restrictions: Characterizations of a Pre-depressive Position, *International Journal of Psychoanalysis*, 45: 358–63

Bion, W. (1959) Attacks on Linking, *International Journal of Psychoanalysis*, 30: 308–15

Bion, W. (1962) *Learning from Experience*. London: Heinemann

Bion, W. R. (1967) *Second Thoughts*. New York: Jason Aronson

Brenner, C. (1970) Panel: Negative Therapeutic Reaction; Olinick, S, reporter; *Journal of the American Psychoanalytic Association*, 18: 655–72

Brenner, C. (1987) Working Through: 1914–1984, *Psychoanalytic Quarterly*, 56: 88–108

Britton, R. (1998) *Belief and Imagination*. London: Routledge, pp. 1–7

Caper, R. (1992) Does Psychoanalysis Heal? A Contribution to the Theory of Psychoanalytic Technique, *International Journal of Psychoanalysis*, 73: 283–92

Caper, R. (1997) Psychic Reality and the Interpretation of Transference, *Psychoanalytic Quarterly*, 66: 18–33

Capozzi, P. and De Masi, F. (2001) The Meaning of Dreams in the Psychotic State: Theoretical Considerations and Clinical Applications, *International Journal of Psychoanalysis*, 82: 5, 933–952

Carere, T. (1999) Copper, Gold, Platinum, panel discussion with the Italian Psychoanalytic Association on Psychoanalysis and Psychotherapy, held 12/5/1999

Carey, F. (2002) Singular Attention: Some Once-a-Week Therapies, in *Challenges to Practice*, ed. B. Bishop. London: Karnac Books, pp. 43–59

Cherry, S. *et al.* (2004) Psychoanalytic Practice in the Early Postgraduate Years, *Journal of the American Psychoanalytic Association*, 52: 3, 851–71

Der Leeuw, P. (1980) 'Modern Times' and the Psychoanalyst Today, *International Review of Psychoanalysis*, 7: 137–45

Dewald, P. (1976) Transference Regression and Real Experience in the Psychoanalytic Process, *Psychoanalytic Quarterly*, 45: 213–30

Dodes, L. (1990) Addiction, Helplessness, and Narcissistic Rage, *Psychoanalytic Quarterly*, 59: 398–419

Dodes, L. (1996) Compulsion and Addiction, *Journal of the American Psychoanalytic Association*, 44: 815–35

Doidge, N., Simon, B., Gillies, L., *et al.* (1994) Characteristics of Psychoanalytic Patients under a Nationalized Health Plan: DSM-3-R Diagnosis, Previous Treatment, and Childhood Trauma, *American Journal of Psychiatry*, 151: 586–90

Feldman, M. (1992) The Manifestation of the Object in the Transference, *Bulletin of the European Psychoanalytic Federation*, 39: 69–75

Feldman, M. (1993) Aspects of Reality and the Focus of Interpretation, *Psychoanalytic Inquiry*, 13: 4, 274–95

Feldman, M. (1997) Projective Identification: The Analyst's Involvement, *International Journal of Psychoanalysis*, 78: 227–41

Feldman, M. (2000) Some Manifestations of the Death Instinct, *International Journal of Psychoanalysis*, 81: 53–67

Fenichel (1939) Problems of Psychoanalytic Technique, *Psychoanalytic Quarterly*, 8: 438–70

Fisher, N. (2004a) The State of the Association, *American Psychoanalyst*, 38: 1, 3

Fisher, N. (2004b) Preaching What We Practice: The Psychotherapy Initiative, *American Psychoanalyst*, 38: 1, 31

Fox, M. (2004) Practicing What We Preach, the Psychotherapy Initiative, *American Psychoanalyst*, 38: 1, 30

Freud, S. (1914) *Remembering, Repeating, and Working-Through (Further Recommendations on the Technique of Psychoanalysis 2)*, S.E. 12

Freud, S. (1920) A Child is Being Beaten: A Contribution to the Study of the Origin of Sexual Perversions, *International Journal of Psychoanalysis*, 1: 371–95

Freud, S. (1930) *Civilization and its Discontents*, S.E. 21

Freud, S. (1937) *Analysis Terminable and Interminable*, S.E. 23

Gabbard, G. (2004) *Long Term Psychodynamic Psychotherapy: A Basic Text*. London: American Psychiatric Press

Galatariotou, C. (2000) "Psychoanalysis, Psychoanalytic Psychotherapy and Supportive Psychotherapy: Contemporary Controversies" by Otto F. Kernberg, A Review, *International Journal of Psychoanalysis*, 81: 385–401

Gibeault, A. in Galatariotou, C. (2000) Review of Psychoanalysis, Psychoanalytic Psychotherapy, and Supportive Psychotherapy by Otto Kernberg, *International Journal of Psychoanalysis*, 81: 385–401

Gifford, S. (2005) Psychoanalysis in Northern America from 1998 to the Present, in *Textbook of Psychoanalysis*, ed. E. Person, A. Cooper, and G. Gabbard. London: American Psychiatric Press, ch. 25, pp. 387–404

Gill, M. (1979) The Analysis of the Transference, *Journal of the American Psychoanalytic Association*, 27(S): 263–88

Gill, M. (1994) *Psychoanalysis in Transition: A Personal View*. London: Analytic Press

Goldberg, S. and Grusky, Z. (2004) The Dark Side of Analytic Conviction, *Journal of the American Psychoanalytic Association*, 25: 4, 1095–125

Greenson, R. (1965) The Problem of Working Through, in *Drives, Affects, Behavior, Essays in Memory of Marie Bonaparte*, Vol. 2, ed. M. Scour. New York: International Universities Press, pp. 277–314

Grinberg, L. (1977) An Approach to the Understanding of Borderline Disorders, in *Borderline Personality Disorders*, ed. Peter Hartocollis. New York: International University Press, pp. 123–41

Grinberg, L. (1979) Countertransference and Projective Counteridentification, *Contemporary Psychoanalysis*, 15: 226–47

Grossman, W. (1991) Pain, Aggression, Fantasy, and Concepts of Sadomasochism, *Psychoanalytic Quarterly*, 60: 22–51

Grossman, L. (1993) The Perverse Attitude toward Reality, *Psychoanalytic Quarterly*, 62: 422–36

Hargreaves, E. and Varchevker, A. (2004) *In Pursuit of Psychic Change: The Betty Joseph Workshop*. London: Brunner-Routledge

Harris, A. (2005) Transference, Countertransference, and the Real Relationship, in *Textbook of Psychoanalysis*, ed. E. S. Person, A. M. Cooper, and G. O. Gabbard. London: American Psychiatric Press, ch. 13, pp. 201–16

Hasui, C. and Kitamuca, T. (2004) Aggression and Guilt during Mourning by Parents Who Lost an Infant, *Bulletin of the Menninger Clinic*, 68: 3, 245–59

Hess, N. (1999) Psychoanalytic Psychotherapy for Chronic Depression, in *Psychoanalytic Psychotherapy in the Kleinian Tradition*, ed. S. Ruszczynski and S. Johnson. London: Karnac Books, pp. 117–34

Hinshelwood, R. (2004) Contrasting Clinical Techniques: A British Kleinian, a Contemporary Freudian, and a Latin American Kleinian Discuss Clinical Material: A Panel Discussion, *International Journal of Psychoanalysis*, 85: 5, 1257–60

Isaacs, S. (1948) The Nature and Function of Phantasy, *International Journal of Psychoanalysis*, 29: 73

Johnson, B. (1999) Three Perspectives on Addiction, *Journal of the American Psychoanalytic Association*, 47: 791–815

Jones, E. E. (1993) How Will Psychoanalysis Study Itself? *Journal of the American Psychoanalytic Association*, 41(S): 91–108

Jones, E. E. (1997) Modes of Therapeutic Action, *International Journal of Psycho-Analysis*, 78: 1135–50

Joseph, B. (1975) The Patient Who is Difficult to Reach, in *Tactics and Techniques in Psychoanalytic Therapy*, vol. 2, ed. P. Giovacchini. New York: Jason Aronson, pp. 205–16

Joseph, B. (1978) Different Types of Anxiety and their Handling in the Analytic Situation, *International Journal of Psychoanalysis*, 59: 223–8

Joseph, B (1983) On Understanding and not Understanding: Some Technical Issues, *International Journal of Psychoanalysis*, 64: 291–8

Joseph, B. (1985) Transference: The Total Situation, *International Journal of Psychoanalysis*, 66: 447–54

Joseph, B. (1988) Object Relations in Clinical Practice, *Psychoanalytic Quarterly*, 57: 626–42

Joseph, B. (1989) *Psychic Equilibrium and Psychic Change: Selected Papers of Betty Joseph*. London: Routledge, p. 157

Joseph, B. (1992) Psychic Change: Some Perspectives, *International Journal of Psychoanalysis*, 73: 237–43

Joseph, B. (2000) Agreeableness as Obstacle, *International Journal of Psychoanalysis*, 81: 641–9

Joseph, B. (2001) *Transference, in Kleinian Theory: A Contemporary Perspective*, ed. Catalina Bronstein. London: Whurr Publications, pp. 181–92

Kernberg, O. (1996) Thirty Methods to Destroy the Creativity of Psychoanalytic Candidates, *International Journal of Psychoanalysis*, 77: 1031–40

Kernberg, O. (1999) Psychoanalysis, Psychoanalytic Psychotherapy and Supportive Psychotherapy, *International Journal of Psychoanalysis*, 80: 1075–91

Kirsner, D. (2001) Off the Radar Screen, in *Psychoanalysis and Psychotherapy: The Controversies and the Future*. London: Karnac, pp. 111–21

Klein, M. (1921) The Development of a Child, in *Love, Guilt and Reparation and Other Works, The Writings of Melanie Klein*, vol. 1. New York: Free Press, 1–53

Klein, M. (1926) The Psychological Principles of Early Analysis, *The Writings of Melanie Klein*, vol. 1. New York: Free Press

Klein, M. (1927) Criminal Tendencies in Normal Children, *The Writings of Melanie Klein*, vol. 1. New York: Free Press

Klein, M. (1935) A Contribution to the Psychogenesis of Manic-Depressive States, The Writings of Melanie Klein, in *Love, Guilt, and Reparation and Other Works 1921–1945, The Writings of Melanie Klein*, vol. 1. London: Free Press, p. 262

Klein, M. (1946) Notes on Some Schizoid Mechanisms, *The Writings of Melanie Klein*, vol. 3. London: Hogarth Press, pp. 1–24

Klein, M. (1950) On the Criteria for the Termination of an Analysis, in *Melanie Klein: Envy and Gratitude and Other Works 1946–1963*. London: Free Press, p. 46

Klein, M. (1955) On Identification, *The Writings of Melanie Klein*, vol. 3. New York: Free Press

Klein, M. (1959) Our Adult World and Its Roots in Infancy, *The Writings of Melanie Klein*, vol. 3. New York: Free Press

Klein, M. (1961) Narrative of a Child Analysis, *The Writings of Melanie Klein*, vol. 3. New York: Free Press

Laplanche, J. and Pontalis, J.-B. (1973) *The Language of Psychoanalysis*. New York: Norton Books

Leichsenring, F., Biskup, J., Kreishe, R., *et al.* (2005) The Gottingen Study of Psychotherapy, *International Journal of Psychoanalysis*, 86: 2, 433–55

Meyer, L (2004) Contrasting Clinical Techniques: A British Kleinian, a Contemporary Freudian, and a Latin American Kleinian Discuss Clinical Material: A Panel Discussion, *International Journal of Psychoanalysis*, 85: 5, 1257–60

Mitchel, S. (1995) Interaction In the Kleinian and Interpersonal Traditions, *Contemporary Psychoanalysis*, 31: 65–90

O'Shaughnessy, E (1983) Words and Working Through, *International Journal of Psychoanalysis*, 64: 281–9

Rangell, L. (1996) The "Analytic" in Psychoanalytic Treatment: How Analysis Works, *Psychoanalytic Inquiry*, 16: 140–66

Rey, J. (1994) *Universals of Psychoanalysis in the Treatment of Psychotic and Borderline States*. London: Free Association Books

Riesenberg-Malcolm, R. (1986) Interpretation: The Past in the Present, *International Journal of Psychoanalysis*, 13: 433–43

Riesenberg-Malcolm, R. (1995) The Rationale of Interpretation: What, Where, When, *International Journal of Psychoanalysis*, 76: 447–56

Riviere, J. (1991) *Joan Riviere: the Inner World and Joan Riviere*, ed. Athol Hughes. London: Karnac Books

Rosenfeld, H. (1960) On Drug Addiction, *International Journal of Psychoanalysis*, 41: 467–75

Rothstein, A. (1991) Sadomasochism in the Neuroses Conceived of as a Pathological Compromise Formation, *Journal of the American Psychoanalytic Association*, 39: 363–75

Rusbridger, R. (2004) Elements of the Oedipus Complex: A Kleinian Account, *International Journal of Psychoanalysis*, 85: 3, 731–47

Safá-Gerard, B. (1998) Bearable and Unbearable Guilt: A Kleinian Perspective, *Psychoanalytic Quarterly*, 67: 351–78

Sandler, J. (1976) Countertransference and Role-Responsiveness, *International Review of Psychoanalysis*, 3: 43–7

Sandler, P. (1997) The Apprehension of Psychic Reality: Extensions of Bion's Theory of Alpha-Function, *International Journal of Psychoanalysis*, 78: 43–52

Schafer, R. (2003) *Bad Feelings*. New York: Other Press

Sechaud, E. (2000) Affective Self-Disclosure by the Analyst, *International Journal of Psycho-Analysis*, 81: 164–5

Segal, H (1967) Melanie Klein's Technique, in *Psychoanalytic Techniques*, ed. B. Wolman. New York: Basic Books, pp. 168–90

Segal, H. (1974) *An Introduction to the Work of Melanie Klein*. New York: Basic Books, pp. 27–8, 68–9

Segal, H (1982) Early Infantile Development as Reflected in the Psychoanalytic Process: Steps in Integration, *International Journal of Psychoanalysis*, 63: 15–21

Segal, H (2001) Yesterday, Today, and Tomorrow, Inaugural lecture for the opening of the Centre for the Advancement fo Psychoanalytic Studies, available at www.melanie-klein-trust.org.uk/segal2002.htm

Spillius, E. (2004) Melanie Klein Revisited: Her Unpublished Thoughts on Technique, on the Melanie Klein Trust Website, at www.melanie-klein-trust.org.uk/spillius2004.htm

Steiner, J. (1984) Some Reflections on the Analysis of the Transference: A Kleinian View, *Psychoanalytic Inquiry*, 4: 443–63

Steiner, J. (1993) *Psychic Retreats: Pathological Organizations in Psychotic, Neurotic, and Borderline Patients*. London: Routledge

Steiner, J (1996) The Aim of Psychoanalysis in Theory and In Practice, *International Journal of Psychoanalysis*, 77: 1073–83

Steiner, J. (2004) Gaze, Dominance, and Humiliation in the Schreber Case, *International Journal of Psychoanalysis*, 85: 269–84

Steiner, J. (2005) The Conflict between Mourning and Melancholia, *Psychoanalytic Quarterly*, 74: 1, 83–104

Strachey, J. (1937) Panel Discussion, *International Journal of Psychoanalysis*, 5: 18

Sulkowicz, K. (2004) Is the Couch Just a Couch?, *Psychiatric News*, 39: 6, 11

Sulzberger-Wittenberg, I. (1970) *Psychoanalytic Insight and Relationships: A Kleinian Approach*. London: Routledge and Kegan Paul

Suman, A. and Brgnone, A. (2001) Psychoanalytic Psychotherapy and Psychoanalysis: A Choice in Step with the Times, in *Psychoanalysis and Psychotherapy: The Controversies and the Future*. London: Karnac, pp. 91–109

Tuckett, D. (1983) Words and the Psychoanalytical Interaction, *International Review of Psychoanalysis*, 10: 407–13

Tuckett, D. (1997) Mutual Enactment in the Psychoanalytic Situation, in *The Perverse Transference and Other Matters: Essays in Honor of R. Horacio Etchegoyen*, ed. J. Ahumada, O. Olagaray, A. K. Richards, *et al.* New York: Jason Aronson, pp. 203–16

Tuckett, D. (2005) Psychoanalysis in Great Britain and Continental Europe, in *Textbook of Psychoanalysis*, ed. E. S. Person, A. M. Cooper, and G. O. Gabbard. London: American Psychiatric Press, ch. 26, pp. 407–21

Valenstein, A. (1983) Working Through and Resistance to Change: Insight and the Action System, *Bulletin of the American Psychoanalytic Association*, 31: 353–73

Volkan, K. (1994) *Addiction from an Object Relations Perspective*. New York: Peter Lang Publishing

Waska, R. (1999) Bargains, Treaties, and Delusions, *Journal of the American Academy of Psychoanalysis*, 27: 3, 451–69

Waska, R. (2002) *Primitive Experiences of Loss: Working with the Paranoid-Schizoid Patient*. London: Karnac

Waska, R. (2004) *Projective Identification: The Kleinian Interpretation*. London: Brunner/Routledge

Waska, R. (2005) *Real People, Real Problems, Real Solutions: The Kleinian Approach to Difficult Patients*. London: Brunner/Routledge

Waska, R. (2006) *The Danger of Change: The Kleinian Approach with Patients who Experience Progress as Trauma*. London: Brunner/Routledge

Weintrobe, S. (2004) Links Between Grievance, Complaints, and Different Forms of Entitlement, *International Journal of Psychoanalysis*, 85: 1, 83–96

Williams, G. (1997) Reflections on Some Dynamics of Eating Disorders: 'No Entry' Defences and Foreign Bodies, *International Journal of Psychoanalysis*, 78: 927–41

Further reading

Arlow, J. (1985) The Concept of Psychic Reality and Related Problems, *Journal of the American Psychoanalytic Association*, 33: 521–35

Asch, S. (1976) Varieties of Negative Therapeutic Reaction and Problems of Technique, *Journal of the American Psychoanalytic Association*, 24: 383–407

Bader, M. (1993) Adaptive Sadomasochism and Psychological Growth, *Psychoanalytic Dialogues*, 3: 279–300

Freud, S. (1923) *The Ego and the Id.* S.E., 19: 3–66

Grinberg, L. (1964) Two Kinds of Guilt: Their Relations with Normal and Pathological Aspects of Mourning, *International Journal of Psychoanalysis*, 45: 366–71

Grotstein, J. (1977) The Psychoanalytic Concept of Schizophrenia: 1. The Dilemma, *International Journal of Psychoanalysis*, 58: 403–25

Joseph, B. (1982) Addiction to Near Death, *International Journal of Psychoanalysis*, 63: 449–56

Klein, M. (1940) Mourning and Its Relationship to Manic-Depressive States, *The Writings of Melanie Klein*, vol. 1. London: Hogarth Press, pp. 34–69

Klein, M. (1952) The Origins of Transference, *International Journal of Psychoanalysis*, 33; reprinted in *The Writings of Melanie Klein*, vol. 3 (1975). London: Hogarth Press, pp. 48–56

Klein, M. (1952) Some Theoretical Contributions Regarding the Emotional Life of the Infant, *The Writings of Melanie Klein*, vol. 3, New York: Free Press

Klein, M. (1957) On Envy and Gratitude, *The Writings of Melanie Klein*, vol. 3, New York: Free Press

Kwawer, J. (1980) Some Interpersonal Aspects of Self Mutilation in a Borderline Patient, *Journal of the American Academy of Psychoanalysis*, 8: 2, 203–16

Limentani, A. (1981) On Some Positive Aspects of the Negative Therapeutic Reaction, *International Journal of Psychoanalysis*, 62: 379–90

Olinick, S. (1970) Panel: Negative Therapeutic Reaction; Olinick, S, reporter; *Journal of the American Psychoanalytic Association*, 18: 655–72

O'Shaughnessy, E. (1964) The Absent Object, *Journal of Child Psychotherapy*, 1: 2, 34–43

Richards, A. (1997) The Relevance of Frequency of Sessions to the Creation of an Analytic Experience, *Journal of the American Psychoanalytic Association*, 45: 1241–51

Riviere, J. (1936) A Contribution to the Analysis of the Negative Therapeutic Reaction, *International Journal of Psychoanalysis*, 17: 304–20

Rosenfeld, H. (1971) A Clinical Approach to the Psychoanalytic Theory of the Life and Death Instincts: An Investigation into the Aggressive Aspects of Narcissism, *International Journal of Psychoanalysis*, 52: 169–78

Rosenfeld, H. (1975) The Negative Therapeutic Reaction, in Tactics and Techniques, in *Psychoanalytic Therapy*, vol. 2, ed. P. Giovacchini. New York: Jason Aronson, pp. 217–28

Rosenfeld, H. (1978) Notes on the Psychopathology and Psychoanalytic Treatment of Some Borderline Patients, *International Journal of Psychoanalysis*, 59: 215–21

Rosenfeld, H. (1987) *Impasse and Interpretation: Therapeutic and Anti-Therapeutic Factors in the Psychoanalytic Treatment of Psychotic, Borderline, and Neurotic Patients.* London and New York: New Library of Psychoanalysis

Roth, P. (2001) The Paranoid-Schizoid Position, in *Kleinian Theory: A Contemporary Perspective*, ed. Catalina Bronstein. London: Whurr Publications, pp. 47–62

Segal, H. (1981) *The Work of Hanna Segal: A Kleinian Approach to Clinical Practice.* Northvale, NJ: Jason Aronson, p. 61

Segal, H. (1993) On the Clinical Usefulness of the Concept of Death Instinct, *International Journal of Psychoanalysis*, 74: 55–61

Segal, H. (1997) *Psychoanalysis, Literature, and War*, London and New York: Routledge

Stein, R. (1990) A New Look at the Theory of Melanie Klein, *International Journal of Psychoanalysis*, 71: 499–511

Steiner, J. (1994) Patient Centered and Analyst Centered Interpretations: Some Implications of Containment and Countertransference, *Psychoanalytic Inquiry*, 14: 406–22

Stephen, K. (1934) Introjection and Projection: Guilt and Rage, *British Journal of Medical Psychology*, 14: 317–31

Symington, N. (2004) Two Sessions with Lawrence, *International Journal of Psychoanalysis*, 85: 2, 253–68

Temperley, J. (2001) The Depressive Position, in *Kleinian Theory: A Contemporary Perspective*, ed. Catalina Bronstein. London: Whurr Publications, p. 50

Valenstein, A. (1973) On Attachment to Painful Feelings and the Negative Therapeutic Reaction, *Psychoanalytic Study of the Child*, 28: 365–92

Index